ALEX KALINOVSKY

COVERT

JAVA

Techniques for Decompiling, Patching, and Reverse Engineering

Covert Java: Techniques for Decompiling, Patching, and Reverse Engineering

International Standard Book Number: 0-672-32638-8

Library of Congress Catalog Card Number: 2003116632

Printed in the United States of America

First Printing: May 2004

07   06   03   04   4   3   2   1

Bulk Sales

Sams Publishing offers excellent discounts on this book when ordered in quantity for bulk purchases or special sales. For more information, please contact

> **U.S. Corporate and Government Sales**
> 1-800-382-3419
> corpsales@pearsontechgroup.com

For sales outside of the United States, please contact

> **International Sales**
> 1-317-428-3341
> international@pearsontechgroup.com

Trademarks

All terms mentioned in this book that are known to be trademarks or service marks have been appropriately capitalized. Sams Publishing cannot attest to the accuracy of this information. Use of a term in this book should not be regarded as affecting the validity of any trademark or service mark.

Warning and Disclaimer

Every effort has been made to make this book as complete and as accurate as possible, but no warranty or fitness is implied. The information provided is on an "as is" basis. The author and the publisher shall have neither liability nor responsibility to any person or entity with respect to any loss or damages arising from the information contained in this book.

Associate Publisher
Michael Stephens

Acquisitions Editor
Todd Green

Development Editor
Sean Dixon

Managing Editor
Charlotte Clapp

Project Editor
Elizabeth Finney

Production Editor
Megan Wade

Indexer
Mandie Frank

Proofreader
Katie Robinson

Technical Editor
Craig Pfeifer

Publishing Coordinator
Cindy Teeters

Multimedia Developer
Dan Scherf

Interior Designer
Gary Adair

Cover Designer
Gary Adair

Page Layout
Brad Chinn

Contents at a Glance

Table of Contents

About the Author

Alex Kalinovsky was born in Ukraine in 1974 and moved to the United States in 1997. He has been in the IT industry for more than 10 years, with experience that ranges from writing C and C++ applications to developing enterprise Java solutions. Since 1997, Alex has worked solely with Java and is proud to be one of its original evangelists. He has taught more than 15 classes on Enterprise Java technologies and worked as a mentor for many teams. Alex has written for various publications, including *JavaWorld*, *Sun JavaSoft*, *Information Week*, and the *Washington Post*. He is a Certified Enterprise Java Architect consulting for leading companies that use Java and J2EE. He is also a lead architect for WebCream, a revolutionary Java product that bridges Swing and HTML. In his spare time, Alex enjoys traveling, reading, windsurfing, snowboarding, and bodybuilding.

Dedication

I would like to dedicate this book to my parents, Stanislav and Lubov Kalinovsky, who have given me everything they could from day one of my life. It is only with age that one starts to truly understand and appreciate the impact that the family has on one's life, and I would like to take this opportunity to thank my parents for all the sacrifices they made and for all the patience they had. This work is also a tribute to the other two people who had a tremendous influence on my life, my brother Andrew Kalinovsky and my second dad and mentor Sergei Boiko. Thanks and I love you all.

Acknowledgments

Throughout the long hours I have spent writing this book, many people have helped me to accomplish this project. I would like to thank my closest friends LaWanda Tetteh and Gleb Tulukin for giving me support and encouragement when I needed it. Special credit goes to Amie Koker for being patient and understanding and to Tricia Riviere for her sense of humor and quick wit. Troy Davis and Yves Noel have been great in sharing their technical and personal views and in reviewing my work. This book would not have been possible without Todd Green, Sean Dixon, and the rest of the team at Sams Publishing who shared their expertise and professionalism. I want to express my appreciation to everyone, mentioned here or not, who has helped me in completing this goal.

We Want to Hear from You!

As the reader of this book, *you* are our most important critic and commentator. We value your opinion and want to know what we're doing right, what we could do better, what areas you'd like to see us publish in, and any other words of wisdom you're willing to pass our way.

As an associate publisher for Sams Publishing, I welcome your comments. You can email or write me directly to let me know what you did or didn't like about this book[md]as well as what we can do to make our books better.

Please note that I cannot help you with technical problems related to the topic of this book. We do have a User Services group, however, where I will forward specific technical questions related to the book.

When you write, please be sure to include this book's title and author as well as your name, email address, and phone number. I will carefully review your comments and share them with the author and editors who worked on the book.

Email: feedback@samspublishing.com

Mail: Michael Stephens
         Associate Publisher
         Sams Publishing
         800 East 96th Street
         Indianapolis, IN 46240 USA

For more information about this book or another Sams Publishing title, visit our Web site at www.samspublishing.com. Type the ISBN (excluding hyphens) or the title of a book in the Search field to find the page you're looking for.

Introduction

There are many good books written on Java. It sometimes amazes me how many books you can see on the same subject. Searching on www.amazon.com for a book on Enterprise JavaBeans (EJB) returns more than 50 results. Come on, people! EJB is a complex technology and today every self-respecting Java developer has to have it on his resume, but *50* books? So, what right do I have to add another tome to the Java bookshelf? Well, I believe that there are a few less-publicized development techniques that, when used correctly, can yield astonishing results. Most of the methods deal with core Java concepts and issues and therefore can be used in a variety of applications. The techniques presented in this book are unorthodox solutions to common problems in Java development. Some of them are controversial and should be used with great care, but all of them are powerful methods of achieving what you want. Learn them, and you will be able to separate yourself from the majority of other developers by delivering a solution when everyone else is grasping to understand what the problem really is. You might have used some of the techniques presented in this book already, and I congratulate you if this is the case, but I am confident that you'll pick up at least a few helpful new tricks as you peruse the advice I give here.

A large portion of the book is dedicated to techniques that are commonly considered to be hacking. *Hacking* is used rather freely in the media and oftentimes with negative connotation. Hackers are frequently portrayed as crazy geeks wanting to boost their self esteem, and for some cases this is certainly true. The methods presented here, however, are intended for professional software developers and each technique has a real-life application.

Who Will Benefit from This Book?

Java developers and architects stand the best chance of learning the most from this work. To truly appreciate the problems and solutions presented in this book, you should have completed at least a few significant Java applications and worked with third-party code. That is not to say that junior developers have nothing to gain from this work. To keep the book concise and focused on the main topics, little coverage is given to the subjects that are expected to be well-known or well-documented. For example, when talking about hacking non-public class members, the book does not explain the limitations imposed by each visibility modifier. Such information can be easily obtained from the Internet or books that cover these topics in detail. *Covert Java: Techniques for Decompiling, Patching, and Reverse Engineering* is about extreme techniques that punch through the commonly expected boundaries.

It is worth noting that the techniques presented here are largely independent of one another. Because the presentation of the material follows a "most common simpler methods first" order, feel free to skip chapters and go directly to the one you are interested in. Chapter 1, "Getting Started," has a section that briefly describes each of the techniques and when to use it, so I recommend familiarizing yourself with it first.

The Moral and Legal Aspects of Hacking

Most of the chapters are strictly technical, but it is extremely important to understand that not all the techniques can be freely applied when working with applications. Not every approach presented in the book is "hacking" but, if used without first checking the legal consequences, it can certainly get you in trouble. Let's start by trying to give a broad definition of hacking and then look at how to tread that treacherous water.

Merriam-Webster's dictionary has the following definition for the term *hacker*: "an expert at programming and solving problems with a computer." However, there is another meaning given right after it: "a person who illegally gains access to and sometimes tampers with information in a computer system." Being an expert at programming is certainly a great thing; fiddling with illegal stuff lands you in jail. The short message is that this book is for the good guys, and if you are a bad guy, please stop reading right now and get a new job with the testing team. Any information or discovery can be used for good or ill. It is not the information but the use of it that determines whether the outcome is considered positive or negative.

By now, there have been a number of high-profile court cases revolving around digital copyrights, reverse engineering, and patent violations. Companies and individuals have lost millions of dollars and sometimes reputations as well. Although the laws are complex and the license agreements are written by lawyers for lawyers, it is not that difficult to steer clear of legal problems. Here are the two basic rules to follow:

- If an author expects you to pay for her work, do so.

- If you are tinkering with something, be sure that it does not hurt the author's interests.

Simple and effective. The first rule is very easy to understand, but the second is the one that is important to remember when applying the methods presented in the book. For example, if you reverse engineer someone's code to find a workaround for a bug, the author isn't likely to prosecute you. However, if you reverse engineer someone's code and make a competitive product based on the same unique principles, you are most likely to see the author in court.

It is important to remember that the software we are working with is written by people just like you and I, and just like you and I they have to pay bills. Open source is a different phenomenon, and because the source code is freely available, you don't need to use extreme methods to learn something about or change something in the product. But most of the software developed today is commercial and most of the innovation is done by commercial vendors. Hacking the software to avoid paying the license fees is counterproductive because it undermines the software market and indirectly hurts the developers. Stealing ice cream from a shop next door will either raise the price of the ice cream or drive the shop out of business. And if you own a bakery, the owner of the ice cream shop might start stealing cookies from you.

The two rules cover the moral aspects of hacking, but what generally covers the legal aspects are the copyright and intellectual property laws and end user license agreements (EULAs). The laws are complex and not easy to read, but EULAs are a must because they generally are more restrictive than the laws. They are written to provide the author with the protection that might not be adequately granted by the respective laws, and users are generally required to explicitly agree to the terms of the agreement before using a product. For example, even though reverse engineering is not prohibited by law, most software products forbid it in the EULA. It is therefore *imperative* to thoroughly study the EULA before using the techniques described in this book on a product. To avoid repetition and to keep the contents of the book strictly technical, the material of the chapters does not mention the legal aspects associated with the techniques. It is *your* responsibility to ensure the legality of your actions.

Special Features of the Text

Several typographic conventions are used in *Covert Java: Techniques for Decompiling, Patching, and Reverse Engineering* to make the text more readable. *Italic font* is used for emphasis and to indicate new terms. `Monospace font` is used for parts of code, filenames, and URLs. `Monospace italic font` indicates placeholders in code syntax.

In addition, a few special elements are used in this book. "Stories from the Trenches" describe my own experiences in working with the various techniques described throughout *Covert Java: Techniques for Decompiling, Patching, and Reverse Engineering* to help you understand how these techniques work out in actual practice. Each chapter ends with an "In Brief" section summarizing the main points of the chapter, as well as a quiz section to help you review the material.

Getting Started

Techniques Overview—When and Why to Use Each Method

Table 1.1 presents a brief overview of techniques that are discussed in more detail in the corresponding chapters. Use this as a road map to getting started with this book.

TABLE 1.1

Techniques Overview

CHAPTER	TECHNIQUE	USEFUL FOR
2	Decompiling classes	Recovering lost source code
		Learning the implementation of a feature or trick
		Troubleshooting undocumented code
		Fixing urgent bugs in production or third-party code
		Evaluating how your code might be hacked
3	Obfuscating classes	Protecting bytecode from decompiling
		Protecting the intellectual property inside the bytecode
		Preventing the applications from being hacked
4	Hacking non-public methods and variables of a class	Accessing functionality that exists but is not exposed
		Changing the values of internal variables
5	Replacing and patching application classes	Changing the implementation of a class without having to rebuild the entire library
		Altering the functionality of a third-party application or framework

TABLE 1.1

Continued

CHAPTER	TECHNIQUE	USEFUL FOR
6	Using effective tracing	Creating applications that are easy to maintain and troubleshoot
		Learning the internal workings of an application
		Inserting debug information into the existing applications to understand the implementation details
7	Manipulating Java security	Adding or removing restrictions on access to critical system resources
8	Snooping the runtime environment	Determining the values of system properties
		Determining the system information, such as the number of processors and memory limits
		Determining a network configuration
9	Cracking code with unorthodox debuggers	Hacking applications that do not have good tracing
		Analyzing the control flow of multithreaded applications
		Cracking obfuscated applications
10	Using profilers for application runtime analysis	Investigating heap usage and garbage collection frequency to improve performance
		Browsing object allocation and references to find and fix memory leaks
		Investigating thread allocation and synchronization to find the locking and data race problems and to improve performance
		Investigating an application at runtime to gain a better understanding of its internal structure
11	Load testing to find and fix scalability problems	Creating automated test scripts that simulate a load on a system
		Analyzing how well the application meets the service level requirements such as scalability, availability, and failover
12	Reverse engineering applications	Hacking the user interface elements such as messages, warnings, prompts, images, icons, menus, and colors
13	Eavesdropping techniques	Intercepting HTTP communication between the browser and the Web server
		Intercepting communication between the RMI client and server
		Intercepting SQL statements and values from the JDBC driver

TABLE 1.1		
Continued		
CHAPTER	**TECHNIQUE**	**USEFUL FOR**
14	Controlling class loading	Implementing a custom class loader to control how and from what source the classes are loaded
		Using the custom class loader to instrument the bytecode on-the-fly
		Creating classes programmatically at runtime
15	Replacing and patching core Java classes	Changing the implementations of system classes to alter core behavior
		Enhancing the core functionality of the JDK to suit the application's needs
		Fixing bugs in the JDK implementation
16	Intercepting control flow	Reacting gracefully to system errors such as out of memory and stack overflow
		Capturing the output to `System.out` and `System.err`
		Intercepting calls to `System.exit()`
		Reacting to JVM shutdown
		Intercepting any method call, object allocation, or thread lifecycle event via JVMPI
17	Understanding and tweaking bytecode	Altering class implementation at the bytecode level
		Programmatically generating bytecode
		Instrumenting bytecode to introduce new logic
18	Total control with native code patching	Patching the implementation of native functions
		Augmenting the JVM behavior on the lowest level
19	Protecting commercial applications from hacking	Protecting sensitive information using Java cryptography
		Securing data integrity with digital signatures
		Implementing secure license policy to unlock features of commercial applications

Improving Productivity with File Managers

The techniques discussed here serve the purpose of increasing the productivity of the development. At the end of the day, quality and productivity are what differentiate expert programmers from novice programmers, and because this book is meant to turn readers into experts, I feel it is my duty to introduce a few productivity tools. Hacking and regular development require manipulation of files and directories, and getting the right tool can make doing so much easier. Obviously, it is up to you to decide whether to use a tool. You should remember that most of the tools require upfront investment in installing, configuring, and learning—not to mention the possible license fees. But as with most tools, the investment pays off very quickly.

We are going to look at two advanced replacements for the combination of Windows Explorer, Notepad/Text Editor, and CMD.EXE. We will focus on Windows because that is where most of the Java development is taking place, but productivity tools might be available on other platforms as well. It might sound silly that we're starting an advanced Java book by talking about Notepad and CMD.EXE, but a large number of the developers I have seen are still using it, so I want to present a better alternative.

Windows Explorer is a simple shell easily understood by regular users, but it is not capable of helping with the tasks a programmer needs to perform. A very simple example is creating and running a .bat file. Using the default Windows interface, you would have to navigate to the target directory, click the mouse through a few dialog boxes to create a new file, and then open that file in Notepad and edit it. To run the file, you could double-click it, but any output or errors would be lost with the CMD window that was automatically opened by Explorer. A better way, therefore, is to open a CMD.EXE, navigate to the directory, and then run the file. In the end, you must deal with three open windows that are not synchronized or interrelated. A better alternative is using integrated file management software that combines a directory navigating interface with a text editor, a command line for running scripts, archive support, and a multitude of features that make common tasks easy.

FAR and Total Commander

File and Archive Manager (FAR) and Total Commander are both advanced file managers for Windows that trace their roots back to the DOS days and Norton Commander. Distributed as shareware, they can be used without time limitation until you are ready to register for a small fee. They are packed with features for searching files, changing file attributes, and working with multiple files and directories. They have built-in networking and FTP support that presents remote FTP sites in a panel that looks just like a local directory panel. FAR has a powerful built-in editor that can be configured for color highlighting. Both environments have extensive sets of keyboard shortcuts, and FAR supports plug-ins. Both tools support browsing the content of archive files, such as JAR and Zip files, in a panel just like browsing a subfolder. This makes software such as WinZip unnecessary, and what is even better is that the user does not have to deal with different current directories and user interfaces, as is the case when working with nonintegrated software. Table 1.2 provides a list of features and a side-by-side comparison of FAR and Total Commander.

TABLE 1.2
FAR Versus Total Commander

FEATURE	FAR	TOTAL COMMANDER
Create, copy, view, edit, and delete for files and folders	Excellent	Excellent
Internal and external viewer/editor	Excellent	Good (no internal editor)
Seamless browsing of archive contents (JAR, Zip, and so on)	Excellent	Excellent
Extensive customization of features and UI	Excellent	Good
Windows-like look and feel	Poor	Good
Customizable user menus	Excellent	Excellent
Built-in Windows network support	Yes	Yes
Built-in FTP client	Yes	Yes
Keyboard shortcuts	Excellent	Good
Filename filters	Excellent	Excellent
Quick View	Fair	Excellent
Command, folder, view, and edit history	Excellent	Good
Customizable file associations	Excellent	Good
Files highlighting	Excellent	Excellent
Memory footprint	4MB–14MB	4MB–10MB
Plug-in API and availability of various plug-ins	Excellent (more than 500 plug-ins)	Not available
Registration cost of one copy	$25	$28
Overall rating	*Excellent*	*Good*

Although both tools provide a better alternative to Windows Explorer reinforced with other software, FAR proves to be more powerful. Even in its default packaging, it provides more features and productivity gains than Total Commander. In addition, with more then 500 plug-ins written by other developers, its functionality is virtually boundless. The downside of FAR is its somewhat unappealing user interface, although it is something you can get used to. Total Commander, shown in Figure 1.1, looks more like Windows Explorer; if you don't need the ultimate customization and functionality, it can be a better choice.

Regardless of your preferences, please try an integrated file manager, even if you feel it is difficult to use. It will pay off in the long run!

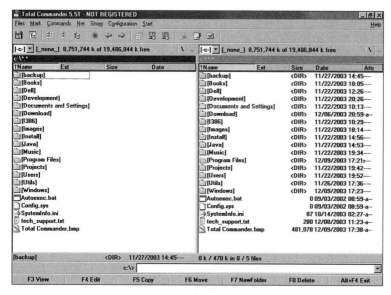

FIGURE 1.1 Total Commander.

Java IDEs

Most of the techniques in this book do not involve a lot of coding, and with a tool like FAR, you can easily accomplish all the required tasks. However, integrated development environments (IDEs) make coding much easier, so this section presents a brief overview of the leading IDEs and a recommendation of the one to use.

Today, when it comes to IDEs the question is not whether you should use IDEs or not, but which IDE you should use. A lot of it has to do with development background and personal preferences, so I won't spend a lot of time talking about them. The two leading free IDEs are Eclipse (http://www.eclipse.org) promoted by IBM and NetBeans (http://www.netbeans.org) promoted by Sun. Both are good, although Eclipse has a little more steam and following. The best commercial IDEs are IntelliJ IDEA, Borland JBuilder, and Oracle JDeveloper.

Because you will be working with low-level coding and hacking, your best bet is a flexible IDE with a small memory footprint. My personal favorite is IDEA because of its flexibility, intuitive interface, and abundance of shortcuts and refactoring features. It is not free, so if you can't afford a license, my second recommendation is Eclipse.

Sample Application Functionality and Structure

Throughout most of this book, we will be working with the same sample application. It is not very sophisticated, but it does contain a basic set of components found in most standalone Java programs. This section describes the application and its implementation.

Chat is a simple TCP/IP chat implementation in Java. It enables users to exchange instant messages via the network. Chat maintains a history of the conversation and uses colors to differentiate between the sent and received messages. It has a menu bar and About dialog box. Chat can be started using chat.bat script in the distrib/bin directory. Figure 1.2 shows Chat running.

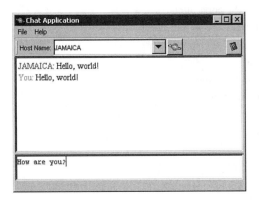

Chat is implemented using Java Swing for the user interface and RMI for network communication. When running, each instance of Chat creates an in-process RMI registry that is used by other instances to post messages to the user. Users are required to enter the hostname of the user to which they want to post a message. When the user sends a message, Chat looks up the remote server object and calls a method on it. For testing purposes, messages can be sent to "localhost", in which case the same message is added to the conversation as was sent and received.

FIGURE 1.2   The Chat application.

The UML class diagram for Chat is shown in Figure 1.3.

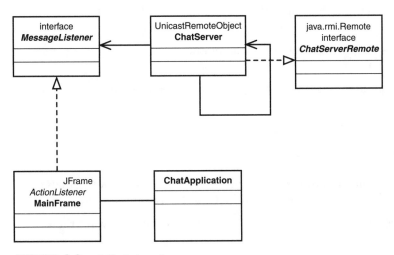

FIGURE 1.3   A Chat class diagram.

The Chat directory structure follows the de-facto standards for Java application development. The "home" folder for the application directories is called CovertJava. The subdirectories it contains are listed in Table 1.3.

TABLE 1.3

Chat Application Directory Structure

DIRECTORY NAME	DESCRIPTION
bin	Contains the scripts and the development and test scripts
build	Contains Ant's build.xml and other build-related files
classes	Compiler output directory for .class files
distrib	Contains the application in its distribution form
distrib\bin	Contains scripts that run the application
distrib\conf	Contains configuration files, such as Java policy files
distrib\lib	Contains libraries used to run the application
distrib\patches	Contains patches for classes
lib	Contains libraries used to build the application
src	Contains application source files

A Chat application can be built by Ant using build.xml in the build directory.

Quick Quiz

1. Which techniques can be used to learn about the internal implementation of an application?

2. Which techniques can be used to change the internal implementation of an application?

3. Which techniques can be used to capture the communication between a client and a server?

4. Which Windows applications are substituted by FAR and Total Commander?

In Brief

■ Various techniques presented in this book can be used to learn about the internals of implementation to hack an application or to work with the JDK at the system level.

■ Integrated file management applications increase productivity and are worth the investment.

Decompiling Classes

2

"When all else fails, read the manual."
Murphy's Technology Laws

Determining When to Decompile

In an ideal world, decompilation would probably be unnecessary, except when learning how other people who don't like to write good documentation implemented a certain feature. In the real world, however, there are often situations where a direct reference to the source code can be the best, if not the only, solution. Here are some of the reasons to decompile:

■ Recovering the source code that was accidentally lost

■ Learning the implementation of a feature or trick

■ Troubleshooting an application or library that does not have good documentation

■ Fixing urgent bugs in third-party code for which no source code exists

■ Learning to protect your code from hacking

Decompiling produces the source code from Java bytecode. It is a reverse process to compiling that is possible due to the standard and well-documented structure of bytecode. Just like running a compiler to produce bytecode from the source code, you can run a decompiler to obtain the source code for given bytecode. Decompiling is a powerful method of learning about implementation logic in the absence of documentation and the source code, which is why many product vendors explicitly prohibit decompiling and reverse engineering in the license agreement. Be sure to check the license agreement or get an explicit permission from the vendor if you are uncertain about the legality of your actions.

Some people might argue that you shouldn't have to resort to extreme measures such as decompiling and that you should rely on vendors of the bytecode for support and bug fixing. In a professional environment, if you are a developer of an application, you are responsible for the functionality being flawless. The users and management do not care whether a bug is in your code or in third-party code. They care about the problem being fixed, and they will hold you accountable for it. Contacting the vendor of the third-party code should be a preferred way. However, in urgent cases when you must provide a solution in a matter of hours, being able to work with the bytecode will give you that extra edge over your peers, and maybe a bonus as well.

Knowing the Best Decompilers

To embark on the task of decompiling, you need the right tools. A good decompiler can produce the source code that will be almost as good as the original source code that was compiled into bytecode. Some decompilers are free, and some are commercially available. Although I support the principles behind commercial software, it needs to offer a useful premium over its free counterparts for me to use it. In the case of decompilers, I have not found the free ones lacking any features, so my personal recommendation is to use a free tool such as JAD or JODE. Table 2.1 lists some of the commonly used decompilers and includes a

STORIES FROM THE TRENCHES

At Riggs Bank we were preparing to go live with a very large and important J2EE application that was deployed into a cluster of application servers from a leading J2EE vendor. Several teams were waiting for the production environment to be ready, but for some strange reason the application server would not start on some of the hosts. The exact same installation would run on some machines but fail on others with an error message about an invalid configuration URL. To make matters worse, the URL in the error message could not be found in any of the configuration files, shell scripts, or environment variables.

Several days were spent trying to fix the problem in vain, and the situation was ready to explode because several teams were about to miss a critical deadline. After copying and reinstalling the application server failed, we finally resorted to finding the class in the application server libraries that was producing the error message. Decompiling it, and a few other classes that were using it, revealed that the URL was programmatically generated based on the server installation directory. The installation directory was determined by executing the pwd Unix command. It turned out that on the failing hosts there were no permissions to execute pwd, but the misleading error message did not make that obvious. Fixing the permissions took a matter of minutes, and the whole process from the time we found and decompiled the class took less than an hour. Thus, a looming disaster was turned into a big win for the IT team.

short description highlighting the quality of each one. The URLs presented might become outdated, so doing a Google search is typically the best way of finding the decompiler's home page and the latest version to download.

A very important criterion is how well the decompiler supports more advanced language constructs such as inner classes and anonymous implementations. Even though the bytecode format has been very stable since JDK 1.1, it is important to use a decompiler that is frequently updated by its authors. The new language features in JDK 1.5 will require an update in decompilers, so be sure to check the release date of the version you are using.

TABLE 2.1

Decompilers

TOOL/RATING	LICENSE	DESCRIPTION
JAD/Excellent	Free for noncommercial use	JAD is a very fast, reliable, and sophisticated decompiler. It has full support for inner classes, anonymous implementations, and other advanced language features. The generated code is clean, and imports are well organized. Several other decompiling environments use command-line JAD as the decompiling engine.
JODE/Excellent	GNU public license	JODE is a very good decompiler written in Java and available with the full source code on SourceForge.net. It might not be as fast and widespread as JAD, but it produces excellent results, at times even cleaner than JAD. Having the source code for the decompiler itself cannot be underestimated for educational purposes.
Mocha/Fair	Free	Mocha is the first well-known decompiler that has generated a lot of legal controversy but also a wave of enthusiasm. Mocha made it obvious that Java source code can be reconstructed almost to its original form, which was cheered by the development community but feared by the legal departments. The public code has not been updated since 1996, although Borland has presumably updated and integrated it into JBuilder.

Although you might find other decompilers on the market, JAD and JODE are certainly good enough and therefore widely used. Many products provide graphical user interfaces (GUIs) but rely on a bundled decompiler to do the actual work. For instance, Decafe, DJ, and Cavaj are GUI tools bundled with JAD and therefore were not included in the review. For the rest of this book, we will use command-line JAD to produce the source code. Most of the time, the command-line decompiler is all you need, but if you prefer to use a GUI, just be sure that it uses a solid decompiler such as JAD or JODE.

Decompiling a Class

In case you haven't used one before, let's see how good a job a decompiler can do. We will
work with a slightly enhanced version of the MessageInfo class, which is used by Chat to
send the message text and the attributes to a remote host. MessageInfoComplex.java, shown
in Listing 2.1, has an anonymous inner class (MessageInfoPK) and a main() method to illustrate some of the more complex cases of decompiling.

LISTING 2.1 MessageInfoComplex Source Code

```java
package covertjava.decompile;

/**
 * MessageInfo is used to send additional information with each message across
 * the network. Currently it contains the name of the host that the message
 * originated from and the name of the user who sent it.
 */
public class MessageInfoComplex implements java.io.Serializable {

    String hostName;
    String userName;

    public MessageInfoComplex(String hostName, String userName) {
        this.hostName = hostName;
        this.userName = userName;
    }

    /**
     * @return name of the host that sent the message
     */
    public String getHostName() {
        return hostName;
    }

    /**
     * @return name of the user that sent the message
     */
    public String getUserName() {
        return userName;
    }
```

```
/**
 * Convenience method to obtain a string that best identifies the user.
 * @return name that should be used to identify a user that sent this message
 */
public String getDisplayName() {
    return getUserName() + " (" + getHostName() + ")";
}



/**
 * Generate message id that can be used to identify this message in a database
 * The format is: <ID><UserName><HostName>. Names are limited to 8 characters
 * Example: 443651_Kalinovs_JAMAICA would be generated for Kalinovsky/JAMAICA
 */
public String generateMessageId() {
    StringBuffer id = new StringBuffer(22);

    String systemTime = "" + System.currentTimeMillis();
    id.append(systemTime.substring(0, 6));

    if (getUserName() != null && getUserName().length() > 0) {
        // Add user name if specified
        id.append('_');
        int maxChars = Math.min(getUserName().length(), 8);
        id.append(getUserName().substring(0, maxChars));
    }

    if (getHostName() != null && getHostName().length() > 0) {
        // Add host name if specified
        id.append('_');
        int maxChars = Math.min(getHostName().length(), 7) ;
        id.append(getHostName().substring(0, maxChars));
    }
    return id.toString();
}



/**
 * Include an example of anonymous inner class
 */
public static void main(String[] args) {
    new Thread(new Runnable() {
```

LISTING 2.1   Continued

```
            public void run() {
                System.out.println("Running test");
                MessageInfoComplex info = new MessageInfoComplex("JAMAICA", "Kalinovsky");
                System.out.println("Message id = " + info.generateMessageId());
                info = new MessageInfoComplex(null, "JAMAICA");
                System.out.println("Message id = " + info.generateMessageId());
            }
        }).start();
    }



    /**
     * Inner class that can be used as a primary key for MessageInfoComplex
     */
    public static class MessageInfoPK implements java.io.Serializable {
        public String id;
    }
}
```

After compiling MessageInfoComplex.java using javac with default options, we get three class files: MessageInfoComplex.class, MessageInfoComplex$MessageInfoPK.class, and MessageInfoComplex$1.class. As you might know, inner classes and anonymous classes have been added to Java in JDK 1.1, but the design goal was to preserve bytecode format compatibility with earlier versions of Java. That is why these language constructs result in somewhat independent classes, although they do retain the association with the parent class. The final step of our test is to run the decompiler on the class file and then compare the generated source code with the original. Assuming that you have downloaded and installed JAD and added it to the path, you can run it using the following command:

jad MessageInfoComplex.class

Upon completion, JAD generates the MessageInfoComplex.jad file. This is renamed to MessageInfoComplex_FullDebug.jad, as shown in Listing 2.2.

LISTING 2.2   MessageInfoComplex Decompiled Code

```
// Decompiled by Jad v1.5.7g. Copyright 2000 Pavel Kouznetsov.
// Jad home page: http://www.geocities.com/SiliconValley/Bridge/8617/jad.html
// Decompiler options: packimports(3)
// Source File Name:   MessageInfoComplex.java
```

```
package covertjava.decompile;

import java.io.PrintStream;
import java.io.Serializable;

public class MessageInfoComplex
    implements Serializable
{
    public static class MessageInfoPK
        implements Serializable
    {

        public String id;

        public MessageInfoPK()
        {
        }
    }


    public MessageInfoComplex(String hostName, String userName)
    {
        this.hostName = hostName;
        this.userName = userName;
    }

    public String getHostName()
    {
        return hostName;
    }

    public String getUserName()
    {
        return userName;
    }

    public String getDisplayName()
    {
        return getUserName() + " (" + getHostName() + ")";
    }

    public String generateMessageId()
```

LISTING 2.2   Continued

```java
    {
        StringBuffer id = new StringBuffer(22) ;
        String systemTime = "" + System.currentTimeMillis();
        id.append(systemTime.substring(0, 6));
        if(getUserName() != null && getUserName().length() > 0)
        {
            id.append('_');
            int maxChars = Math.min(getUserName().length(), 8);
            id.append(getUserName().substring(0, maxChars));
        }
        if(getHostName() != null && getHostName().length() > 0)
        {
            id.append('_');
            int maxChars = Math.min(getHostName().length(), 7);
            id.append(getHostName().substring(0, maxChars));
        }
        return id.toString();
    }

    public static void main(String args[])
    {
        (new Thread(new Runnable() {

            public void run()
            {
                System.out.println("Running test");
                MessageInfoComplex info = new MessageInfoComplex("JAMAICA", "Kalinovsky");
                System.out.println("Message id = " + info.generateMessageId());
                info = new MessageInfoComplex(null, "JAMAICA");
                System.out.println("Message id = " + info.generateMessageId());
            }

        })).start();
    }

    String hostName;
    String userName;
}
```

Take a few moments to review the generated code. As you can see, the code is almost a 100% match to the original! The order of variables, methods, and inner class declarations is different, and so is the formatting, but the logic is absolutely the same. We have also lost the comments, but well-written Java code such as ours is self-evident, isn't it?

Our case produced good results because full debugging information is included by javac when the -g option is used. If the source code was compiled without the debug information (the -g:none option), the decompiled code would lose some of the clarity, such as the parameter names of methods and names of local variables. The following code shows the constructor and a method that uses local variables for MessageInfoComplex with no debugging information included:

```java
public MessageInfoComplex(String s, String s1)
{
    hostName = s;
    userName = s1;
}

public String generateMessageId()
{
    StringBuffer stringbuffer = new StringBuffer(22);
    String s = "" + System.currentTimeMillis();
    stringbuffer.append(s.substring(0, 6));
    if(getUserName() != null && getUserName().length() > 0)
    {
        stringbuffer.append('_');
        int i = Math.min(getUserName().length(), 8);
        stringbuffer.append(getUserName().substring(0, i));
    }
    if(getHostName() != null && getHostName().length() > 0)
    {
        stringbuffer.append('_');
        int j = Math.min(getHostName().length(), 7);
        stringbuffer.append(getHostName().substring(0, j));
    }
    return stringbuffer.toString();
}
```

What Makes Decompiling Possible?

Java source is not compiled to binary machine code like C/C++ source is. Compiling Java source produces intermediate bytecode, which is a platform-independent representation of the source code. Bytecode can be interpreted or compiled after loading, which results in a two-step transformation of the high-level programming language into the low-level machine code. It is the intermediate step that makes decompiling Java bytecode nearly flawless. Bytecode carries all the significant information found in a source file. Even though the comments and formatting are lost, all the methods, variables, and programming logic are obviously preserved. Because the bytecode does not represent the lowest-level machine language, the format of the code closely resembles the source code. The JVM specification defines a set of instructions that match Java language operators and keywords, so a fragment of Java code such as

```java
public String getDisplayName() {
    return getUserName() + " (" + getHostName() + ")";
}
```

is represented by the following bytecode:

```
 0 new #4 <java/lang/StringBuffer>
 3 dup
 4 aload_0
 5 invokevirtual #5 <covertjava/decompile/MessageInfoComplex.getUserName>
 8 invokestatic #6 <java/lang/String.valueOf>
11 invokestatic #6 <java/lang/String.valueOf>
14 invokespecial #7 <java/lang/StringBuffer.<init>>
17 ldc #8 < (>
19 invokevirtual #9 <java/lang/StringBuffer.append>
22 aload_0
23 invokevirtual #10 <covertjava/decompile/MessageInfoComplex.getHostName>
26 invokevirtual #9 <java/lang/StringBuffer.append>
29 ldc #11 <)>
31 invokevirtual #9 <java/lang/StringBuffer.append>
34 invokestatic #6 <java/lang/String.valueOf>
37 invokestatic #6 <java/lang/String.valueOf>
40 areturn
```

Bytecode format is covered in detail in Chapter 17, "Understanding and Tweaking Bytecode," but you can see the resemblance by just looking at the bytecode. The decompiler loads the bytecode and tries to reconstruct the source code based on the bytecode instructions. The names of class methods and variables are typically preserved, whereas the names of method parameters and local variables are lost. If the debugging information is available, it provides the decompiler with parameter names and line numbers—and that makes the reconstructed source file even more readable.

Potential Problems with Decompiled Code

Most of the time, decompiling produces a readable file that can be changed and recompiled. However, on some occasions decompiling does not render a file that can be compiled again. This can happen if the bytecode was obfuscated, and the names given by the obfuscator result in ambiguity at the compilation. The bytecode is verified when loaded, but the verifications assume that the compiler has checked for a number of errors. Thus, the bytecode verifiers are not as strict as compilers and obfuscators can take advantage of that to better protect the intellectual property. For example, here is the JAD output on the anonymous inner class from the `MessageInfoComplex main()` method that was obfuscated by the Zelix ClassMaster obfuscator:

```
static class c
    implements Runnable
{

    public void run()
    {
        boolean flag = a.b;
        System.out.println(a("*4%p\002\026&kj\016\0135"));
        b b1 = new b(a("2\000\006_\";\0"), a("3 'w\005\02778u\022"));
        System.out.println(a("5$8m\n\037$kw\017X¦k").concat(String.valueOf
        ➥(String.valueOf(b1.d()))));
        b1 = new b(null, a("2\000\006_\";\0"));
        System.out.println(a("5$8m\n\037$kw\017X¦k").concat(String.valueOf
        ➥(String.valueOf(b1.d()))));
        if(flag)
            b.c = !b.c;
    }

    private static String a(String s)
    {
        char ac[];
        int i;
        int j;
        ac = s.toCharArray();
        i = ac.length;
        j = 0;
        if(i > 1) goto _L2; else goto _L1
_L1:
        ac;
        j;
```

```
_L10:
            JVM INSTR dup2 ;
            JVM INSTR caload ;
            j % 5;
            JVM INSTR tableswitch 0 3: default 72
    //                          0 52
    //                          1 57
    //                          2 62
    //                          3 67;
                goto _L3 _L4 _L5 _L6 _L7
_L4:
            0x78;
              goto _L8
_L5:
            65;
              goto _L8
_L6:
            75;
              goto _L8
_L7:
            30;
              goto _L8
_L3:
            107;
_L8:
            JVM INSTR ixor ;
            (char);
            JVM INSTR castore ;
            j++;
            if(i != 0) goto _L2; else goto _L9
_L9:
            ac;
            i;
              goto _L10
_L2:
            if(j >= i)
                return new String(ac);
            if(true) goto _L1; else goto _L11
_L11:
        }

    }
```

As you can see, it is a total fiasco, not even closely resembling Java source. What's more disturbing, JAD produced source code that cannot be compiled. The other two decompilers have reported an error on the class file. Needless to say, the JVM recognizes and loads the bytecode in question with no problems. Obfuscation is covered in detail in Chapter 3, "Obfuscating Classes."

A powerful way of protecting the intellectual property is encoding the class files and using a custom class loader to decode them on loading. This way, the decompilers cannot be used on any of the application classes except for the entry point and the class loader. Although not unbreakable, encoding makes hacking much more difficult. A hacker would first have to decompile the class loader to understand the decoding mechanism and then decode all the class files; only then could he proceed with decompiling. Chapter 19, "Protecting Commercial Applications from Hacking," provides information on how to best protect the intellectual property in Java applications.

Quick Quiz

1. What are the reasons to decompile bytecode?

2. Which compiler options affect the quality of decompilation, and how?

3. Why is decompiled Java bytecode almost identical to the source code?

4. How can you protect the bytecode from decompiling?

In Brief

- Decompiling produces the source code from bytecode, which is almost identical to the original.

- Decompiling is a powerful method of learning about implementation logic in the absence of documentation and source code. However, decompiling and reverse engineering might be explicitly prohibited in the license agreement.

- Decompiling requires downloading and installing a decompiler.

- Decompiling Java classes is effective because the bytecode is an intermediate step between the source code and machine code.

- A good obfuscator can make decompiled code very hard to read and understand.

Obfuscating Classes

3

"Any sufficiently advanced technology is indistinguishable from magic."

Murphy's Technology Laws

Protecting the Ideas Behind Your Code

Reverse engineering and hacking have been around since the early days of software development. As a matter of fact, stealing or replicating someone else's ideas has always been the easiest way of creating competitive products. There is, of course, a perfectly acceptable method of building on previous discoveries by others—and as long as the others don't mind, it works fine. Most inventors and researchers, however, would like to get credit and possibly a financial reward for their work. In simpler terms, they also have mortgages to pay and vacations to take.

A good way of protecting intellectual property is for the author to obtain copyrights and patents on the unique features of the work. This is certainly recommended for inventions and major discoveries that required a lot of investment into research and development. Copyrighting software is a rather easy and cost-effective process, but it protects only the "original" code of the application, not the ideas behind it. Others would not be able to take copyrighted code and use it in their applications without the author's permission, but if they have their own implementation of the same feature, it would not be considered a violation to use that. Patents provide a much better protection because they cover the ideas and algorithms rather than a specific implementation, but they are expensive to file and can take years to obtain.

Is the risk of having your application hacked real? If it has good ideas, then absolutely. Most of the widely publicized reverse engineering cases at the time of this writing did not occur with Java products, but here's an excerpt from a Java vendor (DataDirect Technologies):

> ROCKVILLE, MD., July 1, 2002—DataDirect Technologies, Inc., an industry-leading data connectivity vendor has filed a lawsuit against i-net Software GmbH alleging copyright infringement and breach of contract. DataDirect Technologies is seeking both preliminary and permanent injunctive relief to prevent i-net from engaging in further efforts to market and sell products which DataDirect Technologies believes were illegally reverse-engineered from its products.

DataDirect Technologies claims that a competitor reverse engineered its product, and yet even today its product has only minimal protection from decompiling.

In the real world, copyrighting the code and getting a patent for an approach cannot provide adequate protection if a competitor or hacker can easily learn the implementation from the source code. The issues of legal protection are discussed in a separate chapter, but for now, let's focus on smart ways to protect the intellectual property (IP) of Java applications.

Obfuscation As a Protection of Intellectual Property

Obfuscation is the process of transforming bytecode to a less human-readable form with the purpose of complicating reverse engineering. It typically includes stripping out all the debug information, such as variable tables and line numbers, and renaming packages, classes, and methods to machine-generated names. Advanced obfuscators go further and change the control flow of Java code by restructuring the existing logic and inserting bogus code that will not execute. The premise of the obfuscation is that the transformations do not break the validity of the bytecode and do not alter the exposed functionality.

Obfuscation is possible for the same reasons that decompiling is possible: Java bytecode is standardized and well documented. Obfuscators load Java class files, parse their formats, and then apply transformations based on supported features. When all the transformations are applied, the bytecode is saved as a new class file. The new file has a different internal structure but behaves just like the original file.

Obfuscators are especially necessary for products and technologies in which the implementation logic is delivered to the user. That is the case for HTML pages and JavaScript where the product is distributed in source code form. Java doesn't fare much better because, even though it is typically distributed in binary bytecode, using a decompiler as described in the previous chapter can produce the source code—which is almost as good as the original.

Transformations Performed by Obfuscators

No standards exist for obfuscation, so the level of protection varies based on the quality of the obfuscator. The following sections present some of the features commonly found in obfuscators. We will use ChatServer's sendMessage method to illustrate how each transformation affects the decompiled code. The original source code for sendMessage is shown in Listing 3.1.

LISTING 3.1   Original Source Code of sendMessage

```
public void sendMessage(String host, String message) throws Exception {
    if (host == null || host.trim().length() == 0)
        throw new Exception ("Please specify host name");

    System.out.println("Sending message to host " + host + ": " + message);
    String url = "//" + host + ":" + this.registryPort + "/chatserver";
    ChatServerRemote remoteServer = (ChatServerRemote)Naming.lookup(url);

    MessageInfo messageInfo = new MessageInfo(this.hostName, this.userName);
    remoteServer.receiveMessage(message, messageInfo);
    System.out.println("Message sent to host " + host);
}
```

Stripping Out Debug Information

Java bytecode can contain information inserted by the compiler that helps debug the running code. The information inserted by javac can contain some or all of the following: line numbers, variable names, and source filenames. Debug information is not needed to run the class but is used by debuggers to associate the bytecode with the source code. Decompilers use this information to better reconstruct the source code. With full debug information in the class file, the decompiled code is almost identical to the original source code. When the debug information is stripped out, the names that were stored are lost, so decompilers have to generate their own names. In our case, after the stripping, sendMessage parameter names would appear as s1 and s2 instead of host and message.

Name Mangling

Developers use meaningful names for packages, classes, and methods. Our sample chat application's server implementation is called ChatServer and the method that sends a message to another user is called sendMessage. Good names are crucial for development and maintenance, but they mean nothing to the JVM. Java Runtime (JRE) doesn't care whether sendMessage is called goShopping or abcdefg; it still invokes it and executes it. By renaming the meaningful human-readable names to meaningless machine-generated ones, obfuscators make the task of understanding the decompiled code much harder. What used to be ChatServer.sendMessage becomes d.a; when many classes and methods exist with the same names, the decompiled code is extremely hard to follow. A good obfuscator takes advantage of polymorphism to make matters worse. Three methods with different names and signatures doing different tasks in the original code can be renamed to the same common name in the obfuscated code. Because their signatures are different, it does not violate the Java language specification but adds confusion to the decompiled code. Listing 3.2 shows an example of a decompiled sendMessage after obfuscation that stripped the debugging information and performed name mangling.

LISTING 3.2   Decompiled sendMessage After Name Mangling

```
public void a(String s, String s1)
    throws Exception
{
    if(s == null || s.trim().length() == 0)
    {
        throw new Exception("Please specify host name");
    } else
    {
        System.out.println(String.valueOf(String.valueOf((
            new StringBuffer("Sending message to host ")
            ).append(s).append(": ").append(s1))));
        String s2 = String.valueOf(String.valueOf((
            new StringBuffer("//")).append(s).append(":")
            .append(b).append("/chatserver"))));
        b b1 = (b)Naming.lookup(s2);
        MessageInfo messageinfo = new MessageInfo(e, f);
        b1.receiveMessage(s1, messageinfo);
        System.out.println("Message sent to host ".concat(
                String.valueOf(String.valueOf(s))));
        return;
    }
}
```

Encoding Java Strings

Java strings are stored as plain text inside the bytecode. Most of the well-written applications have traces inside the code that produce execution logs for debugging and audit trace. Even if class and method names are changed, the strings written by methods to a log file or console can betray the method purpose. In our case, `ChatServer.sendMessage` outputs a trace message using the following:

```
System.out.println("Sending message to host " + host + ": " + message);
```

Even if `ChatServer.sendMessage` is renamed to `d.a`, when you see a trace like this one in the decompiled message body, it is clear what the method does. However, if the string is encoded in bytecode, the decompiled version of the class looks like this:

```
System.out.println(String.valueOf(String.valueOf((new
StringBuffer(a("A\025wV6¦\0279_:a\003xU:2\004v\0227}\003m\022"))
).append(s).append(a("(P")).append(s1))));
```

If you look closely at the encoded string, it is first passed to the `a()` method, which decodes it and returns the readable string to the `System.out.println()` method. String encoding is a powerful feature that should be provided by a commercial-strength obfuscator.

Changing Control Flow

The transformations presented earlier make reverse engineering of the obfuscated code harder, but they do not change the fundamental structure of the Java code. They also do nothing to protect the algorithms and program control flow, which is usually the most important part of the innovation. The decompiled version of `ChatServer.sendMessage` shown earlier is still fairly understandable. You can see that the code first checks for valid input and throws an exception upon error. Then it looks up the remote server object and invokes a method on it.

The best obfuscators are capable of transforming the execution flow of bytecode by inserting bogus conditional and `goto` statements. This can slow down the execution somewhat, but it might be a small price to pay for the increased protection of the IP. Listing 3.3 shows what `sendMessage` has become after all the transformations discussed earlier have been applied.

LISTING 3.3   Decompiled `sendMessage` After All Transformations

```
    public void a(String s, String s1)
        throws Exception
    {
        boolean flag = MessageInfo.c;
        s;
        if(flag) goto _L2; else goto _L1
_L1:
        JVM INSTR ifnull 29;
           goto _L3 _L4
_L3:
        s.trim();
```

LISTING 3.3   Continued

```
_L2:
        if(flag) goto _L6; else goto _L5
_L5:
        length();
        JVM INSTR ifne 42;
           goto _L4 _L7
_L4:
        throw new Exception(a("\002)qUe7egDs1,rM6:*g@6<$yQ"));
_L7:
        System.out.println(String.valueOf(String.valueOf((
            new StringBuffer(a("\001 zP\177<\"4Ys!6uSsr1{\024~=6`\024"))
            ).append(s).append(a("he")).append(s1))));
        String.valueOf(String.valueOf(
            (new StringBuffer(a("}j"))).append(s).append(":")
            .append(b).append(a("}&¦Ub! fBs "))));
_L6:
        String s2;
        s2;
        covertjava.chat.b b1 = (covertjava.chat.b)Naming.lookup(s2);
        MessageInfo messageinfo = new MessageInfo(e, f);
        b1.receiveMessage(s1, messageinfo);
        System.out.println(a("\037 gGw5 4Gs<14@yr-{Gbr").concat(String.valueOf
        ➥(String.valueOf(s))));
        if(flag)
            b.c = !b.c;
        return;
    }
```

Now that's a total, but powerful, mess! sendMessage is a fairly small method with little conditional logic. If control flow obfuscation was applied to a more complex method with for
loops, if statements, and local variables, the obfuscation would be even more effective.

Inserting Corrupt Code

Inserting corrupt code is a somewhat dubious technique used by some obfuscators to prevent
obfuscated classes from decompiling. The technique is based on a loose interpretation of the
Java bytecode specification by the Java Runtime. JRE does not strictly enforce all the rules of
bytecode format verification, and that allows obfuscators to introduce incorrect bytecode into
the class files. The introduced code does not prevent the original code from executing, but an
attempt to decompile the class file results in a failure—or at best in confusing source code full
of JVM INSTR keywords. Listing 3.3 shows how a decompiler might handle corrupt code. The
risk of using this method is that the corrupted code might not run on a version of JVM that

more closely adheres to the specification. Even if it is not an issue with the majority of JVMs today, it might become a problem later.

Eliminating Unused Code (Shrinking)

As an added benefit, most obfuscators remove unused code, which results in application size reduction. For example, if a class called A has a method called m() that is never called by any class, the code for m() is stripped out of A's bytecode. This feature is especially useful for code that is downloaded via the Internet or installed in unsecured environments.

Optimizing Bytecode

Another added benefit touted by obfuscators is potential code optimization. The vendors claim that declaring nonfinal methods as final where possible and performing minor code improvements can help speed up execution. It is hard to assess the real performance gains, and most vendors do not publish the metrics. What is worth noting here is that, with every new release, JIT compilers are becoming more powerful. Therefore, features such as method finalization and dead code elimination are most likely performed by it anyway.

Knowing the Best Obfuscators

Plenty of obfuscators are available, and most of them contain the same set of core features. Table 3.1 includes just a few of the most popular products, both free and commercial.

TABLE 3.1

Popular Obfuscators

PRODUCT	KLASSMASTER	PROGUARD	RETRO GUARD	DASH-O	JSHRINK
Version	4.1	1.7	1.1.13	2.x	2.0
Price	$199–$399	Free	Free	$895–$2995	$95
Stripping out of debug information	Yes	Yes	Yes	Yes	Yes
Name mangling	Yes	Yes	Yes	Yes	Yes
Encoding of Java strings	Yes	No	No	No	Yes
Changing of control flow	Yes	No	No	No	No
Insertion of corrupt code	Yes	No	No	No	No
Elimination of unused code (shrinking)	Yes	Yes	No	Yes	Yes
Optimizing of bytecode	No	No	No	Yes	Yes
Flexibility of scripting language and obfuscation control	Excellent	Excellent	Good	Not rated	Good
Reconstruction of stack traces	Yes	Yes	No	No	No

For commercial applications that contain intellectual property, I recommend Zelix KlassMaster primarily because of its unique control flow obfuscation. This technique makes the obfuscated code truly hard to crack, so the product is worth every dollar you will pay for it. At the time of writing, it is the only obfuscator known to have this feature. ProGuard is available free from `www.sourceforge.net` and is the best choice for the budget-conscious user with applications that do not require commercial-strength protection.

Potential Problems and Common Solutions

Obfuscation is a reasonably safe process that should preserve application functionality. However, in certain cases the transformations performed by obfuscators can inadvertently break code that used to work. The following sections look at the common problems and recommended solutions.

Dynamic Class Loading

The renaming of packages, classes, methods, and variables works fine as long as the name is changed consistently throughout the system. Obfuscators ensure that any static references within the bytecode are updated to reflect the new name. However, if the code performs dynamic class loading using `Class.forName()` or `ClassLoader.loadClass()` passing an original class name, a `ClassNotFound` exception can result. Modern obfuscators are pretty good with handling such cases, and they attempt to change the strings to reflect the new names. If the string is created at runtime or read from a properties file, though, the obfuscator is incapable of handling it. Good obfuscators produce a log file with warnings pointing out the code that has potential for runtime problems.

STORIES FROM THE TRENCHES

The most innovative product from CreamTec is WebCream, which is available for a free download from the Web. The free edition is limited to five concurrent users; to get more users, you must buy a commercial license. Having grown up in the Ukraine, I knew many people who would prefer to crack the licensing to turn the free edition into an unlimited edition that would normally be worth thousands of dollars. At CreamTec, we used a simple, free obfuscator that didn't do much more than name mangling. We thought it was good enough until a friend of mine, who views limited-functionality commercial software as a personal insult, cracked our licensing code in less than 15 minutes. The message was clear enough, and we decided to purchase Zelix KlassMaster to protect the product as well as we could. After we used the aggressive control flow obfuscation with a few extra tricks, our friend has not been able to get to the licensing code with the same ease as before—and because he didn't want to spend days figuring it out, he has given up.

The simplest solution is to configure the obfuscator to preserve the names of dynamically loaded classes. The content of the class, such as the methods, variables, and code, can still be transformed.

Reflection

Reflection requires compile-time knowledge of method and field names, so it is also affected by obfuscation. Be sure to use a good obfuscator and to review the log file for warnings. Just as with the dynamic class loading, if runtime errors are caused by obfuscation, you must exclude from obfuscation the method or field names that are referenced in `Class.getMethod` or `Class.getField`.

Serialization

Serialized Java objects include instance data and information about the class. If the version of the class or its structure changes, a deserialization exception can result. Obfuscated classes can be serialized and deserialized, but an attempt to deserialize an instance of a nonobfuscated class by an obfuscated class will fail. This is not a very common problem, and it can usually be solved by excluding the serializable classes from obfuscation or avoiding the mixing of serialized classes.

Naming Conventions Violation

The renaming of methods can violate design patterns such as Enterprise JavaBeans (EJB), where the bean developer is required to provide methods with certain names and signatures. EJB callback methods such as `ejbCreate` and `ejbRemove` are not defined by a super class or an interface. Providing these methods with a specific signature is a mere convention prescribed by EJB specification and enforced by the container. Changing callback method names violates the naming convention and makes the bean unusable. You should always be sure to exclude the names of such methods from obfuscation.

Maintenance Difficulties

Last, but not least, obfuscation makes maintaining and troubleshooting applications more difficult. Java exception handling is an effective way of isolating the faulty code, and looking at the stack trace can generally give you a good idea of what went wrong and where. Keeping the debugging information for source filenames and line numbers enables the runtime to report the exact location in code where the error occurred. If done carelessly, obfuscation can inhibit this feature and make debugging harder because the developer sees only the obfuscated class names instead of the real class names and line numbers.

You should preserve at least the line number information in the obfuscated code. Good obfuscators produce a log of the transformations, including the mapping between the original class names and methods and the obfuscated counterparts. The following is an excerpt from the log file generated by Zelix KlassMaster for the ChatServer class:

```
Class: public covertjava.chat.ChatServer    =>    covertjava.chat.d
    Source: "ChatServer.java"
    FieldsOf: covertjava.chat.ChatServer
        hostName    =>    e
        protected static instance    =>    a
        messageListener    =>    d
        protected registry    =>    c
        protected registryPort    =>    b
        userName    =>    f
    MethodsOf: covertjava.chat.ChatServer
        public static getInstance()    =>    a
        public getRegistry(int)    =>    a
        public init()    =>    b
        public receiveMessage(java.lang.String, covertjava.chat.MessageInfo)
        ➥NameNotChanged
        public sendMessage(java.lang.String, java.lang.String)    =>    a
        public setMessageListener(covertjava.chat.MessageListener)    =>    a
```

So, if an exception stack trace shows the covertjava.chat.d.b method, you can use the log and find out that it was originally called "init" in a class that was originally called covertjava.chat.ChatServer. If the exception occurred in covertjava.chat.d.a, you would not know the original method name for sure because multiple mappings exist (witness the power of overloading). That's why line numbers are so important. By using the log file and the line number in the original source file, you can quickly locate the problem area in the application code.

Some obfuscators provide a utility that reconstructs the stack traces. This is a convenient way of getting the real stack trace for the obfuscated stack trace. The utility typically uses the same method as we used earlier, but it automates the job—so why not save ourselves some time? It also allows scrambling the line numbers for extra protection.

Using Zelix KlassMaster to Obfuscate a Chat Application

Even though each obfuscator has its own format of configuring the transformations, they all support a common set of features. The Chat application does not contain state-of-the-art algorithms or patent-pending inventions, but it is dear to our hearts so we are going to use Zelix KlassMaster to protect it from the prying eyes of hackers and thieves.

First, we obtain a copy of Zelix KlassMaster and install it on a local machine. Remember that we refer to the Chat application's home directory as CovertJava. Next, we copy ZKM.jar from KlassMaster's installation directory to our project lib directory so we can script against it. The easiest way to create the obfuscation script is with KlassMaster's GUI. Using the command

```
java -jar ZKM.jar
```

from the lib directory, we run the GUI. Then, in the initial helper dialog box that appears, we select the Set Classpath option. We now select the runtime libraries of the JDK we're using and, in the Open Classes dialog box that appears next, we select CovertJava/lib/chat.jar. After that, KlassMaster should load all the classes of the Chat application and we should be able to view the internal structure of the bytecode. The screen should look similar to Figure 3.1.

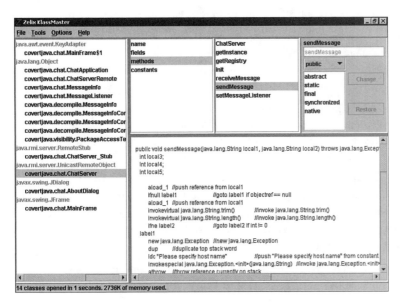

FIGURE 3.1 Chat classes loaded into the KlassMaster GUI.

While working with the GUI, you can easily see just how flexible KlassMaster is. You can manually change the names of classes, methods, and fields; modify the visibility of classes or methods; make methods final; change text strings; and do other cool stuff. KlassMaster attempts to propagate the changes throughout the loaded code, so if other classes refer to a method and you change its name, the referring classes are updated to reflect the change. After making all your changes, you can save the classes as is or trim and obfuscate them first. Classes loaded into the GUI environment can be further modified after the obfuscation, even though I can't think of a reason why someone would need to do so. For details of KlassMaster's features and how to use it, please refer to its user manual.

A well-written Java application provides scripts to build it, so let's integrate obfuscation into our build script. We start by using KlassMaster's GUI to create the obfuscation script. Then, we update it manually to make it more flexible. It is entirely possible to write the script manually or copy and modify a sample script. We run the GUI and select ZKM Script Helper from the Tools menu. Then, we do the following:

1. Read the instructions on the Introductory Page and click Next.

2. On the Classpath Statement page, select rt.jar and click Next.

3. On the Open Statement page, navigate to CovertJava/distrib/chat.jar and click > to select it for opening. We only need one file because all our application classes are packaged in it. Click Next.

4. On the TrimExclude Statement page, the default exclusions are preset to exclude the cases where obfuscation is likely to result in an error. For example, renaming methods of an EJB implementation class makes it unusable, so EJBs are excluded by default.

5. On the Trim Statement page, select the Delete Source File Attributes check box and the Delete Deprecated Attributes check box to get rid of the debug information; then click Next.

6. In the Don't Change Main Class Name combo box on the Exclude Statement page, select covertjava.chat.ChatApplication to preserve its name. This keeps JAR manifest entries valid and enables users to continue invoking the chat using a human-readable name.

7. On the Obfuscate Statement page, select Aggressive in the Obfuscate Control Flow combo box. Then select Aggressive in the Encrypt String Literals combo box, and select Scramble in the Line Number Tables combo box. This ensures adequate protection for the code but enables us to translate stack traces later. Make sure that Produce a Change Log File is checked and click Next.

8. On the SaveAll Statement page, navigate to CovertJava/distrib and create a subdirectory called obfuscated. Select the newly created directory for output and click Next.

9. The next page should show the script text and allow us to save it to a directory. Save it as obfuscate_script.txt in the CovertJava/build directory and exit the GUI.

The resulting script should look similar to Listing 3.4.

LISTING 3.4 Obfuscation Script Generated by the GUI

```
/***********************************************************************/
/* Generated by Zelix KlassMaster 4.1.1 ZKM Script Helper 2003.08.13 17:03:43 */
/***********************************************************************/
```

```
classpath    "c:\java\jdk1.4\jre\lib\rt.jar"
             "c:\java\jdk1.4\jre\lib\sunrsasign.jar"
             "c:\java\jdk1.4\jre\lib\jsse.jar"
             "c:\java\jdk1.4\jre\lib\jce.jar"
             "c:\java\jdk1.4\jre\lib\charsets.jar";


open         "C:\Projects\CovertJava\distrib\chat.jar";


trim         deleteSourceFileAttributes=true
             deleteDeprecatedAttributes=true
             deleteUnknownAttributes=false;


exclude      covertjava.chat.^ChatApplication^ public static main(java.lang.String[]);


obfuscate    changeLogFileIn=""
             changeLogFileOut="ChangeLog.txt"
             obfuscateFlow=aggressive
             encryptStringLiterals=aggressive
             lineNumbers=scramble;


saveAll      archiveCompression=all "C:\Projects\CovertJava\distrib\obfuscated";
```

A good idea would be to replace the absolute file paths with the relative ones, so that instead of opening C:\Projects\CovertJava\distrib\chat.jar, the script opens distrib\chat.jar. Finally, we will integrate obfuscation into the build process by declaring a custom task and adding a target that calls it. KlassMaster is written in Java and can be called from any build script. Conveniently, it provides a wrapper class for Ant integration, so all we have to do is add the following to Chat's build.xml:

```
<!-- Define a task that will execute Zelix KlassMaster to obfuscate classes -->
<taskdef name="obfuscate" classname="ZKMTask" classpath="${basedir}/lib/ZKM.jar"/>
...
<!-- Define a target that produces obfuscated version of Chat -->
<target name="obfuscate" depends="release">
    <obfuscate scriptFileName="${basedir}/build/obfuscate_script.txt"
        logFileName="${basedir}/build/obfuscate_log.txt"
        trimLogFileName="${basedir}/build/obfuscate_trim_log.txt"
        defaultExcludeFileName="${basedir}/build/obfuscate_defaultExclude.txt"
        defaultTrimExcludeFileName="${basedir}/build/obfuscate_defaultTrimExclude.txt"
        defaultDirectoryName="${basedir}"
    />
</target>
```

We can now run Ant on obfuscate target. If the build is successful, a new file (chat.jar) is created in CovertJava/distrib/obfuscated. This file contains the obfuscated version of Chat that can still be invoked using the java -jar chat.jar command. Take a few moments to look inside that JAR and try decompiling some of the classes.

Before we close the subject of using KlassMaster, I'd like to give a few more examples of script file syntax for excluding classes and class members from obfuscation. The format shown in Table 3.2 can be used for statements of obfuscation script that take in names as parameters. ZKM script language supports wildcards, such as * (any sequence of characters) and ? (any one character), and boolean operations, such as ¦¦ (or) and ! (not). For a detailed explanation and full syntax, please refer to KlassMaster documentation.

TABLE 3.2

Commonly Used Name Patterns for KlassMaster

SYNTAX	WHAT IT MATCHES
package1.package2.	Package names package1 and package2. Other package names and children of package2 are not matched.
*.	All package names in the application.
Class1	The name of the class Class1.
package1.Class1	The name of Class1 in package package1 but *not* package1's name.
package1.^Class1	The names of Class1 *and* package1.
package1.^Class1^ method1()	The names of package1, Class1, and method1 with no parameters.
package1.^Class1^ method1(*)	The names of package1, Class1, and all overloaded versions of method1.

Cracking Obfuscated Code

Now that we have spent so much time talking about how to protect intellectual property through obfuscation, a few words are due on the strength of the protection. Does a good obfuscator make it hard to hack an application? Absolutely. Does it guarantee that the application will not be hacked? Not at all!

Unless flow control obfuscation is used, reading and working with the obfuscated code is not that difficult. The key point is finding a good starting point for decompiling. Chapter 2, "Decompiling Classes," presented several techniques for reverse engineering of applications, but obfuscation can defeat many of them. For example, the most effective way of locating a starting point is text searching through the class files. With string encoding, the search will yield no results because the strings are not stored as plain text. Package names and class names can no longer be used to learn about the application structure and to select a good starting point. It is still technically possible to decompile the application entry point and work your way through the control flow for a decent-size application, but it is not feasible.

For flow-obfuscated code, the most sensible method of learning the application implementation is using a good old debugger. Most IDEs come with debugging capabilities, but our case will require a heavyweight debugger capable of working without the source code. To find a good starting point for decompiling, the application needs to be run in debug mode. Java has a standard API for debuggers called Debugger API (duh!) that is capable of local as well as remote debugging. Remote debugging enables the debugger to attach itself to an application running in debug mode and is a preferred way of cracking the application. Good debuggers display in-depth information about running threads, call stacks for each thread, loaded classes, and objects in memory. They enable you to set a breakpoint and trace the method executions. A key for working with obfuscated applications is to use the regular interface (UI or programming API) to navigate to a feature of interest and then to rely on the debugger to learn about the class or classes that implement the feature. After the classes are identified, they can be decompiled and studied as described in Chapter 2. Working with debuggers is covered in detail in Chapter 9, "Cracking Code with Unorthodox Debuggers."

Quick Quiz

1. What are the means of protecting intellectual property in Java applications?

2. Which transformations provided by obfuscators offer the strongest protection?

3. For each of the potential problems listed in this chapter, which transformation(s) can cause it?

4. What is the most efficient way to study the obfuscated code?

In Brief

- Obfuscation can be the best way to protect the intellectual property in Java bytecode.

- Obfuscators perform some or all of the following transformations: stripping out debug information, name mangling, encoding strings, changing control flow, inserting corrupt code, eliminating unused code, and optimizing bytecode.

- Obfuscation introduces maintenance difficulties that can be minimized by configuring the obfuscator.

- Obfuscated code is still readable unless control flow obfuscation and string encoding is used.

Hacking Non-Public Methods and Variables of a Class

4

"Anything can be made to work if you fiddle with it. If you fiddle with something long enough, you'll break it."

Murphy's Technology Laws

The Problem of Encapsulation

Encapsulation is one of the pillars of object-oriented programming. The purpose of encapsulation is separation of the interface from implementation and modularity of application components. It is generally recommended that you make data members private or protected and provide public accessor and mutator functions (also known as *getter* and *setter* functions). It is also sometimes recommended that you make internal implementation methods private or public to protect a class from being used incorrectly. Following the principle of encapsulation helps create a better application, but occasionally it can prove to be an obstacle for usage that was not foreseen by the class developer.

We will use java.awt.BorderLayout in our experiments. Maybe at some point this will encourage JavaSoft engineers to add public methods. We will obtain the source code for BorderLayout from src.jar in the JDK installation directory.

Accessing Packages and Protected Class Members

We will start by demonstrating how to easily access package-visible variables and methods. Our example uses a package-visible variable, but the technique works equally well for protected visibility. A variable or method is *package visible* when no specific visibility keyword such as `public`, `protected`, or `private` is used for declaration. `BorderLayout` stores the component that was added using the `BorderLayout.CENTER` constraint in a `center` variable declared as follows:

```
package java.awt;

public class BorderLayout implements LayoutManager2, java.io.Serializable {
    ...
    Component center;
    ....
}
```

Recall that package-visible members are accessible to the class that declared them and all classes within the same package. In our example, any class in the `java.awt` package can access the `center` variable directly. A simple solution therefore is to create a helper class, `AwtHelper`, in the `java.awt` package and use it to access package-visible members of `BorderLayout` instances. `AwtHelper` has a public function that takes in an instance of `BorderLayout` and returns the component for a given layout constraint:

STORIES FROM THE TRENCHES

WebCream is a product that converts Java AWT and Swing applications into interactive HTML Web sites. It does it by emulating a graphical environment for the graphical user interface (GUI) application running on the server side and capturing and converting the currently displayed top window to an HTML page. To generate the HTML, WebCream iterates all containers and tries to mimic Java layouts with HTML tables. One of the layouts WebCream needs to support is `BorderLayout`. For a container with `BorderLayout`, the HTML rendering module needs to know which child component has been added to the South section, which one to the North, and so on. `BorderLayout` stores this information in the member variables `south`, `north`, and so on, and it even has a `getChild()` method that can be used to obtain the component. The problem is that the variables are declared with package visibility and the `getChild` method is declared as private. To get around the absence of public access to `BorderLayout`'s child components, WebCream engineers had to rely on the hacking techniques described in this chapter.

```
package java.awt;

public class AwtHelper {

    public static Component getChild(BorderLayout layout, String key) {
        Component result = null;

        if (key == BorderLayout.NORTH)
            result = layout.north;
        else if (key == BorderLayout.SOUTH)
            result = layout.south;
        else if (key == BorderLayout.WEST)
            result = layout.west;
        else if (key == BorderLayout.EAST)
            result = layout.east;
        else if (key == BorderLayout.CENTER)
            result = layout.center;
        return result;
    }
}
```

Let's write a test class called covertjava.visibility.PackageAccessTest that uses AwtHelper to obtain the split pane instance from Chat's MainFrame. The following source code excerpt is what we are mostly interested in:

```
Container container = createTestContainer();
if (container.getLayout() instanceof BorderLayout) {
    BorderLayout layout = (BorderLayout)container.getLayout();
    Component center = AwtHelper.getChild(layout, BorderLayout.CENTER);
    System.out.println("Center component = " + center);
}
```

We obtain the layout for the container and, if it is BorderLayout, we use AwtHelper to get the center component. Chat's MainFrame has the split pane in the center; therefore, if the code is written correctly, we should see an instance of JSplitPane on the system console. Running PackageAccessTest, we get the following exception:

```
java.lang.SecurityException: Prohibited package name: java.awt
```

The exception is thrown because java.awt is considered to be a system name space that should not be used by regular classes. This would not have happened if we were trying to hack a package-visible member of a third-party class, but we have intentionally picked a system class to illustrate a real-life example. The only potential problem with using this technique for a nonsystem name space such as `com.mycompany.mypackage` occurs if the package is sealed. Adding a helper class to a sealed package requires the same technique as is explained for adding a patched class in Chapter 5, "Replacing and Patching Application Classes."

Adding system classes is a little trickier because they are loaded and treated differently from application classes. Chapter 16, "Intercepting Control Flow," provides a comprehensive discussion of system classes. For now, though, it would suffice to say that to add a class to the system package, the class has to be placed on the boot class path. A directory or JAR file can be prepended or appended to the boot class path using the `-Xbootclasspath` parameter to the `java` command line. Because we already have a `patches` subdirectory for the Chat application, we will use it for system classes as well. We modify `build.xml` to move the `java.lang` directory with `AwtHelper` to `distrib/patches` and create a new script (`package_access_test.bat`) in `distrib/bin`, as follows:

```
@echo off
set CLASSPATH=..\lib\chat.jar
java -Xbootclasspath/p:..\patches covertjava.visibility.PackageAccessTest
```

Running `package_access_test.bat` produces the following output:

```
C:\Projects\CovertJava\distrib\bin>package_access_test.bat
Testing package-visible access
Center component = javax.swing.JSplitPane[,0,0,0x0,...]
```

Having to place classes on the system boot class path makes deployment a little more involved because it requires modification of the startup script. For example, a Web application that is deployed into a Web container, such as Tomcat or WebLogic, can no longer be simply deployed through a console or the application deployment directory. The script that starts the application server must be modified to include the `-Xbootclasspath` parameter. Another disadvantage of this technique is that it does not work for private members. Last, but not least, adding classes to packages can violate the license agreement. This is the case with `BorderLayout` because a section in Sun's Java license agreement explicitly prohibits adding classes to packages that begin with `java`. The next section presents another alternative that solves some of these problems.

Accessing Private Class Members

Private members are accessible only to the class that declares them. That is one of the ground rules of the Java language that ensures encapsulation. But is it really so? Is it really enforced all the time? If you said, "Well, this guy is writing about it, so there has to be a loophole of some sort," you'd be right. The Java compiler enforces the privacy of private members at compile time. Thus, there can be no static references by other classes to private methods and variables of a class. However, Java has a powerful mechanism of reflection that enables querying instance and class metadata and accessing fields and methods at runtime. Because reflection is dynamic, compile time checks are not applicable. Instead, Java runtime relies on a security manager—if one exists—to verify that the calling code has enough privileges for a particular type of access. The security manager provides enough protection because all the functions of the reflection API delegate to it before executing their logic. What undermines this protection is the fact that the security manager is often not set. By default, the security manager is not set, and unless the code explicitly installs a default or a custom security manager, the runtime access control checks are not in effect. Even if a security manager is set, it is typically configured through a policy file, which can be extended to allow access to the reflection API.

If you looked at the BorderLayout class carefully, you might have noticed that it already has a method that returns a child component based on the position key. Not surprisingly, it is called getChild and has the following signature:

```
private Component getChild(String key, boolean ltr)
```

This sounds like good news because you don't really have to write your own implementation. The problem is that the method is declared as private and there is no public method you can use to call it. To leverage the existing JDK code, you must call BorderLayout.getChild() using the reflection API. We will use the same test structure as in the previous section. This time, though, instead of using AwtHelper, the test class delegates to its own helper function (getChild()):

```
public class PrivateAccessTest {

    public static void main(String[] args) throws Exception {
        Container container = createTestContainer();
        if (container.getLayout() instanceof BorderLayout) {
            BorderLayout layout = (BorderLayout)container.getLayout();
            Component center = getChild(layout, BorderLayout.CENTER);
            System.out.println("Center component = " + center);
        }
        ...
    }

    public static Component getChild(BorderLayout layout, String key) throws Exception {
        Class[] paramTypes = new Class[]{String.class, boolean.class};
        Method method = layout.getClass().getDeclaredMethod("getChild", paramTypes);
        // Private methods are not accessible by default
        method.setAccessible(true);
        Object[] params = new Object[] {key, new Boolean(true)};
        Object result = method.invoke(layout, params);
```

```
        return (Component)result;
    }

    ...

}
```

The getChild() implementation is the core of the technique. It obtains the method object through reflection and then calls setAccessible(true). A value of true is set to suppress the access control checking and allow method invocation. The rest of the method is plain reflection API usage. Running covertjava.visibility.PrivateAccessTest produces the same output you saw in the previous section:

```
C:\Projects\CovertJava\distrib\bin>private_access_test.bat
Testing private access
Center component = javax.swing.JSplitPane[,0,0,0x0,...]
```

This was alarmingly easy. We might have to do a little more work if a security manager is set using System.setSecurityManager or via a command line, which is the case for most application servers and middleware products. If we run our test passing -Djava.security.manager to the java command line, we get the following exception:

```
java.security.AccessControlException: access denied
(java.lang.RuntimePermission accessDeclaredMembers)
```

For our code to work with a security manager installed, we have to grant the permissions to access declared members through reflection and to suppress access checks. We do so by adding a Java policy file that grants these two permissions to our code base:

```
grant {
    permission java.lang.RuntimePermission "accessDeclaredMembers";
    permission java.lang.reflect.ReflectPermission "suppressAccessChecks";
};
```

Finally, we create a new test script (private_access_test.bat) in the distrib\bin directory that adds a command-line parameter (java.security.policy) to install our policy file:

```
set CLASSPATH=..\lib\chat.jar
set JAVA_ARGS=%JAVA_ARGS% -Djava.security.manager
set JAVA_ARGS=%JAVA_ARGS% -Djava.security.policy=../conf/java.policy

java %JAVA_ARGS% covertjava.visibility.PrivateAccessTest
```

If a policy file is already installed, our grant clause needs to be inserted into it. Java security files allow inclusion of additional policy files using the policy.url.n attribute. See Chapter 7, "Manipulating Java Security," for a detailed discussion of Java security and policy files.

The technique that relies on the reflection API can be used to access package and protected members as well. This makes inserting helper classes into third-party packages unnecessary. The drawback of the reflection API is that it is notoriously slow because it has to deal with runtime information and might have to go through a number of security checks. When speed is an issue, it is preferable to rely on the helper classes for package and protected members. Yet another alternative is serializing an instance into a byte array stream and then parsing the stream to obtain the values of the member variables. Obviously, this is a tedious process that does not work for transient fields.

Quick Quiz

1. Which technique can be used to obtain a value of a protected variable?

2. Which technique can be used to obtain a value of a private variable?

3. What are the advantages and disadvantages of each technique?

In Brief

■ Methods and variables that are not declared `public` can still be accessed.

■ A member with `package` or `protected` visibility can be accessed by inserting a helper class into its package or using the reflection API.

■ A member with `private` visibility can be accessed using the reflection API.

■ If a security manager is installed, the Java policy needs to be altered to allow unrestricted access for the reflection API.

Replacing and Patching Application Classes

"How many software engineers does it take to change a light bulb?"

"None. We'll document it in the manual."

"None. It's a hardware problem."

"One, but he's not available till the year 2010."

"Two. One always leaves in the middle of the project."

"Four. One to design the change, one to implement it, one to document it, and one to maintain it afterward."

What Do We Do When We Have Tried Every Road but Failed?

Just about every developer at some point has used a library or a component developed by someone else. Just about every developer at some point has also gotten frustrated with the library to the point of being willing to find the guy who decided to make a method `private` and talk some sense into him. Well, most of us wouldn't go that far, but it would certainly be nice to be able to change things that make our lives miserable. It's not that libraries are written by mean people; it's just that even the brightest designers are unable to foresee all the possible ways that other developers would want to use their code.

Certainly, it is always better to resolve matters peacefully. If you can get the vendor to change his code, or if you are in a position to do it yourself, then certainly do so. But the sheer fact that you are reading this book proves that in real life the conventional approach does not always work. And this is where things get interesting. Having said that, when should you resort to replacing and patching classes? The following are several of the situations that call for a hacker approach:

▶ **You are using a third-party library that has the capability you need, but it is not exposed through a public API**—For example, until JDK 1.4, Java Swing did not provide a method to obtain a list of JComponent listeners. The component would store the listeners in a package-visible variable with no public access to it, so there was no way to find out programmatically whether a component had event listeners.

▶ **You are using a third-party class or an interface, but the functionality exposed is not flexible enough for your application**—A simple change in the API can save you days of work or might be the only solution to your problem. In this case, you are happy with 99% of the library, but the remaining 1% prevents you from being able to use it effectively.

▶ **There is a bug in the product or API you are using and you cannot wait for the vendor to fix it**—JRun 3.0, for instance, had a bug in the JVM version detection on HP UX. While parsing the version string reported by Java Runtime, it would erroneously conclude that it was running under an older version of JDK and refuse to run.

▶ **You need a very close integration with a product, but its architecture is not open enough to satisfy your requirements**—Many frameworks separate interfaces from implementation. Internally interfaces are used to access functionality and concrete classes are instantiated to provide the implementation. Java core libraries for the most part allow specifying implementation classes through system properties. This is the case for AWT Toolkit and SAX parser, where implementation classes can be specified using the java.awt.toolkit and org.xml.sax.driver system properties, respectively. Hacking would be required if you needed to provide a different implementation class for a library that does not provide means of customization.

▶ **You are using third-party code, but the expected functionality is not working**—You are not sure whether it is because you are not using it correctly or because of a bug in the code. The documentation does not refer to the problem and you do not have a workaround. Temporarily inserting debug traces and messages into the third-party code can help you understand what is happening in the system.

▶ **You have an urgent production issue that has to be fixed**—You also cannot afford to go through risky redeployment of the new code to the production environment. The solution to the problem requires a small change in the code that affects only a few classes.

If dealing with third-party code, you might be violating the license agreement, so be sure to read it and run it by your legal department to be safe. Copyright laws can be strictly enforced, and changing third-party code is often illegal. Get the vendor's permission to implement a solution rather than assuming responsibility for the hack. The good news is that by using the method presented in this chapter, you aren't making direct changes to the library or the product you are using. You aren't tampering with the code, but rather providing replacement functionality for the one you are not happy with. In a way, it is like deriving your class from the vendor's class to override a method, although this can be a slippery slope. Legal issues aside, let's see how you can go about doing this.

Finding the Class That Has to Be Patched

First, you have to determine what code has to be patched. Sometimes it's fairly obvious and you will know the specific class or interface right away. If you feel you are too smart to be told how to locate the code, then by all means skip to the section that talks about how to patch. Otherwise, sit back, relax, and learn several approaches to achieving the result.

The General Approach

The general method of locating a class to be patched consists of finding a starting point and navigating the execution sequence until you get to the code you want to change. If you do not encounter the code you want to change in the vicinity of the starting point, you must

STORIES FROM THE TRENCHES

AT&T Wireless was upgrading its order entry system for cell phone activation. Written in Java, it had to be migrated from JDK 1.2 to 1.3. The upgrade was crucial because of the bug fixes in Swing and other Java packages and the fact that users were waiting for a better option. The performance improvement and optimized memory consumption of JDK 1.3 were among other important factors in making the upgrade decision. The development was done on Windows systems, but the production environment was HP UX. When all the bugs were fixed and the unit tested under JDK 1.3, the new version of Java was installed on the staging HP UX server to begin formal integration testing.

Unfortunately, it turned out that the application server used for J2EE services had a bug in detecting the JDK version. There was an error in parsing the version string from the system properties, but because it was different on Windows and Unix, the bug didn't surface until the integration testing phase. The application server refused to run on HP, believing that it was running on an earlier version of Java. At that point, it was too late to go back to JDK 1.2, but there was no fix for the problem. To save the project, the engineers resorted to decompiling the class from the application server that was doing the version checking and fixing the bug themselves. After the patch was deployed, the server was started and worked flawlessly in production. Unfortunately, none of the engineers were sent to Jamaica as a reward—as was promised by management—but such is life.

obtain a new starting point and repeat the process. A good starting point is crucial for quick results. Sometimes picking a class to start is fairly obvious. For example, for API or logic patching the entry point would be the interface or class you want to change. If you want to make a private method of a class into a public method, the starting point is the class in question. If you need to fix a bug that results in a Java exception, the starting point is the class at the top of the stack trace.

Regardless of the situation, after establishing a starting class you should obtain the source code (decompiling the bytecode if you must) and, if necessary, traverse to the class that actually needs to be patched. This process is similar to traversing a sequence diagram, starting from the method just described and examining each class that is invoked on the way. In large systems with hundreds of classes, you might have to identify several starting points and pick the one that provides the shortest route to the code you need to change.

Searching for Text Strings

A large, sophisticated system has dozens of packages and hundreds of classes. If you don't have a clear starting point, you can easily get lost while trying to traverse the application logic. Think about the startup code for an application server such as WebLogic. During startup, WebLogic performs hundreds of tasks and uses many threads to accomplish them— and even with an unlimited supply of caffeine, I would not advise you to try to crack it by traversing from the `weblogic.Server` class.

The most reliable approach for such cases is a text-based search for a string that is known to be close to the target class. Well-written products and libraries can be configured to produce extensive debug information into a log file. Besides the obvious benefits for maintenance and troubleshooting, this makes locating the code responsible for the functionality in question easier. When you configure the application to write a detailed log of the execution sequence and a problem occurs somewhere, you can use the last successful (or the first erroneous) log message to identify the entry point. As you might know, the bytecode stores strings as plain text, which means you can search through all `.class` files for a substring that you have seen in a log file. Suppose while using the security framework, an exception with the text `Invalid username` is thrown on certain names. The reason for rejection is unknown, and so is the solution. The easiest way to get to the code if the stack trace is unavailable is by searching for `Invalid username` in all the `.class` files of the framework. Most likely it will be one or two instances in the entire code, and by decompiling the class file, you will be able to understand the root of the problem. Likewise, you can search all the class files for a method or class name, a GUI label, a substring of an HTML page, or any other string you think is embedded in the Java code.

Working with Obfuscated Code

A worse scenario is when you have to deal with the obfuscated code. A good obfuscator renames packages, classes, methods, and variables. The best products on the market even encode Java strings, so searching for a trace message can yield no results. This turns your task into a hellish toil of understanding the application piece by piece. Here you have to use a more creative approach; otherwise, it is like trying to find a needle in a haystack. Knowing the principles of obfuscation can help you in the navigation. Although the obfuscator has the freedom to change the application class and method names, it cannot do so for system classes. For example, if a library checks for the presence of a file and throws an exception if the file is not there, doing a binary search on the exception string might yield no results if the obfuscator was smart enough to encode it. However, doing a search on `File` or `FileInputStream` can lead you to the related code. Similarly, if the application incorrectly reads the system date or time, you can search for the `java.util.Date` or `getTime` method of the `Calendar` class. The biggest problem is that obfuscated classes cannot always be recompiled after decompilation. Refer to Chapter 2, "Decompiling Classes," for more information.

A Sample Scenario That Requires Patching

We are going to modify the Chat application presented earlier to show the username and hostname instead of just the hostname in the conversation window. As you recall, the original application displays the hostname followed by a colon for each message that is received, as shown in Figure 5.1.

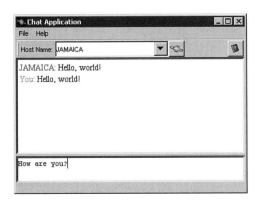

FIGURE 5.1 The main window of the original Chat.

This makes the implementation of the utility easy, but users will certainly prefer to see from which person they are getting messages rather than which computer is used to send the messages. Chat is free and open for enhancements, but no source code exists for it.

As is common with Java applications, the bytecode is shipped in one or several JAR files, so the first task is to create a working directory and unjar all the libraries into it. This allows easy navigation and direct access to the `.class` files, which are the target of our research. After creating a working directory executing `jar xf chat.jar`, we see the following files:

```
images
AboutDialog.class
ChatApplication.class
ChatServer.class
ChatServerRemote.class
MainFrame.class
MainFrame$1.class
MessageInfo.class
MessageListener.class
```

Let's try all the approaches of locating the starting point presented earlier and see which one works best for this application.

Using the Class Name

Luckily, the bytecode is not obfuscated, so we can look at the class names and see whether we can pick the winner. A 5-second examination should lead to the conclusion that `MainFrame` is the best candidate for a first look. Browsing through the decompiled code, we see that all recording of the conversation is done via the `appendMessage` method that looks like this:

```
void appendMessage(String message, MessageInfo messageInfo) {

    if (messageInfo == null) {
        this.conversation.append("<font color=\"red\">");
        this.conversation.append("You");
    }
    else {
        this.conversation.append("<font color=\"blue\">");
        this.conversation.append(messageInfo.getDisplayName());
    }
    this.conversation.append(": ");
    this.conversation.append("</font>");

    this.conversation.append(message);
    this.conversation.append("<br>");
    this.txtConversation.setText(this.conversation.toString() +
                "</BODY></HTML>");
}
```

The implementation of the method uses the `getDisplayName()` method of the `MessageInfo` class to obtain the name of the sender. This leads us to decompiling the `MessageInfo` class to obtain the implementation of `getDisplayName`, shown here:

```
public String getDisplayName() {
    return getHostName();
}
```

Bingo! We have found out that the Chat user interface relies on `MessageInfo` and that the current implementation uses just the hostname. Our task is therefore to patch `MessageInfo.getDisplayName()` to use both the hostname and username.

Searching for Text Strings

Let's pretend that Chat is a large application with more than 500 classes in many different packages. Hoping to guess the right class based on its name is like hoping your code will run correctly after the first compile. You need to use a more reliable method to obtain a starting point. The Chat utility writes pretty decent log messages, so let's try to use it. After starting it, we send a message to another user, get a reply, and get the following output on the Java console:

```
Initializing the chat server...
Trying to get the registry on port 1149
Registry was not running, trying to create one...
ChatApplication server initialized
Sending message to host JAMAICA: test
Received message from host JAMAICA
```

It is not hard to guess that appending a new message to the conversation history occurs when a message is sent or received. It is also fairly obvious that information such as the host that sent or was a destination for a message would not be a part of a static string. Therefore, we will use `Received message from host` as a search criteria for all the `.class` files in the working directory. The search produces one file, `ChatServer.class`, which we promptly decompile to get `ChatServer.jad`. Searching for the string inside the decompiled source code leads us to the `receiveMessage()` method, which is as follows:

```
public void receiveMessage(String message, MessageInfo messageInfo)
    throws RemoteException
{
    System.out.println("Received message from host " + messageInfo.getHostName());
    if(messageListener != null)
        messageListener.messageReceived(message, messageInfo);
}
```

Searching `ChatServer.jad` for `messageListener`, we get to know that it is an interface and a method called `setMessageListener()` sets the listener instance. Now we have two options: One is to find the classes that implement `MessageListener` and see which one (if several exist) is associated with `ChatServer`. Another approach is based on the fact that Java method names are stored as text inside the bytecode. Because the code is not obfuscated, we can search for `setMessageListener()` in all the class files. We will use the latter method and run the search. In our case, it returns two classes, `ChatServer` and `MainFrame`. We conclude that only `MainFrame` acts as a listener on `ChatServer` and proceed to decompile it. The rest of the investigation is performed exactly as in the previous section where we used the class name to find `MainFrame`. In our sample application, guessing the starting point from the class name proved to be faster, but a certain factor of luck is involved. Using log messages is a more reliable approach that works better for most real-life applications.

Using the Call Stack to Navigate Application Logic

Many problems in Java manifest themselves through exceptions. Exceptions can be thrown by Java runtime classes or by the application itself, and of course the error message provided by the exception together with the exception type is usually sufficient to solve the problem. But the reason this book exists is because not all things are simple in life. You can get a NullPointerException or an exception with no error message, and if you are dealing with third-party code, you will have no clue as to how to work around it. As long as the license does not prevent you from decompiling the source code, or if you have the source code itself, you can embark on a search using a much less painful method.

The easiest and most certain way to understand what is causing an exception is to rely on the call stack. You should be aware that operating systems use a stack to keep track of the method calls. If method A calls method B, A's information is placed on the stack. If B further calls method C, B's information is placed on the stack as well. As each method returns, the stack is used to determine which method should resume execution. Anyway, in Java you can access the call stack either through a debugger (by calling printStackTrace() on the exception) or by using the Thread.dumpStack() method. Using a debugger usually proves too burdensome for server-side applications, so for our example, I suggest using the latter two methods. Exception's printStackTrace() is widely used and should not surprise anyone. Thread's dumpStack is not as common but can be extremely helpful if you want to see who is calling a method at runtime. Simply add

```
Thread.dumpStack();
```

to the method body you are investigating and run the application. Every time the method is called, you will know exactly how the execution got to it and which other methods to inspect.

The call stack is addressed in more detail in Chapter 16, "Intercepting Control Flow."

Patching a Class to Provide New Logic

Now that you know what needs to be patched, the actual job is relatively easy. Obtain the source file either directly from the distribution or by decompiling the .class file (make sure the license does not prevent that). For ease of maintenance, you should keep all your patched classes in a separate directory—for example, in patches. Re-create the directory structure to match the package structure of the class and use your favorite IDE or plain-old editor and command-line compiler to make changes to the class. Keep in mind that you are likely to upgrade the library at some point, so you should write comments for every piece of code you insert. That way, when you get the new version of the original class, you can easily repeat the steps. For the same reason, you should isolate your changes and keep them all together in the file. If you are adding a reasonable amount of code, consider creating a helper class and delegating to it so that you make as few changes to the patched file as possible.

In our example we must provide a new implementation for the getDisplayName() method that will use the UserName (HostName) pattern. Then we create a new directory called patches with a subdirectory called covertjava.chat in the application installation directory and copy MessageInfo.jad to it, renaming it to MessageInfo.java. MessageInfo already contains the getUserName() method, so our task is just to concatenate the two strings together. We rewrite the getDisplayName() method to look as follows:

```
public String getDisplayName() {
    return getUserName() + " (" + getHostName() + ")";
// *** original logic patched by Alex Kalinovsky to meet new requirements
//    return getHostName();
}
```

Then we compile MessageInfo.java. Having done this, we can now update the application to put the new logic into effect. We should also document our changes so we can maintain the code in the future.

Reconfiguring the Application to Load and Use the Patched Class

This is the task that actually makes the trick work. We need to ensure that the JVM uses the patched version of the class we provided in place of the old version. This brings us to the cornerstone of Java programming, which is setting the right CLASSPATH. Yes, it's as simple as that. You just need to ensure that the archive (Zip or JAR) or directory that contains the patched version of the class appears in the class search path *before* the archive or directory that contains the original version. In the script file that starts up your application and configures its CLASSPATH, you should make this archive or directory the first entry. Keeping all your patches together but separate from the products and libraries they patch allows for easy maintenance. When you get a new version of a library, you can overwrite the old library JAR files without being afraid of loosing your patches. You must retest, of course, and because the patch relies not only on public interfaces but also on private implementations, you might have to update your patch to match the new library. Last, but not least, if you need to explain to somebody what the heck you have done with the system, you can point to the patches directory and the documentation.

As the saying goes, "All is not what it seems." Sometimes you might *think* the system is loading your new class, but in fact the old version of the class is loaded. The best way to ensure that the new version is used is to add a debug trace or even a crude

System.out.println() for the new class. When you run the application, be sure you see the trace, after which you can remove it. In our sample code we have added a static initializer that prints a message indicating that the patches are in effect, as shown in the following code:

```
static {
    // Log the fact that patch is in effect
    System.out.println("Loaded patched MessageInfo");
}
```

To see our changes in action, we update the start script for the Chat application to include the patches directory. We copy bin/chat.bat to bin/chat_patched.bat and open it in an editor. We then change the CLASSPATH initialization so it includes the patches directory before the application chat.jar file:

```
set CLASSPATH=..\patches;..\lib\chat.jar
```

Next, we save the file and run it. We send a few test messages to localhost and, if all is done correctly, the new screen should look like Figure 5.2.

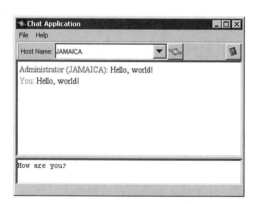

If the class you are patching is a system class, the job is more difficult. The system class is the one that was loaded from the boot class path—for example, java.lang.String. Even if you place the patched version of the class as the first one in the CLASSPATH, it will not replace the original class. To learn how to patch system classes, see Chapter 15, "Replacing and Patching Core Java Classes."

Patching Sealed Packages

FIGURE 5.2   The main window of the patched Chat.

Java supports a notion of *sealed* packages. If a package is sealed, all classes from that package must be loaded from the same JAR file. For application developers and tool vendors, this is a great feature that was supposed to prevent the technique you have just learned. To seal a package, you have to specify an attribute called Sealed with a value of true in the JAR manifest file. When the Chat application's chat.jar is sealed, running bin\chat_patched.bat produces the following exception:

```
Exception in thread "main" java.lang.ExceptionInInitializerError
        at sun.reflect.NativeConstructorAccessorImpl.newInstance0(Native Method)
        at sun.reflect.NativeConstructorAccessorImpl.newInstance
```

```
➥(NativeConstructorAccessorImpl.java:39)
    at sun.reflect.DelegatingConstructorAccessorImpl.newInstance
➥(DelegatingConstructorAccessorImpl.java:27)
    at java.lang.reflect.Constructor.newInstance(Constructor.java:274)
    ...
Caused by: java.lang.SecurityException: sealing violation: package covertjava.chat is
➥sealed
    at java.net.URLClassLoader.defineClass(URLClassLoader.java:225)
    at java.net.URLClassLoader.access$100(URLClassLoader.java:54)
    at java.net.URLClassLoader$1.run(URLClassLoader.java:193)
    at java.security.AccessController.doPrivileged(Native Method)
```

Unfortunately for vendors and fortunately for hackers and inquisitive people like us, sealed packages are frequently easy to break. All you have to do is change the value of the `Sealed` attribute to `false` inside the JAR's manifest or extract the contents of the JAR to a working directory and modify the start script to use this directory instead of the original JAR file. This is an example of a good intention that was never implemented seriously.

Quick Quiz

1. Which approaches can be used in finding a class to be patched?

2. Why is it possible to use a text-based search in locating a class, and when would it not work?

3. How can you obtain a call stack for an arbitrary point in the application (not inside a `catch` block)?

4. What are the requirements for installing a patch?

In Brief

To patch application logic you need to

■ Locate the class that contains the logic

■ Obtain the source for the class

■ Modify the source to implement new logic

■ Compile and deploy the new class file

■ Update the application startup environment to load the new class first

Using Effective Tracing

6

"A complex system that does not work is invariably found to have evolved from a simple system that works just fine."

Murphy's Technology Laws

Introduction to Tracing

Tracing is writing debug messages to an output stream during the execution of an application. It provides a recorded track of operations performed by the running application in real time. Tracing does not require the application to be running in debug mode. Also, because the trace messages are typically written to a log file, tracing provides information for studying the behavior and troubleshooting the application. Tracing has been used for many years, but it became especially popular in server-side programming. When the application is small, it can easily be loaded into a debugger and stepped through to investigate a problem. Distributed systems tend to be much more complex on the server side and often run inside middleware products such as an application or a Web server. This makes using a debugger impractical, and stepping through code can interfere with multithreading. Debugging is not an option at all for running production applications, so tracing is the only plausible method for providing information about what is going on in the system.

Traces are inserted in code almost like comments, and good tracing makes comments unnecessary. Because tracing results in method calls and messages written to a stream, it can become expensive—especially if placed inside loops and frequently called methods. Logging frameworks are designed to add minimum overhead to code execution, and they can be configured to reduce the level of trace messages that are written to the output stream. It is important to realize, however, that tracing that is not very well optimized is still better than no tracing at all. If a problem exists in a production application without traces, the only source of information is user feedback, which as we all know, is often unreliable or inaccurate. Good use of traces allows tracking the user's action and the application's response to it, which should be adequate to identify the source of the problem in most cases. You should include some sort of user identification in each trace so the log file can be filtered on operations performed by a specific user.

Java did not have a standard logging API until JDK 1.4. This is somewhat unfortunate given the popularity and importance of logging for J2EE applications. As a result of this late standardization, each vendor and many application developers had to create their own version of the tracing and logging API. Today, it is common to see various versions of the logging API, sometimes even in the same application. For example, a J2EE application running inside WebLogic might be using Log4J for its own debug traces but using WebLogic logging API to report system-level critical errors. All logging APIs support a concept of log message levels that control how many messages are written to the log file.

STORIES FROM THE TRENCHES

A couple of years ago, I was called by our major client to make an assessment of the current state of its project and provide recommendations on improvements. Things were not going well at the client side, and both the management and the development team were frustrated with the slow progress and inability to quickly fix defects. Examination of the code revealed that there was no systematic use of traces. The developers at best would use an occasional `System.out` to print the value of a variable, but the running application was akin to a black hole—nobody knew what was going on at any point in time. Even a simple problem was hard to fix because the conditions that lead to it and sometimes even the origin of the problem were unknown.

My first recommendation was to therefore invest three days in inserting logging into the code. The entire team stopped doing their current tasks and went through the code, adding traces that printed the names of methods being called and the business parameters such as usernames, order numbers, and database record IDs. These three days paid off almost immediately. With the effective tracing, identifying and fixing defects was easy without even having to debug the code. Even if part of the application was written by someone else, the traces provided the insight into the execution process. What is more important, when the system was put into production, the log file was the main source of information about the current state of the system and operations performed throughout the day.

Tracing As an Effective Method of Learning the Software

We already talked about the importance of tracing for the troubleshooting of large systems. The information provided in trace logs is also invaluable for understanding the execution flow of an application and identifying the starting points for reverse engineering. Because traces are designed to provide a human-readable history of operations performed by a product, they are easier to read than decompiled Java code. The log file presents a snapshot of the work done so far. Thus, if a bug results in an exception with no stack trace, you can turn on the most detailed level of tracing, re-create the bug, and find the last message that made it into the log file before the exception. The same technique can be used to locate code that needs to be patched. If the application does not provide adequate tracing, you can add trace messages and even thread stack dumps to classes using patching. Although tedious, it can be the only effective way of studying obfuscated code, especially if control flow obfuscation was used. Tracing takes the guessing out of the picture because trace messages provide undisputable evidence that a certain piece of code executed at a given moment in time.

If the application is not printing log messages already, inserting traces can be time-consuming, and—let's admit it—it is not the type of challenge a good developer is looking for. A quick-and-dirty way of getting a glimpse at the runtime state is printing the call stack of the current thread from a method under investigation, as described in Chapter 5, "Replacing and Patching Application Classes." Recall that adding a call to the `dumpStack()` method of `java.lang.Thread` causes it to print the names of methods that form the call stack. With just one line of code, you can get a good understanding of which calls led to the invocation of the method in question.

Tracing and Logging Tools and APIs

There are two dominant logging APIs today. The first one is Apache's Log4J, which dates back to 1999 when it was started by IBM's AlphaWorks group. It has come a long way and today is probably the most advanced and flexible logging API. It is free and can be distributed as a standalone JAR file, which is compatible with all versions of JDK starting from 1.1. Because of the Apache group's brand recognition and the great set of features found in Log4J, it has gained enormous popularity among Java developers and can be considered the de facto standard for Java logging.

The second framework is Sun's Java Logging API, which has been made the official standard. For better or worse, JCP has decided not to use Log4J but to create a new standard. The Java Logging API is also powerful and flexible, although it lacks some of the advanced features found in Log4J, including

- Logging to system logs such as the Windows NT Event log and Unix Syslog

- Log file rotation based on the date

- C language `printf`-like formatting patterns

- Reloading the configuration file

Reloading the configuration file is an important feature for highly available applications. Typically, the configuration is read when a framework is initialized, which is usually at the application startup. Changes to the log levels and categories are not picked up until the application is restarted. Troubleshooting a running production system rules out the possibility of frequent restarts, so without the reloading feature the logging level has to be decided before you start the application.

For the purposes of hacking and reverse engineering, Log4J is clearly a better choice because it can be used with all versions of JDK. The download and online documentation are available at `http://jakarta.apache.org/log4j`.

Tracing Do's and Don'ts

Tracing is extremely important for large distributed applications, but if it's not used carefully, it can significantly degrade the application performance. Following is a set of simple rules for effective tracing.

Tracing Do's

- Do use tracing as much as possible.

- Make sure each trace includes the time, class, and method name that produced the trace.

- Do write traces before and after critical parts of code, such as external system calls, database calls, and disk access. This enables easy identification of the point of failure.

- Do include values of parameters and context variables that will help you understand the execution context at the time of the trace. For example, including the user ID in each trace helps filter the log file on operations performed on behalf of a specific user.

- Do trace out exceptions with the stack trace when it is first caught.

- Do be sure to use different trace levels when writing messages. Use the critical level for system and error messages and the debug level for noisy messages that are not very important for troubleshooting the system. This enables you to control the size of the log file and the overhead on the application.

Tracing Don'ts

- Don't use `System.out.println` to write traces. This imposes permanent overhead on the application and does not allow flexibility. Use a logging framework instead.

- Don't use `Exception.printStackTrace()` to output an exception because it always writes the output to the `System.out`. Use methods provided by the logging framework.

- Don't insert traces into loops with hundreds or thousands of repetitions.

- Don't insert traces into small methods that are called frequently.

Another practice to avoid is using the + operator to concatenate strings when passing parameters to the logging framework. Even if the tracing level is raised, the runtime will still perform the expensive operation of allocating a new buffer for a resulting string and copying the argument strings into it. Thus, instead of using

```
logger.debug("Message received from host: " + host + ", text: " + text)
```

use

```
if (logger.isDebugEnabled() == true)
    logger.debug("Message received from host: " + host + ", text: " + text)
```

The cost of executing the second piece of code is much lower because the string concatenation does not take place unless the debugging traces are enabled.

Quick Quiz

1. How is tracing different from debugging?

2. How can tracing be used to hack an application?

3. Why is the reloading of the logging configuration at runtime important?

4. Why is using + for string concatenation dangerous?

In Brief

- Tracing is writing debug messages to an output stream during the execution of an application.

- Traces are inserted as API calls into the application code.

- Traces add performance overhead, but it is justified by the improved troubleshooting.

- Adding traces to an application helps in understanding its execution flow.

- Log4J and Java Logging API are both good choices for logging frameworks. Log4J is more advanced and can be used with JDKs prior to 1.1, which makes it a better choice for hacking.

Manipulating Java Security

7

"An expert is one who knows more and more about less and less until he knows absolutely everything about nothing."

Murphy's Technology Laws

Java Security Overview

From the beginning Java was designed to be secure. Security includes language features such as array index range checks, bytecode verification, and controlled access to critical system resources such as files and user information. At the beginning the security model assumed that all locally installed classes should be granted access to system resources and that all bytecode downloaded via the network should be restricted from sensitive information and operations. As Java matured, the distinction between the local and remote classes somewhat blurred. Application servers and Web servers rely on the security model to ensure that one component, such as a Web application, does not violate another. Signed applets allow downloaded code to access local files, the clipboard, and system properties.

Various core classes at runtime use the security framework to check whether the caller should be allowed to perform the requested operation. At the center of the security model is an instance of java.lang.SecurityManager that acts as a facade for the java.security package. Java uses the concept of a *permission* to represent access to system information or a resource. For example, PropertyPermission represents access to system properties. Before executing the method logic, core classes use the security manager to check whether the caller is granted the appropriate permissions. An easy way to understand how the mechanism works is to look at the implementation of the System.setProperty() method, shown in Listing 7.1.

LISTING 7.1 System.setProperty

```java
public static String setProperty(String key, String value) {
    if (key == null) {
        throw new NullPointerException("key can't be null");
    }
    if (key.equals("")) {
        throw new IllegalArgumentException("key can't be empty");
    }
    if (security != null)
        security.checkPermission(new PropertyPermission(key, "write"));
    return (String) props.setProperty(key, value);
}
```

The implementation first obtains the system security manager. If one is installed and the parameters are valid, it then uses the security manager to verify that PropertyPermission to write into the given key is granted. The security manager's checkPermission method throws a SecurityException exception if the permission is not granted. The system property is set to the new value only if checkPermission returns successfully. Table 7.1 lists the operations governed by the security manager.

TABLE 7.1

Operations Protected by the Security Manager

TYPE	PROTECTED OPERATIONS
System	Access packages
	Access member variables and methods of a class
	Load native libraries
	Exit the system
	Start and stop threads
	Create custom class loaders
Input, Output, Network	Create, remove, read, and write files
	Traverse directories
	Create sockets
	Load classes from a network URL
AWT/Swing	Access the clipboard
	Access the system event queue
	Display windows without a warning message
	Get a print job

The information on which permissions are granted to which classes is stored in Java policy files. The systemwide java.policy file is loaded first from the ${java.home}/lib/security directory, where ${java.home} is the JRE installation directory. If it exists, the ${user.home}/.java.policy file is loaded next. A custom Java policy file can be specified at the command line using the -Djava.security.policy parameter. A detailed discussion of Java security and permissions can be found at http://java.sun.com/j2se/1.3/docs/guide/security/permissions.html.

Java security includes APIs for encryption (JCE), authentication and authorization (JAAS), secure sockets support (JSSE), and many others. These additional APIs provide powerful means of protecting the information, but they are not used directly in a typical application. We are going to focus on the security features an application developer is most likely to face.

Bypassing Security Checks

From the perspective of this book, we are mostly interested in bypassing the security checks performed by Java runtime. The three configuration scenarios that determine the strictness of the security model are as follows:

- The security manager is not installed.
- The security manager is installed with a default policy.
- The security manager is installed with a custom policy.

STORIES FROM THE TRENCHES

We were planning to use a third-party deployment technology to roll out our Swing application to thousands of user desktops. The product we were going to use supported automatic updates, which required the application to be started by the product's launcher rather than as a standalone application. To implement the automatic update via HTTP, the product was installing its own HTTP handler that conflicted with the SSL-enabled HTTP handler used by our application. Java does not support the dynamic switching of protocol handlers because it stores and reuses the implementation instances from a private cache. The only way to get around the problem was to forcefully clear the cache upon application startup. We used the technique for accessing private members described in Chapter 4, "Hacking Non-Public Methods and Variables of a Class," which requires a security manager and a custom policy file. We shipped the policy file, allowing unrestricted access to class members via the reflection API with our application, and after clearing the cache at the startup, we got the product to coexist with our code.

The Security Manager Is Not Installed

If the security manager is not installed, the checks are simply not going to be performed. As you have seen in Listing 7.1, the permission checking is done only if the system security manager instance is not null. By default, Java applications (but not applets or Web start applications) run without a security manager, which means the code has virtually unrestricted access to system information and resources. For instance, without a security manager, any class can read the name of the user account from the user.name system property. Not having a security manager installed is therefore not recommended for applications that require a secure environment.

The Security Manager Is Installed with a Default Policy

Installing a security manager enables permission checking for information and resource access. This is the default model for applets and Web start applications that run in a sandbox. The security manager can be installed by setting the -Djava.security.manager command-line option to java or by calling System.setSecurityManager(). If no custom policy file is specified, the default file is loaded and used. The default policy allows just a handful of permissions, resulting in a relatively secure runtime environment. Following is a shortened version of the default policy file that shows which permissions are granted:

```
grant codeBase "file:${java.home}/lib/ext/*" {
    permission java.security.AllPermission;
};

grant {
    // Allows any thread to stop itself using the java.lang.Thread.stop()
    // method that takes no argument.
    permission java.lang.RuntimePermission "stopThread";

    // allows anyone to listen on un-privileged ports
    permission java.net.SocketPermission "localhost:1024-", "listen";

    // "standard" properties that can be read by anyone
    permission java.util.PropertyPermission "java.version", "read";
    ...
}
```

If permission is not explicitly granted, it is not allowed. For instance, accessing a private method through reflection requires a RuntimePermission of type accessDeclaredMembers and a ReflectPermission of type suppressAccessChecks. If you try to run the test shown in Chapter 4 with the security manager installed, the application fails with a security exception.

There are several ways of granting permissions to code. The easiest one is to create a custom Java security policy file that contains all the required permissions and specify it on the command line using the -Djava.security.policy property. This approach was shown in Chapter 4.

The Security Manager Is Installed with a Custom Policy

What if the security manager is installed and a custom policy file is already specified using the -D option? This is often the case with application servers and Web servers that rely on Java security to isolate J2EE applications. Two more alternatives are available for granting additional permissions. Obviously, you can just edit the custom policy file of the product that runs your code or the system policy file, but this is not a clean solution.

A better way is to name your policy file .java.policy and place it in the user's home directory. The Java runtime first loads the system policy file from ${java.home} and then loads the user policy file from ${user.home}. You wouldn't have to change any existing scripts or files, which isolates your changes and ensures easy maintenance.

Another alternative is to include a reference to your policy file into the java.security file that can be found in the ${java.home}/lib/security subdirectory. This file describes the security configuration and specifies which policy files to load and in what order. You can find references to the system policy file and the user policy file there; to include your policy file, you should add the following line:

```
policy.url.3=file:/C:/Projects/CovertJava/distrib/conf/java.policy
```

Be sure to use the path that corresponds to the file location on your computer. "3" is the next available index in the policy file URLs list.

Quick Quiz

1. Which class acts as a facade for Java security framework?

2. What role do permissions play?

3. Which files are loaded to determine the permissions to be granted, and in what order?

In Brief

- Java security controls access to system information and resources through permissions.

- The security manager is in the center of the security model. If it is not installed, no checks are performed.

- Permissions can be granted in Java policy files.

- Policy files can be specified on the command line or through the Java security configuration file.

Snooping the Runtime Environment

"Logic is a systematic method of coming to the wrong conclusion with confidence."

Murphy's Technology Laws

The Value of Understanding the Runtime Environment

Hacking systems and troubleshooting applications often require manipulation of various system parameters. For example, to install a patched version of a class in Chapter 5, "Replacing and Patching Application Classes," we modified the value of the CLASSPATH variable. In Chapter 7, "Manipulating Java Security," you saw how to use a system property to install the security manager. Understanding the runtime environment and knowing the exact values of system parameters enables you to base your work on knowledge instead of assumptions. In this chapter, you learn how to obtain the values of system properties, check whether a security manager is installed, and get various memory and network information.

Most of the useful information is easily accessible through Java API classes, as long as you know where to look. Because of the cross-platform nature of Java, the information about the underlying hardware and physical resources is limited. In this chapter, we create a snoop class that consolidates and prints all the useful environment information. It can be called from a running application or run separately using either covertjava.snoop.RuntimeInfo as the main class or snoop_re.bat. For example, application servers are usually started through a series of batch files or shell scripts that configure the environment variables and application parameters. Server startup code can change the default state of the environment, and the only reliable way of knowing the current values is to trace them out.

System Properties

System properties are name-value pairs that provide information about the runtime environment. They include data on the operating system and the JVM vendor and version, the paths for class and library loading, the user's home and current directories, and other useful properties. The meaning of each property can be found on the Net, and I encourage you to familiarize yourself with it. A good place to start is the JavaDoc for the `java.lang.System` class, which can be found at `http://java.sun.com/j2se/1.4.1/docs/api/java/lang/System.html`. Listing 8.1 shows how to print all the system properties.

LISTING 8.1   printSystemProperties Source Code

```
public void printSystemProperties(PrintStream stream) {
    StringBuffer buffer = new StringBuffer(1000);
    Properties props = System.getProperties();
    for (Enumeration keys = props.keys(); keys.hasMoreElements();) {
        String key = (String)keys.nextElement();
        buffer.append(key);
        buffer.append("=");
        buffer.append(System.getProperty(key));
        buffer.append('\n');
    }
    stream.print(buffer.toString());
}
```

Running this method produces output similar to the following:

```
java.vm.version=1.4.1-b21
java.vm.vendor=Sun Microsystems Inc.
java.vendor.url=http://java.sun.com/
java.vm.name=Java HotSpot(TM) Client VM
...
```

System properties can be changed using the System.setProperty() method. If a security manager is installed, it is used to ensure that the caller has the write permission for the required property. Some properties are read only at initialization, which makes them behave as if they were read-only. For example, the java.class.path property describes the path that is used to load classes. Even though you can alter the value of this property, doing so does not produce the desired effect because the system class loader reads it only one time and therefore does not see the change. Manipulating Java security was discussed in detail in Chapter 7.

System Information

System properties cover the environment information very well. However, a few more key aspects of the system deserve our attention. We want to see whether a security manager is set to determine how secure the environment is. We also want to know which class loader was used to load the class to see how much room for manipulation of class loading we have. Finally, we want to see how many CPUs are available for licensing and performance considerations. Listing 8.2 shows the source code that obtains this information.

LISTING 8.2   printSystemInfo Source Code

```java
public void printSystemInfo(PrintStream stream) {
    StringBuffer buffer = new StringBuffer(200);
    buffer.append("Security manager: ");
    buffer.append(System.getSecurityManager() == null?
            "null": System.getSecurityManager().getClass().getName());
    buffer.append('\n');

    buffer.append("Class loader for this class: ");
    ClassLoader classLoader = this.getClass().getClassLoader();
    buffer.append(classLoader == null?
            "null": classLoader.getClass().getName());
    buffer.append('\n');

    buffer.append("Number of available processors to JVM: ");
    buffer.append(Runtime.getRuntime().availableProcessors());
    buffer.append('\n');

    stream.println(buffer.toString());
}
```

Memory Information

The JVM manages the memory available to a Java application. When the application requests more memory, the JVM first checks whether it can satisfy the request from the free memory that is already allocated for the process. If there is not enough free memory, the JVM might force garbage collection in an attempt to free up the memory used by dead objects. If garbage collection fails to free enough memory, the JVM tries to obtain more memory from the operating system, thus increasing the total allocated memory. It keeps getting more memory from the OS until the allowed maximum, which is 16MB by default but can be specified using the -Xmx parameter.

Memory management is crucial to the health and performance of Java applications. The details of garbage collection and effective memory usage are beyond the subject of this book, but you will learn how to obtain the size of various memory pools. The best way to monitor the application's memory usage is via a profiler, such as JProble or OptimizeIt. However, they require the application to be run in a debug mode, which is not acceptable for production systems. The new breed of tools, such as Wily Introscope and Borland Server Trace, can monitor and display the memory usage of any running application with minimal overhead. However, they rely on the same method as we will use and can be too expensive for many Java applications. Listing 8.3 shows the implementation of a method that prints the current memory profile of the JVM.

LISTING 8.3   printMemoryInfo Source Code

```
public void printMemoryInfo(PrintStream stream) {
    StringBuffer buffer = new StringBuffer(200);
    buffer.append("Maximum memory allowed for JVM: ");
    buffer.append(toMb(Runtime.getRuntime().maxMemory()));
    buffer.append(" Mb\n");
    buffer.append("Memory currently allocated in JVM: ");
    buffer.append(toMb(Runtime.getRuntime().totalMemory()));
    buffer.append(" Mb\n");
    buffer.append("Free memory in JVM: ");
    buffer.append(toMb(Runtime.getRuntime().freeMemory()));
    buffer.append(" Mb\n");
    stream.println(buffer.toString());
}
```

The helper function toMb converts the given value in bytes to megabytes with two precision points. It can be found in the RuntimeInfo class.

Network Information

There is not a whole lot that can be learned about the network environment by a Java application. Java is a cross-platform, high-level language, which makes it a less-than-ideal choice for implementing low-level OS utilities and drivers. About the only useful information that can be obtained from the runtime is the local hostname and IP address. This can be used for licensing purposes, where licenses are issued per server and are node locked. More information about the underlying network and hardware configuration can be obtained using the JNI and C libraries that make native calls to the OS. Listing 8.4 shows how to obtain the host information.

LISTING 8.4   printNetworkInfo Source Code

```
public void printNetworkInfo(PrintStream stream) {
    StringBuffer buffer = new StringBuffer(200);
    InetAddress localhost = null;
    try {
        localhost = java.net.InetAddress.getLocalHost();
        buffer.append("Local host name: ");
        buffer.append(localhost.getHostName());
        buffer.append('\n');
        buffer.append("Local host IP address: ");
        buffer.append(localhost.getHostAddress());
    }
    catch (UnknownHostException ex) {
        buffer.append("*** Failed to detect network properties " +
                    "due to UnknownHostException: ");
        buffer.append(ex.getMessage());
    }
    stream.println(buffer.toString());
}
```

Accessing Environment Variables

Environment variables provide a good way to parameterize an application. For example, the application installation directory might be different from host to host, and Java does not have a reliable way to find out where the application was installed. That is why a common practice is to define the APP_HOME environment variable and pass it to the Java application.

You shouldn't use too many environment variables because doing so complicates batch file and shell script programming. A better alternative is to rely on configuration files in Java properties or XML format and an environment variable that specifies the location of the configuration files. The correct way of accessing the environment variables in Java is to pass it on the command line using the -D switch. I like prepending all environment variable names with the env prefix for clarity. The following example shows how to pass the values of the TEMP and COMPUTERNAME environment variables on Windows to the snoop utility we are developing in this chapter:

```
set JAVA_ARGS=%JAVA_ARGS% -Denv.temp=%TEMP%
set JAVA_ARGS=%JAVA_ARGS% -Denv.computername=%COMPUTERNAME%

java %JAVA_ARGS% covertjava.snoop.RuntimeInfo
```

The Java application can then obtain the value of the variable using the System.getProperty() method, with the name that was defined on the command line. In our example, the value of the TEMP variable can be obtained using System.getProperty("env.temp").

Quick Quiz

1. When would you snoop the runtime environment?

2. What information about the runtime environment is available through the standard Java API?

3. How can OS- or hardware-specific information that is unavailable through standard APIs be retrieved?

In Brief

- Obtaining a snapshot of environment values is a reliable way of understanding the runtime configuration of a running application.

- System properties available through the System.getProperty() method provide most of the information on the runtime environment.

- A snapshot of memory sizes can help in understanding the effectiveness of the application memory management in a production environment.

- Network information is limited to the name and IP address of the local host.

- Environment variable values can be passed to a Java application using the -D command-line parameter.

Cracking Code with Unorthodox Debuggers

"Any simple theory will be worded in the most complicated way."
Murphy's Technology Laws

Understanding the Internals of Unknown Applications

Writing a chapter on using a conventional debugger is on the border of insulting the reader's intelligence. If you can't figure out how to use a debugger on your own, you probably should think of a career change. Rather, the focus of this chapter is on using an unorthodox tool that offers a different approach to looking inside the running applications. Even though I talk about *debugging*, what you really are going to learn are the internals of unknown applications. Working with the source code is generally a preferred way of doing it, but in certain cases a debugger is irreplaceable, including when

■ You are working with a large application that does not have good tracing.

■ Reading application source code does not provide a clear understanding of the internal logic because of a sophisticated object hierarchy and kludgy programming practices.

■ You are working with an application that was aggressively obfuscated.

Conventional Debuggers and Their Limitations

Java was designed with debugging in mind from the start. The standard Java Debug API relies on the concept of a remote viewer to the process being debugged. This standard allows vendors to implement their own debuggers with a wide range of features. Some of them do not go much further than allowing the developer to place breakpoints and step through the application code. More advanced debuggers provide additional features, such as conditional breakpoints that stop the execution when a variable has a certain value or when a certain exception is thrown.

The conventional debuggers help in coding and fixing bugs, but they are not effective for reverse engineering or troubleshooting a complex application. The biggest problem with these debuggers is that they display information only for the current moment, and as soon as the moment is gone, the information is irrevocably lost. To be effective, conventional debuggers require strategically placed breakpoints throughout the code, which is obviously a tedious process—especially if the code is not very well known.

For example, say you obtained the Chat application and wanted to learn how it processes incoming messages. Although you can load and run it in a debug mode, how do you know where to place the breakpoint? Even with a small application such as Chat, stepping through the code won't help you because the messages are delivered on an RMI thread asynchronously. Only decompiling and carefully studying the code can lead you to the `receiveMessage` method defined in `ChatServerRemote` and implemented in `ChatServer`. If you try to reverse engineer the version of Chat that was obfuscated with Zelix KlassMaster, the task becomes difficult, to say the least. You need a better tool to help you with the task. Enter the Omniscient debugger.

Hacking with an Omniscient Debugger

Omniscient debugging enables you to record the state of the executing program and then go back in time to examine the states. It is different from conventional debugging because the user application is not run in debug mode and therefore it cannot be paused. The idea behind the omniscient debugger is to record as much information as possible about the threads and variables, their values, the standard input and output streams, and the loaded classes. After the information is recorded, the application can be stopped or closed. The debugger can then be used to trace the execution from the start or from the end, or starting from a particular moment in time identified by a method call or a message written to the standard output stream. This makes setting the breakpoints unnecessary, and you can be sure that you won't miss operations processed asynchronously.

Currently, the only implementation of this approach I know of is Omniscient Debugger (ODB) by Bil Lambda. It is distributed under GPL license and can be downloaded from `http://www.lambdacs.com/debugger/debugger.html`. It still needs quite a bit of work, especially on the UI side, but it does the jobs of recording and investigating amazingly well. ODB uses a bytecode decoration technique to insert the code that records the information required for debugging. We are going to pretend that we know nothing about the internal implementation of Chat and use Bil's Omniscient Debugger to learn how Chat processes incoming messages.

Recording Chat Execution

We begin by recording the execution of Chat in ODB. Covert Java distribution includes the latest version of ODB at the time of writing. It is placed in the `lib` directory and is used by default. You can check for a newer version of ODB and use it if you find one. Run `debugChat.bat` located in the `distrib\bin` directory; this batch file configures the environment for ODB and tells it to run `covertjava.chat.ChatApplication` on startup. After ODB has loaded, it opens its main window and runs Chat. When prompted for the source code location of `ChatApplicaton`, we click the No Source Available button to restrict our work to bytecode. Figure 9.1 shows the debugger window after the initialization step.

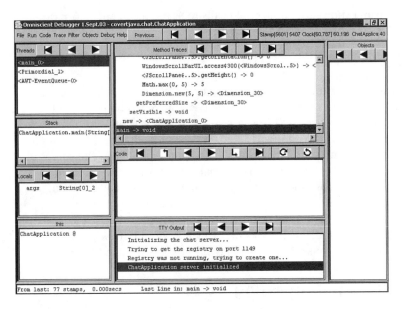

FIGURE 9.1 The ODB window after initialization.

The ODB user interface is not the most intuitive, but after you get used to it, you'll be able to navigate it effectively. To the left of the menu at the very top is the Stamp toolbar. ODB records program execution in a sequence of time stamps, and the Stamp toolbar enables you to go back and forward through this sequence. A number of panels display the information about the application state:

- ▶ **Threads**—This panel shows all the recorded threads. If the name of a thread is prepended with ··, that means that, at the current time stamp, the thread has not been created yet. If the thread is dead, it is shown as Dead.

- ▶ **Stack**—This panel shows the call stack for the currently selected thread.

- ▶ **Locals**—This panel shows the names and values of local variables for the selected method in the call stack or Method Traces panel.

- ▶ **This**—This panel shows the result of calling toString() on the object whose method is currently selected.

- ▶ **Method Traces**—This panel shows the sequence of method calls, including the nested calls that are indented.

- ▶ **Code**—This panel shows the source code if it is available.

- ▶ **TTY Output**—This panel shows the intercepted calls to System.out.println (no other methods of output are currently supported by ODB).

- ▶ **Objects**—This panel shows the stringified versions of objects that are being watched.

Let's try to comprehend the information displayed in Figure 9.1. We can see that, after the initialization, the Chat application has three threads. One is <main_0>, which is currently selected and doesn't have a call stack because it has actually finished execution; however, we can see the methods that run on this thread in the Method Traces panel. Scrolling through the Method Traces panel gives us the complete log of method names and even the values of the parameters. Clicking a method in the Method Traces panel takes us to the moment in time that the method was executed and updates the other panels with the corresponding information. Similarly, clicking a message in the TTY Output panel enables us to see who printed it and when. To trace the program execution from the start, click the First Timestamp of Any Thread button in the Stamp toolbar (it looks like a VCR Rewind button), and then click the Next Timestamp button (it looks like a VCR Play button) to advance step by step.

Navigating the Message Processing Code

We are now ready to crack the message processing code of the Chat application. First, we must work around a bug in ODB that prevents it from capturing information on dynamically loaded classes. Press Alt+Tab to go to the Debug Controller window that has a Stop Recording button and a few check boxes that specify the recording options. Click the Stop Recording button; when its label changes to Start Recording, click it again. Then press Alt+Tab to open the Chat application window. Type **localhost** in the Host Name combo box and type **Hello** in the message text field. Press Enter to send the message and ensure that it appears in the Chat conversation field. Because we ran Chat from the debugger, our input and the application response to it have been recorded, and we can now go back to the debugger window to examine the traces. Click the Last Timestamp Recorded (Any Thread) button in the Stamp toolbar to fast forward the display to the end of the recorded sequence. The TTY Output panel should now show more lines. Click the line that says Received message from host.... The debugger window should look similar to Figure 9.2.

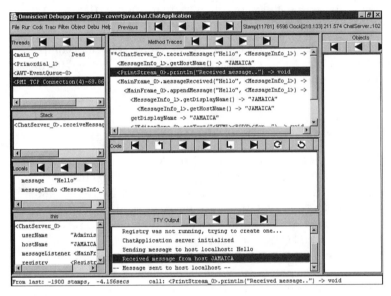

FIGURE 9.2 The ODB window after the message is sent.

From the information displayed in the debugger panels, we can gather that the message was printed by the ChatServer.receiveMessage method running on an RMI TCP Connection thread. This makes sense because, as we know, Chat relies on RMI to deliver the messages. Scrolling through the Method Traces panel, we can see exactly what was done before and after the System.out.println call. We can see that the message text is obtained from the MessageInfo class and appended to JEditorPane inside MainFrame. Even without the source code, we have a pretty good understanding of the Chat message processing logic.

Our task was made easy because we saw a trace message, Received message from host..., which led us directly to the method responsible for message processing. What if this clue was not available? Several approaches can lead us to the same results. After recording the actions, we could look at the Threads panel first. Knowing Java architecture should help us decide which threads to look at. For example, knowing that remote communication between Java applications is likely to use RMI and that RMI processes incoming calls on its own thread, we can look for such threads. Not surprisingly, after fast forwarding the debugger to the end of message sending, we can see a new thread—RMI TCP Connection.... Clicking the thread in the Threads panel displays the methods that executed on it, and—voilá—we again see ChatServer.receiveMessage at the top of the trace.

Another good way of finding the message processing logic is to use the Search feature of ODB. Although not very sophisticated, it allows searching for a test string in a trace panel. In our case, we know that the message text was Hello. If we are unsure about which thread was used to run the message processing logic, we can turn on the Any Thread OK option in the Code menu of the debugger. Then we can select Search from the Trace menu and type **Hello**. Pressing Enter will tell the debugger to find and select the trace that contains the search string, which in our case is... you guessed it, ChatServer.receiveMessage.

After the class and the method are located, we can use either the source code or decompiled code to study the implementation logic. A conventional debugger can now be used to run the application in debug mode and see "live" data because we know where to place the breakpoints.

Using ODB to Crack the Obfuscated Version of Chat

Chapter 3, "Obfuscating Classes," and Chapter 4, "Hacking Non-Public Methods and Variables of a Class," discussed the obfuscation and the difficulties in cracking the applications that were aggressively obfuscated. Decompiling obfuscated code can be tedious, and understanding the inner workings of a large application can prove to be impossible. Using a debugger such as ODB is the best way of working with such applications because, rather than trying to imagine the sequence of method calls, you can simply study its recorded version. The same approaches that were used to locate the starting point for regular classes can be used for obfuscated code. To illustrate the point, let's do the same exercise in understanding Chat's message processing, but this time on the obfuscated version.

We change the CLASSPATH inside debugChat.bat to use lib\obfuscated\chat.jar instead of lib\chat.jar. We then run the debugger and follow the same recording steps as described in the previous sections. After the message is sent, we fast forward the debugger to the end of the recording using the Stamp toolbar. Comparing the information displayed in the debugger panels with the information displayed for unobfuscated Chat, we can see that it is fundamentally the same. Although the names of the Chat classes and methods have changed, the call stacks and parameter values have not. Neither has the system information, such as the Java core classes and thread names. Listing 9.1 shows the contents of the Method Traces panel for obfuscated Chat.

LISTING 9.1   Method Traces Panel Contents

```
**<d_0>.receiveMessage("Hello", <MessageInfo_1>) -> void
  <MessageInfo_1>.a() -> "JAMAICA"
  <PrintStream_0>.println("Received message..") -> void
  <f_0>.a("Hello", <MessageInfo_1>) -> void
    <f_0>.b("Hello", <MessageInfo_1>) -> void
      <MessageInfo_1>.b() -> "JAMAICA"
        <MessageInfo_1>.a() -> "JAMAICA"
      b -> "JAMAICA"
      <JEditorPane_0>.setText("<HTML><BODY><fon..") -> void
    b -> void
  a -> void
receiveMessage -> void
```

We can still use the debugger to find out which method has printed the Received message from host... message or which method trace line includes the Hello string. This gives us a great advantage in locating the starting point for studying the application.

Quick Quiz

1. What are the reasons to use a debugger in hacking?

2. What are the limitations of conventional debuggers?

3. What is the principle behind the implementation of ODB?

4. Which approaches can be used to locate implementation logic in ODB?

In Brief

- A debugger can provide a shortcut to locating the implementation logic in a large application or obfuscated code.

- Conventional debuggers' main limitations are the necessity to set breakpoints in key locations and the lack of history of state changes and method calls.

- ODB records time stamps of the executing application and enables you to navigate it to understand the internal logic.

- ODB is the best approach to cracking obfuscated applications.

Using Profilers for Application Runtime Analysis

"No bug can be fixed correctly after 4:30 p.m. on Friday. The correct solution will become self-evident at 9:15 a.m. on Monday."

Murphy's Technology Laws

Why and When You Should Use Profiling

The term *profiling* is traditionally used to describe the process of measuring the method execution times to find and fix performance bottlenecks. However, in the Java world this term has been expanded to include collecting various metrics and allowing runtime thread and object debugging. The following are some of the reasons to use a profiler for a Java application:

- To investigate heap usage and garbage collection frequency to improve performance

- To browse object allocation and references to find and fix memory leaks

- To investigate thread allocation and synchronization to find locking and data race problems, and to improve performance

- To identify expensive methods to improve performance

- To investigate an application at runtime to gain a better understanding of its internal structure

Profiling is generally done after the development phase, and if you haven't used a profiler yet, it can be an eye opener. The three main high-level goals in using a profiler are to improve application performance, fix bugs that are hard to find in the code, and understand what is going on in the application at runtime as it performs the business logic.

The Best Profilers for Java

To be effective, you need the right tools. The three best-known profilers for Java are JProbe Suite by Quest Software (originally developed by KLGroup), OptimizeIt Suite by Borland, and JProfiler by ej-technologies. All three are good and can do the job almost equally well. I like that JProfiler integrates all the functionality into one application, as opposed to having separate tools for profiling, memory debugging, and thread debugging. JProbe was probably the first tool of this kind and is still the best. Besides providing the functionality available in other tools, it provides a neat heap graph window that shows objects as rectangular nodes and allows navigating the object graphs in a variety of ways. The other tools show the object graph only as a tree, which simplifies the display but is not as visual. This, as well as the other extra features of JProbe, make it my tool of choice for memory debugging. We are going to primarily use it throughout the rest of this chapter, but you are free to select the tool you prefer or have a license for.

Investigating Heap Usage and Garbage Collection Frequency to Improve the Performance

Garbage collection is a great feature of Java that frees developers from having to explicitly release the allocated objects. The price paid for this simplicity is the performance overhead that is incurred when the garbage collection runs. The latest versions of JVM use generational garbage collection, which can run asynchronously; even after these improvements, though, the overhead is still significant. It is easy to underestimate the effect of garbage collection on application performance.

JProbe, as well as the other profilers, shows the runtime heap summary graph for a running application. It enables the monitoring of the total size of the allocated memory and the available free memory, as shown in Figure 10.1.

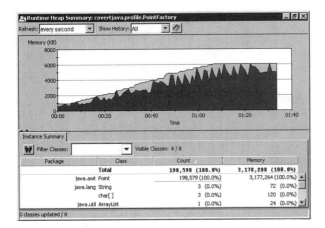

FIGURE 10.1 A runtime heap summary graph for an unoptimized heap size.

When there is not enough free memory to satisfy the allocation request, the JVM runs the first-generation garbage collection to free up the memory taken up by the unused objects. The first generation looks only at objects that were allocated recently to avoid time-consuming iteration of the entire object graph. If enough memory was not freed, the full garbage collection is run. The full garbage collection starts from the roots of the object tree, which are generally the objects referenced by active threads and static variables, and it identifies all the objects that can be reached from the root. The objects that are not reachable from the root (that is, the objects that are not part of a reference graph that starts from the root object) are marked for garbage collection. If the full garbage collection fails to free up enough memory, JVM checks whether it is allowed to allocate more memory from the operating system. If it has reached the maximum allowed limit or the operating system fails to supply more memory, an OutOfMemory exception is thrown.

As you can see, creating many new objects can result in complex and time-consuming operations. Instead of performing the business logic, the JVM might spend processor time on memory management. The graph in Figure 10.1 shows the memory usage of an application that does not have the maximum heap size optimized. Each drop in the amount of used heap

STORIES FROM THE TRENCHES

One of the Java applications we were using at Riggs Bank stopped coming up after the amount of data it was supposed to display sharply increased. Users waited for up to 30 minutes for the application to initialize itself, but it would still not finish. Investigating the application startup showed symptoms of endless garbage collection cycles—high CPU usage with no disk or network traffic. When the maximum allowed heap size was increased from 128MB to 256MB, the application would initialize in less than 30 seconds!

is a result of a garbage collection. You can see that the JVM has to run garbage collection frequently because little free memory exists. The maximum value of the heap size is set using the -Xmx parameter to the java command line. Increasing the maximum heap size from 5MB to 16MB produces the heap summary graph shown in Figure 10.2.

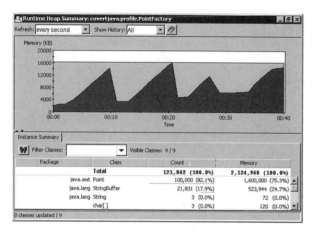

FIGURE 10.2   A runtime heap summary graph for an optimized heap size.

The performance of the application has significantly improved because the garbage collection was run only 3 times, compared to almost 30 times before. There is no fixed rule that can be used to determine the optimal size of the heap. Sometimes running several garbage collection cycles can be almost as fast as running one cycle that has to iterate more objects. Experimenting with the values for the initial and maximum heap sizes for a particular application is the only reliable way to find the best setting for it.

Browsing Object Allocation and References to Find and Fix Memory Leaks

It is no longer a novelty that Java applications have memory leaks. They are not the same type of leaks that riddle lower-level languages such as C++, but they are leaks nonetheless because the memory allocated is not released back into the free pool. As you learned earlier, Java garbage collection releases the memory held by unreachable objects. If an object has a reference to it, it is not eligible for garbage collection, even if it is never used again. For example, if an object is placed into an array and never removed from it, it always stays in memory. These objects, sometimes referred to as *lingering objects*, over time can eat away all available free memory and result in an OutOfMemory exception. The problem is magnified when the object refers to a large tree of other objects, which is often the case in applications.

Another hazard is lingering objects that represent resources, such as database connections or temporary files. The longer an object sits in memory, the more expensive the garbage collection becomes because it has more objects to traverse. Profilers offer the best means of locating lingering objects and identifying what prevents them from being garbage collected.

Let's look at a simple example that produces lingering objects and use JProbe to find it. Suppose we are building a graphical editor and need a factory that provides an abstraction layer for the creation of `Point` objects. The factory implementation fragment is shown in Listing 10.1.

LISTING 10.1   Implementation of `PointFactory`

```java
public class PointFactory {
    protected ArrayList points = new ArrayList();

    public Point createPoint(int x, int y) {
        Point point = new Point(x, y);
        this.points.add(point);
        return point;
    }

    public void removePoint(Point point) {
        this.points.remove(point);
    }
}
```

The `createPoint` method creates instances of `Point` and places them into an array. `removePoint` removes the point from the array, and `PointFactory` comes with a test method that creates several points through the factory. The code for the test method is shown in Listing 10.2.

LISTING 10.2   A Method That Tests Point Creation

```java
public void printTestPoints() {
    for (int i = 0; i < 5; i++) {
        Point point = createPoint(i, i);
        System.out.println("Point = " + point);
    }
}
```

The main method of `PointFactory` displays a dialog box with a Print Test Points button. Clicking a button results in a call to the `printTestPoints()` method of `PointFactory`. The implementation of `printTestPoints` seems like perfectly valid Java code, but running it results in memory leaks. If we increase the size of the object we allocated and the number of iterations in the loop, we can quickly exhaust all the available memory. You have undoubtedly understood what is causing the leak in our example. It is easy to see because we have one class with less than 50 lines of code, but if we had hundreds of classes with complex logic, the problem would not be so evident. This is where profilers become indispensable.

To investigate the memory management of the sample code, we should configure `covertjava.profile.PointFactory` as a standalone application in the JProbe Memory Debugger. After running it in JProbe, the initial view shows a runtime heap summary and a class view. Because the application is small, we see only a few classes in the class view, but in a large application a filter can be applied based on the class or package name. When the application dialog box appears, looking at the classes and the instance count reveals that no `java.awt.Point` objects have been created yet. We click the Print Test Points button in the application and go back to the class view. We now see that five instances of `Point` and five instances of `StringBuffer` have been created. This is the obvious result of calling the `printTestPoints` method, which is no surprise. JProbe enables the enforcing of the garbage collection, so we do that next. After the garbage collection finishes, you should notice that the `StringBuffer` instances are gone but that the points are still in the memory. Repeating the test starting from the Print Test Points button increases the number of `Point` instances to 10. This confirms our claim that memory leaks exist, and we are now going to find out why the points are lingering in memory.

After you have identified the instance that is not being released, you have several options for finding what prevents it from being garbage collected: examining the source code manually, browsing the reference tree in a profiler, and finding all the paths to the root in a profiler.

Going through the source code and finding all the places where the instance is created can help you figure out whether some of the references to it do not go out of scope and are not nullified. Profilers can usually show the allocation point for an instance, which can help with the task. This is a brute-force approach that can be time-consuming. A more sophisticated way, and sometimes the only feasible way, is to take a runtime heap snapshot and then browse through it looking at the object in question. Instead of manually tracking the possible references to an instance in the source code, browsing the heap snapshot enables you to navigate the runtime references that are actually holding the object in memory. Most profilers show the *referrers* (the objects pointing to the object in question) and *references* (the objects pointed to by the object in question). A very powerful feature is the capability of the profiler to show all the paths from the object to the root. Object graphs on the snapshot can be complex and hard to navigate. If you are interested in only a particular object, you do not need to see the entire graph; rather, you just need to see which objects are preventing it from being garbage collected. Recall that the garbage collector reclaims an object only if it is not reachable from the roots. Thus, if you can identify and eliminate all the paths to the root from a given object, it is eligible for garbage collection.

Before taking a heap snapshot, it is always a good idea to request a garbage collection. This removes objects that are not referenced anymore and makes the job of tracking down memory leaks easier. In JProbe you can do this by selecting Request Garbage Collection from the Program menu. After that, take a heap snapshot by selecting Take Heap Snapshot from the Program menu. After JProbe has captured the snapshot, select Class View from the Snapshot menu. You now can look at the state of the heap and the object graphs. In our case, we are interested in `java.awt.Point` objects, so we right-click it in the Class View and select Instance Detail View from the pop-up menu. The new screen displays all the instances of `Point` in memory and enables us to browse the referrer and reference trees. The referrer tree is composed of a hierarchy of ancestors that have the instance as a child directly or indirectly—that is, all its immediate parents, parents of its parents, parents of the parents of its parents, and so on. Navigating the tree gives us a good idea of which references are held. In the case of our `Point` instance, we can see that it is referred to by an `ArrayList` that is referred to by `PointFactory`.

JProbe has another view that I actually prefer to use. It is called Reference Graph and is a better visualization of the object graph. To view the Reference Graph for a `Point`, you right-click a `Point` instance and select Instance Referrers and References from the pop-up menu. This displays a new window showing all the objects as named rectangles with the selected object in the center. Because we are trying to find out why the points are lingering in memory, click the Paths to Root icon in the graph toolbar. The resulting window is shown in Figure 10.3.

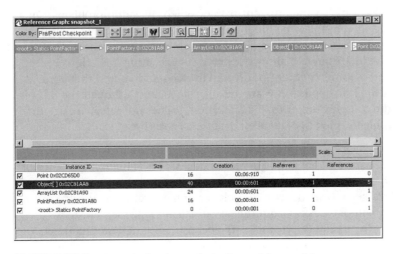

FIGURE 10.3 A graph showing paths to the root for a point.

Once again, we can see that the Point object is referred by the ArrayList of PointFactory. We can conclude that the reason the points stay in memory is because they are never removed from the array. Looking at the implementation of printTestPoint(), we can see that it calls createPoint, which stores the instantiated Point object in the points array. To fix the problem, we need to add a call to removePoint to printTestPoint so that it looks as shown in Listing 10.3.

LISTING 10.3   Corrected Implementation of the Point Creation Test

```java
public void printTestPoints() {
    for (int i = 0; i < 5; i++) {
        Point point = createPoint(i, i);
        System.out.println("Point = " + point);
        removePoint(point);
    }
}
```

Investigating Thread Allocation and Synchronization

Writing multithreaded applications has the inherent risks of synchronization problems. On a single thread the code is executed in the same order as it is written in the source file. With multiple threads of execution, several concurrent operations can be performed at the same time, and each thread can be interrupted to allow the processor executing operations of the next thread. The order and the points of interruption are virtually random and therefore can't be predicted. Most of the Java applications are multithreaded, and although the built-in concept of threads hides the complexities of thread allocation, it does not safeguard against the common threading problems, such as data races, deadlocks, and thread stalls.

A *data race* condition occurs when two threads are simultaneously trying to access and modify a shared resource. A typical example of a potential data race is changing a balance of a bank account without synchronization. Say you have a BankAccount class with getBalance() and setBalance() methods to get and set the current balance, respectively. You also have a deposit() method to add or withdraw funds from the account. The implementation of deposit() first obtains the current balance, then adds the deposit amount, and finally sets the new balance. If two threads—thread1 and thread2—are making a deposit at the same time, thread1 can read the current balance and increment the amount, but before it has a chance to set the new balance it can get interrupted by thread2. thread2 reads the old balance and increments it before being interrupted in favor of thread1. thread1 updates the balance with the amount it has calculated, but after that, thread2 resumes execution and overrides the balance set by thread1 with its own value. In this example, the amount deposited by thread1 would be lost. Customers might well enjoy having this kind of anomaly for withdrawals, but they will not tolerate it for deposits to their accounts. Profilers such as JProbe Threadalizer can catch and report various types of data races. A typical solution to a data race is to add synchronization that protects access to the data. To fix the implementation of bank account deposits, the method that makes a deposit must be declared with a keyword: synchronized. Synchronization ensures that only one thread can obtain the lock, and any other thread attempting to obtain the same lock is blocked until the lock is released by its owner. An alternative to making methods synchronized is to declare a "lock" object and use it as a parameter to a synchronized block, as shown in Listing 10.4.

LISTING 10.4   Safeguarding Data Access with a Synchronized Block

```
protected Object balanceLock = new Object();
protected double balance;

...

public void deposit(double amount) {
    synchronized (balanceLock) {
        double balance = getBalance();
        balance += amount;
        setBalance(balance);
    }
}
```

Using synchronization adds overhead, so it must be applied only when necessary. Also note that not every data race reported by a profiler is a problem that needs to be fixed. For example, even if multiple threads read the balance at the same time, there is no harm in that; therefore, the getBalance() method does not necessarily have to be synchronized. In a multi-tiered application, synchronization can be deferred to other layers. For example, the database transaction isolation level can be used to prevent concurrent reads and writes of the same data.

Deadlock occurs when a thread is waiting for a lock that is acquired by another thread but is never released. It is a common problem in multithreaded applications that can cause the application to stop functioning completely. For example, if thread1 obtains lock1 and then waits for lock2 that is currently held by thread2, a deadlock occurs if thread2 attempts to obtain lock1 without releasing lock2 first. To illustrate the problem, let's look at the sample class with two locks and two methods that use the locks to synchronize the work they perform. In Listing 10.5, the actual work performed is not important because the focus is on the synchronization logic.

LISTING 10.5   Code That Has the Potential for a Deadlock

```
public Object lock1 = new Object();
public Object lock2 = new Object();

public void method1() {
    synchronized (lock1) {
        synchronized (lock2) {
            doSomething();
        }
    }
}

public void method2() {
    synchronized (lock2) {
        synchronized (lock1) {
            doSomething();
        }
    }
}
```

As you can see, both methods use locks lock1 and lock2, but they obtain them in a different order. If run on separate threads, method1 could enter the first synchronized block and get a lock on lock1. However, if it is interrupted by method2, method2 can enter its own outer synchronized block and get a lock on lock2. At this point the deadlock occurs as the threads continue execution because they are both waiting for locks indefinitely. The ThreadTest class from the covertjava.profile package provides an example of this scenario. Running it produces a deadlock that prevents graceful JVM shutdown because the two threads spawned by the main() method never return.

In our example, spotting the problem is easy if you closely examine the code of ThreadTest, but in a real-life application with hundreds of classes it would not be so simple. Good profilers detect deadlocks and provide information on what lead to it. JProbe Threadalizer from Quest and OptimizeIt Thread Debugger from Borland can both detect the deadlocks, but OptimizeIt also provides a visual timeline of thread execution, so we are going to use it for our work. Run OptimizeIt and configure ThreadTest as an application with covertjava.profile.ThreadTest as the main class. Be sure to check the Auto-start Analyzer option in the application settings dialog box to automatically start analyzing the running program for problems. Start ThreadTest using a menu or a toolbar button; after it runs for a few seconds, OptimizeIt should display the threads, as shown in Figure 10.4.

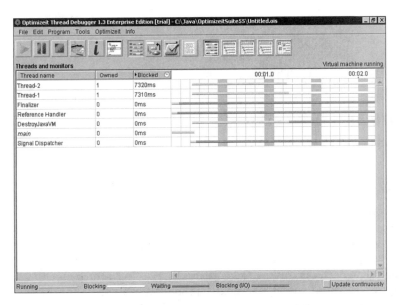

FIGURE 10.4 OptimizeIt's threads view of running ThreadTest.

The view displays all the threads and the timeline of their execution status. Green indicates that the thread is running; yellow indicates that the thread is blocked while waiting for a lock that is owned by another thread; red indicates that the thread is waiting to be notified; and purple indicates that the thread is blocked in native code. ThreadTest spawns two threads that get the default names of Thread-1 and Thread-2. By examining the execution timeline of these two threads, you can see that after running for a short period of time, they became blocked indefinitely. All other threads are started internally by JVM to perform system tasks, so we will keep the focus on the threads created by the application. OptimizeIt allows the viewing of the locks held by each thread and the locks for which the thread is waiting. Because we opted to use the analyzer, we can take advantage of it to get a hint about the problem. We switch to the Analyzer view using the File menu. Then we click the Stop Recording button; we should see one deadlock detected by the tool with the description Locking order mismatch. Selecting the deadlock item displays the detailed information about the threads involved and the locks held. In our case the detailed description text is Thread Thread-2 enters monitor java.lang.Object 0xabf9280 first and then java.lang.Object 0xabf72f0 while thread Thread-1 enters the same monitors in the opposite order. OptimizeIt even shows the lines of code where the locks were acquired. This makes the job of fixing the problem easy.

To avoid deadlock, the order in which the locks are acquired should be the same. In our case, we should change method2 to first get lock1 and then lock2. The last thing to remember is that, even though the analyzer can detect many common errors that can lead to a deadlock, it can't detect every possible situation. Good design and solid coding practices go a long way in preventing problems in the future.

Thread stall is a term used to describe threads that are waiting to be notified when the notification never comes. This happens when a thread calls the wait() method on an object but no other threads call the notify() method on the same object. Thread stall is another example of a multithreading problem that can be detected by a profiler.

Identifying Expensive Methods to Improve Performance

Performance optimization is a complex subject that goes well beyond the scope of this chapter. Java performance has come a long way, and modern JITs deliver excellent speed and code optimizations. The most important factor affecting the ultimate execution speed is the quality of application design and implementation. Some well-known pitfalls and common workarounds can increase performance by hundreds of percentage points. Often, rewriting a few key methods can result in applications responding 10 times faster than before. Performance optimizations begin with identifying the bottlenecks. Naturally, the performance should be considered even during the design phase, although it is not recommended to sacrifice clean design for anticipated minor performance gains. As the code is developed and the unit tested, it should be profiled to see which methods are taking the most time. The integration testing is where most of the profiling is typically done.

Profiling collects various execution statistics that gives an idea about where the time is actually spent. These are the most useful metrics produced by the JProbe profiler:

▶ **Method time**—Shows the time spent executing a given method, excluding the time spent in methods it called.

▶ **Method number of calls**—Shows the number of times the method was called. It can be used to identify the methods where optimization will produce the most dramatic effect on overall performance.

▶ **Average method time**—Shows the average time it took to execute the method. This is equivalent to method time divided by the number of calls and can be used to identify the slowest methods.

▶ **Cumulative time**—Shows the total time spent executing a given method, including the methods it called. It can be used to identify which methods of an application use most of the processing time.

▶ **Average objects per method**—Shows the average number of objects created inside a method. Because garbage collection in Java greatly affects application performance, reducing the object creation can increase the execution speed.

After the statistics are collected and analyzed, steps can be taken to optimize the poorly performing portions of the application.

Investigating an Application at Runtime Using a Thread Dump

Because running an application in a profiler requires the JVM to be started in a debug mode, it is not feasible for production applications. It would be nice to be able to get a snapshot of threads and what they are doing for any application, even if it was started in a normal execution mode. Luckily, a JVM can be told to produce a full thread dump that displays all the threads with the states and the call stack. To obtain a thread dump on Unix, you must execute a `kill -3 <pid>` command, where `<pid>` is the process ID of the JVM (`kill -QUIT <pid>` works on Solaris). On Windows it can be done by pressing Ctrl+Break in the console window. A thread dump for Chat is shown in Listing 10.6.

LISTING 10.6 A Partial Runtime Thread Dump for Chat

```
Full thread dump:
"RMI ConnectionExpiration-[10.241.11.244:14512]" daemon prio=7
tid=0x8ad0b68 nid=0x748 waiting on monitor [0x119df000..0x119dfdbc]
        at java.lang.Thread.sleep(Native Method)
        at sun.rmi.transport.tcp.TCPChannel$Reaper.run(TCPChannel.java:522)
        at java.lang.Thread.run(Thread.java:479)


"TimerQueue" daemon prio=5 tid=0x8ac15d8 nid=0x8a0
waiting on monitor [0x1177f000..0x1177fdbc]
        at java.lang.Object.wait(Native Method)
        at javax.swing.TimerQueue.run(TimerQueue.java:228)
        at java.lang.Thread.run(Thread.java:479)


"AWT-EventQueue-0" prio=7 tid=0x8a1ac28 nid=0x148
waiting on monitor [0x10f3f000..0x10f3fdbc]
        at java.lang.Object.wait(Native Method)
        at java.lang.Object.wait(Object.java:415)
        at java.awt.EventQueue.getNextEvent(EventQueue.java:255)
        at java.awt.EventDispatchThread.pumpOneEventForHierarchy(EventDispatchThread...)
        at java.awt.EventDispatchThread.pumpEventsForHierarchy(EventDispatchThread...)
        at java.awt.EventDispatchThread.pumpEvents(EventDispatchThread.java:88)
        at java.awt.EventDispatchThread.run(EventDispatchThread.java:80)


"Signal Dispatcher" daemon prio=10 tid=0x802388 nid=0x2b0
waiting on monitor [0..0]
```

LISTING 10.6   Continued

```
"Finalizer" daemon prio=9 tid=0x7fe368 nid=0x640
waiting on monitor [0x8c4f000..0x8c4fdbc]
        at java.lang.Object.wait(Native Method)
        at java.lang.ref.ReferenceQueue.remove(ReferenceQueue.java:103)
        at java.lang.ref.ReferenceQueue.remove(ReferenceQueue.java:118)
        at java.lang.ref.Finalizer$FinalizerThread.run(Finalizer.java:157)

...
```

Listing 10.6 shows some of the threads running inside the Chat JVM. For instance, we can see that an RMI connection thread is sleeping inside the run method of the sun.rmi. transport.tcp.TCPChannel$Reaper class. The AWT-EventQueue thread is waiting for the next event, and the finalizer thread is waiting on a monitor using the wait() method.

Thread dumps can be very handy if a deadlock has occurred in a running application and it is not obvious what has caused it. Knowing which threads are waiting for which monitors is the best clue one can get. On Unix the dump also includes the environment variables, OS information, monitors dump, and a lot of other useful information.

Quick Quiz

1. What are the reasons to profile an application?

2. Why does the garbage collection dramatically affect application performance?

3. What can cause memory leaks in a Java application?

4. How would you find and fix memory leaks?

5. What are the common problems in multithreaded applications?

6. Which process would you use to improve the performance of an application?

In Brief

- profilers provide a sophisticated means of solving problems such as memory leaks, data races, deadlocks, and performance issues.

- Investigating heap usage and garbage collection frequency offers knowledge on how to improve performance.

- Browsing object allocation and references at runtime helps you find and fix memory leaks.

- Investigating thread allocation and synchronization helps in finding thread locking and data race problems and improves performance.

- Identifying expensive methods during profiling improves application performance.

- Investigating an application in a profiler provides an insight into its internal structure.

- A thread dump produced by the JVM in response to a SIGQUIT provides useful information on threads and monitors for an application that is not running in debug mode.

Load-Testing to Find and Fix Scalability Problems

"Software bugs are impossible to detect by anybody except the end user."

Murphy's Technology Laws

The Importance of Load-Testing

Server-side applications have service-level requirements that specify the availability, scalability, and failover:

▶ **Availability**—Specifies the up-time requirements that describe how long the application needs to be capable of running without restarting

▶ **Scalability**—Specifies the capability of the application to provide the same level of service as the number of requests increases

▶ **Failover**—Specifies the capability of the application to continue providing the same level of service when one of the application components fails

A typical development cycle allocates time for unit testing and integration testing, which generally focuses on functionality, but it does not always provide time for load-testing. The purpose of load-testing is to assess how the system performance meets service-level requirements under load. Obviously, every system's response time degrades as the load increases, but as long as it meets the specified requirements, the system is considered to be scalable.

Ignoring the load-testing is a risky practice, especially if an application is expected to serve hundreds or thousands of users. With a large user community, a small problem becomes a big problem because it affects a large group of people. Some failures do not appear unless there is a certain load. This might be the case for operations that depend on resources such as threads, database connections, and memory. Most of the problems inherent to multithreaded applications occur when there is a particular number of concurrent requests. Only load-testing and running the system for a prolonged amount of time mimics the production operating environment, so it is absolutely crucial to perform this test before a system goes live. Last, but not least, load-testing an application enables you to see how it will respond to denial-of-service attacks and hacking attempts. Load-testing reveals not how the application is built, but whether it is built to last. It can be used to get more value out of the techniques presented in other chapters. For example, profiling an application under load produces a different picture than without the load.

Simulating a load on the system is not a trivial task, so it is important to leverage the right tools. Plenty of load-testing products are available on the market, most of which are designed to work with Web sites serving HTML content via HTTP. Besides HTTP, Java server applications also work with various other protocols, such as JRMP for RMI clients and IIOP for CORBA and RMI clients. The best tools cost a lot of money, but some open-source alternatives can deliver most of the basic functionality. We are going to load-test an RMI-based Chat application using the open-source JUnit framework. Later we will use another open-source tool called JMeter to load-test WebCream, a Web-based application that has browser-based clients.

STORIES FROM THE TRENCHES

We were building a Web application that was going to be used by 5,000 users. The first release of the application had missed several deadlines, so when the development and unit testing was finished, no time was left to write automated test scripts or do a load test with a proper testing tool. Several testers manually simulated some load and, with fingers crossed, the deployment received a "go." The application was put into production at a conspicuous time of 2 a.m. because of the server maintenance window, and the exhausted development team went home hoping to enjoy a few days of rest. However, by 11 a.m. the next day when users had started accessing the Web site, the application server stopped responding to requests. Restarting it helped for a few hours, but then the deadlock occurred again. Management was furious, and threats of finding "who done it" and firing the perpetrator were made. When the problem was finally located, it turned out that the culprit was multithreaded code handling exceptions and failover. The code was written so that, if an exception was detected during the request processing, the exception was analyzed and in some cases a recovery was attempted followed by a retry of the operation. The problem was that, with multiple concurrent requests, the analysis/recovery/retry code turned into an endless loop. Had a proper load test been done earlier, the error would have been found and fixed without affecting thousands of users or the reputation of the development team.

The principles behind simulating a load are virtually the same. A test case is first created by recording the running application or programmatically. When the test case is ready, it is used to create virtual users or clients, which are then run on multiple threads to simultaneously access the server. To the server application, the virtual users appear as the real traffic, and monitoring the server response's correctness and time produces the test results.

Load-Testing RMI-Based Servers with JUnit

JUnit is an open-source Java project that provides a framework for writing and executing unit tests. It promotes writing test code that asserts the validity of the application functionality. A JUnit test case is a Java class that is compiled and executed to test the application code. This approach provides the benefits of automated retesting with the ease of maintaining the testing code in sync with the application code. Last, but not least, developers get to write Java code instead of click buttons in debuggers and test tools, which is probably a significant contributor to the popularity of the framework.

To use JUnit, a developer must write a test case that extends `junit.framework.TestCase` or implements `junit.framework.Test`. The test case consists of calls to the classes that are being tested and assertions that the return values match the expected result. For example, a test case for a bank account can get the current balance, make a deposit, and then verify that the new balance matches the old balance plus the deposit amount. The quality of the test case is directly proportional to the zeal of the developer. The idea is to try to cover all possible scenarios, including the erroneous ones. After the tests are written, they are compiled and executed individually or in groups. JUnit is a well-documented and easy-to-learn framework, and if you haven't worked with it yet, please invest a couple of hours in reading the manual and the examples. (Don't forget to update your résumé because good managers will view it as a sign of a quality developer.) The framework and its related documentation can be downloaded for free from `http://www.junit.org`. The rest of this section focuses on developing a load test for Chat based on JUnit.

Chat was certainly not built to be indestructible, but it was not meant to scale to hundreds of users either. As long as it can handle between three and six simultaneous users, it is probably enough to satisfy the concurrency requirements for a demo application. For any load test, you should set the high mark a little above the anticipated maximum load. So, for our example, we will use 10 as the number of virtual clients it should support. Our goal is to simulate this number of clients simultaneously sending messages to the same Chat application. We also want to stagger the calls to mimic real-life experience. *Staggering* means that, instead of sending the requests at the same time, they are sent around the same time. Sometimes the term *simultaneous* is used to describe the clients that are sending a request at the same time and *concurrent* is used to describe the clients that maintain a conversation with the server but are sending requests around the same time. On a single CPU system, there is really no distinction between concurrent and simultaneous execution because there can be no true parallel processing, making the terms interchangeable.

We will begin by developing a test case that simulates a user sending one message to the target host. Then we will build a harness that uses the test case to create a number of virtual users repeatedly sending the messages. To be flexible, we will allow parameterization of the test by specifying the number of simultaneous users to simulate, the number of times to repeat the test, and the lag time to use for staggering the calls.

The test case is written in `covertjava.loadtest.ChatTestCase`. It extends `TestCase` and implements the core logic in its `testSendMessage()` method, which is shown in Listing 11.1.

LISTING 11.1   testSendMessage Source Code

```
public void testSendMessage() {
    logger.info("Sending test message...");
    try {
        StringBuffer message = new StringBuffer();
        message.append("[ChatTestCase@");
        message.append(Integer.toHexString(this.hashCode()));
        message.append("] Test ");
        message.append(messagesSent++);
        ChatServer.getInstance().sendMessage(this.host, message.toString());
        logger.info("Sent message successfully");
    }
    catch (Exception e) {
        e.printStackTrace();
        assertTrue("Exception: " + e.getMessage(), false);
    }
}
```

`ChatTestCase` creates a test message and uses `ChatServer` to send it to the target host. The key aspect of this method is a call to `assertTrue()` in the `catch` statement with `false` as the second parameter, which tells JUnit that this test has failed. Otherwise, the method simply returns, which would mean success. This way of testing is certainly far from perfect to ensure that the Chat server has processed the message correctly. It does not test whether the message has been parsed and appropriately added to the conversation history window. However, it provides a fairly decent tactic of testing the network communication and the throughput of the remote server and therefore will suffice to illustrate the point.

The next step is creating a test suite that contains `ChatTestCase` instances. This is accomplished in the `ChatLoadTest` class; the code is shown in Listing 11.2.

LISTING 11.2   Creation of a Test Suite

```
ActiveTestSuite suite = new ActiveTestSuite();
for (int i = 0; i < clientsNumber; i++) {
```

```
        Test test = new ChatTestCase ();
        test = new DelayedTest(test, (int)(Math.random()*lagTime));
        test = new RepeatedTest(test, repeatRuns);
        suite.addTest(test);
}
```

The parameters, such as `clientsNumber` and `lagTime`, are read from the properties file to support customization. JUnit test suites serve as containers for test cases and make running multiple tests easier. `ActiveTestSuite` runs all its tests simultaneously and then waits for them to finish before returning the result. JUnit uses a decorator pattern to attach additional functionality to tests. `RepeatedTest`, for example, runs a given thread repeatedly for a given number of times. To provide staggering execution for a test, we have added the `DelayedTest` decorator class that sleeps for a given period of time before running the test. The end result of the code in Listing 11.2 is a `clientsNumber` number of clients that will simultaneously send messages after sleeping for a random time.

You can run a JUnit test in several ways, but we will use the Swing GUI to get visual feedback on the testing progress. If an instance of Chat is not running on the localhost yet, we start it using `CovertJava\distrib\bin\chat.bat`. Then we use the `loadtestJUnit.bat` file located in the `CovertJava\bin` directory to open the JUnit GUI and execute our test suite. Shortly after the tests begin running, the JUnit GUI should look similar to Figure 11.1.

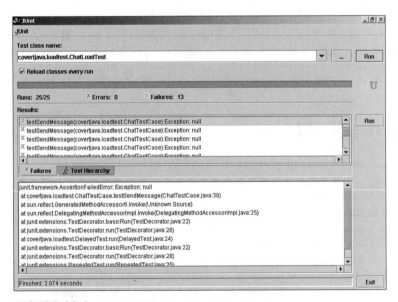

FIGURE 11.1   The JUnit GUI showing the testing progress.

Most of the tests failed, and looking at the result panel, we can see the error message: `testSendMessage(covertjava.loadtest.ChatTestCase): Exception java.lang.NullPointerException: null`. Examining the Chat application shows that the conversation history component contains a mess and that several `NullPointerExceptions` are in the console window. Guess what? We are starting to reap the benefits of load testing. Reducing the number of clients to two makes the tests run successfully, so the problem must come from multithreading. Chapter 9, "Cracking Code with Unorthodox Debuggers," and Chapter 10, "Using Profilers for Application Runtime Analysis," have provided techniques for finding and fixing the problems that arise from concurrent execution. You can try applying these to find out what is wrong with Chat.

For those who feel knowledgeable enough, I will disclose that the problem comes from the way the new messages are appended to the conversation history. Swing is not thread safe, and it is generally recommended to interact with Swing components from the AWT event dispatch thread. The designers of Swing have sacrificed robustness for speed, and we can't really blame them because Swing performance has long been under scrutiny. Chat receives the incoming messages on an RMI thread and delegates message processing to the `MainFrame` class. `MainFrame`'s `appendMessage` method, which appends a new message to the conversation `JEditorPane`, does not use synchronization. Therefore, if several users try to send a message to the same host at the same time, several threads will be trying to set data to the same `JEditorPane`. This is a classic data overrun problem that can be solved by making the `appendMessage` method synchronized. After making this change, rerunning the load test produces a clean result that allows us to happily consider the job done.

The benefit of using JUnit for load-testing is that it is simple and enables you to leverage any test cases that might already have been written. It is also an effective method of testing RMI-based servers because automatic script recording by load-testing tools does not always produce maintainable results.

Load-Testing with JMeter

The previous section showed how to load test Java applications using JUnit. The development of the test was simple and, although we didn't get any fancy graphs or charts, the basic job was done pretty well. However, this approach is rather limited because it requires writing a virtual client manually, and the only thing JUnit can do is run the test case on multiple threads. What if we wanted to test a Web-based application that has HTML front end? That would typically require that the users be running a Web browser, and the server would have to rely on servlets and JSPs to implement the user interface. JUnit is simply not an option because the virtual users should support the functionality of the browser, such as session management, cookies, HTTP forms, and others. Another shortcoming of JUnit is that it doesn't produce tangible evidence of the test's success or failure. A seasoned developer knows the power that reports, charts, and graphs have on management. In short, we need a better tool.

Load-testing is a huge and lucrative market, and many good products are available. At this point in time, they offer virtually the same core functionality, which includes the capability to record virtual users automatically, the capability to create test scripts programmatically, support for multiple programming languages and communication protocols, and—you guessed it—lots of fancy graphs and reports. Often it's the graphs that influence the final decision on what to purchase. I will highlight two products that are deemed to be the market leaders: Mercury Load Runner and Rational Test Suite. Load Runner is an excellent and time-proven tool that provides the ultimate flexibility and has practically any feature you can find in a load-testing tool. An important factor is its capability to record and customize the virtual user scripts, which can make writing code unnecessary. It can even record at the protocol level for HTTP and RMI clients. Because load tests have a high perceived value (and rightfully so), the prices for the tools can be very steep. Testing a cluster of servers with hundreds of virtual users can result in license fees of thousands of dollars. We are going to look at JMeter, an open-source alternative that can be obtained for free from Apache's Web site. Although not nearly as polished or versatile, it offers similar core functionality and is sufficient for most Web-based applications. And make no mistake; you'll learn how to produce a few graphs and a report as well.

JMeter Overview

JMeter is a tool for load-testing and measuring the performance of Web sites and Java applications. It supports servers that accept HTTP and FTP connections but can be used to test databases, Perl scripts, and Java objects as well. JMeter supports basic script recording via a proxy server and requires a thorough understanding of the underlying protocol and server implementation. Creating a test plan demands manual work, but just like JUnit, it is the kind of challenging work that developers actually enjoy. Because most of the new applications built today have a thin client interface, we will use JMeter to load test a Web-based product called WebCream.

JMeter has a GUI that can be used to create a test plan and an engine that executes the test plan to generate the load. The test plan is a container for the configuration elements and logical controllers that represent settings and actions to be performed. The test creation is visual, and the end result is a tree of nested elements that describes the test and its execution. Using HTTP Proxy Server, which records the browsing actions, is a good way to quickly create a draft test plan. Whether you start by recording the test plan or by creating it manually, you need to know the elements used by JMeter to make the test plan work. The following nodes can be added to a test plan:

- **Thread group**—This defines the number of virtual users that will be concurrently executing the nested nodes. It also enables you to specify the ramp-up time for staggering and the duration of the test.

- **Listeners**—This can be added to provide visualization of the test results and to track the progress of the test execution. For example, to have a graph of the response times, the graph results listener can be added to a test plan.

- **Configuration elements**—These are used to add protocol-specific managers and default settings for samplers, which are discussed later. For instance, for virtual clients to support HTTP session via cookies, the HTTP Cookie Manager element must be added.

- **Assertions**—These are used to test the validity of the server response. Getting a response is not enough to say that a test has passed. Assertions enable you to check the response for a certain substring or an exact match, and if the check fails, the assertion fails. Failed assertions can be viewed using the assertion results listener.

- **Preprocessors**—These are executed before an operation is performed. For example, the user parameters preprocessor can be used to define and initialize variables for an HTTP request.

- **Postprocessors**—These are executed after an operation is performed. For example, the regular expression extractor can be added to parse the page title from an HTML page that was returned by the server.

- **Timers**—These are used to introduce scheduled running and staggered execution of operations.

A thread group can have these additional nodes:

- **Logic controllers**—These can be added to specify the control flow for nested nodes. For example, adding a loop controller enables the execution of nested nodes in a loop for a given number of times.

- **Samplers**—These enable the sending of a request to the application being tested. Samplers perform the actual calls to the server. JMeter currently supports FTP, HTTP, SOAP, Java, JDBC, and LDAP requests.

After a test plan is created, it can be executed on the local machine. You can also configure several machines to act as remote JMeter servers, which can be controlled from the same GUI environment. This allows simulating more virtual clients than one machine can handle.

WebCream Overview

WebCream is a unique tool for Java that provides automated Web enabling for GUI-based Java applications and applets. WebCream allows developers to implement a GUI front end using AWT and Swing and, at the same time, automatically get HTML access to the application. In a way, WebCream can be thought of as a dynamic Java-to-HTML converter that transforms GUI frames and dialog boxes to HTML on-the-fly. It then emulates Web page actions as GUI events to retain the application's original logic. WebCream is unique in that it requires no modifications to existing forms or business logic and does not require programmers to learn any APIs. Because WebCream uses a browser-based interface, generates dynamic content, and maintains a session, it is a good choice for HTTP load-testing with JMeter.

WebCream comes with a built-in Tomcat Web server and a demo application; you should play with it a little bit to become familiar with the product. Use the WebCream demo application and be sure to check the HTML source the product generates for each page. Try to understand the URLs used by the product and how it passes the data back to the server, and look for common patterns in generated pages. The standard edition of WebCream is free but limited to five concurrent users, so you might have to restart Tomcat during your tests if you don't want to wait for the sessions to time out. The WebCream demo's main page displays a frame with three buttons—Login Dialog, Tabs and Table, and Tree Dialog (see Figure 11.2).

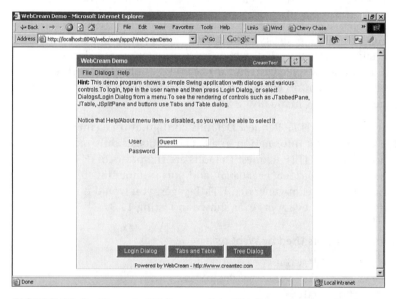

FIGURE 11.2   The main HTML page of the WebCream demo application.

Clicking the Login Dialog button displays the next page, which shows a dialog box allowing the user to enter her username and password and to select a domain. If the OK button is clicked on this page, the login information is passed to the main page. For the purposes of testing, we will limit ourselves to this functionality of the demo.

Creating a Web Test Plan

Now is the time to actually do some work. Download and install JMeter and WebCream. Run the JMeter GUI using the `JMeter\bin\jmeter.bat` file. Because we are going to be testing WebCream, start the built-in Tomcat using `WebCream\bin\startServer.bat`.

The initial tree in the JMeter GUI shows an empty test plan and a WorkBench. The WorkBench is just a placeholder for the temporary nodes and testing, so we will focus on the test plan. Because we want to simulate multiple simultaneous users, we must add a thread group by right-clicking the Test Plan node and selecting Add, Thread Group. Initially, we set the number of threads to 1 to simplify the testing, but later we will change it to 5. To simulate real-life user interactions with the server, we need to ensure that the user makes pauses before sending the requests to the server. One hundred concurrent users in real life does not mean one hundred simultaneous requests on the server because users spend time interpreting the server response and filling out data on forms (sometimes even taking a coffee break). JMeter provides the Gaussian Random Timer for the simulation of user delays. We add it to our thread group and specify a constant delay of 300 milliseconds with 100 milliseconds deviation. This means that JMeter will pause a thread for at least 300 milliseconds before trying to execute the next step of the test plan.

Before we embark on devising the HTTP requests to simulate, we need to take a few preparatory steps. WebCream maintains an HTTP session, which relies on cookies stored in the browser. We are simulating a browser-based client, so we add HTTP Cookie Manager to the thread group. Just adding this configuration element is enough to tell JMeter to store cookies, and we don't have to define any cookies manually.

Last, but not least, we want to use the HTTP Request Defaults configuration element. It is a convenient way to provide the common information in all HTTP requests only once. Obvious choices for inclusion into the HTTP Request Defaults are the protocol (HTTP), server name (localhost), path (/webcream/apps/WebCreamDemo), and port number (8040). If you looked carefully at the source of WebCream-generated HTML pages, you would notice that three hidden parameters are present on every page, as shown in Listing 11.3.

LISTING 11.3   Common Form Parameters Used by WebCream

```
<input type="hidden" name="__RequestId" value="1">
<input type="hidden" name="__WindowTitle" value="WebCream Demo">
<input type="hidden" name="__Action" value="">
```

As the user goes through the pages, the values of these parameters change to reflect the consecutive request number and the current window title. The __Action parameter is used to tell the server which action to perform on the application. For example, to close a window, the client code sets __Action to close. Because these parameters are sent with every request, it is prudent to include them in the HTTP Request Defaults. We use the JMeter GUI to add the three parameters, leaving the values blank for now. We will return to specify the values after you learn a little more about JMeter. Figure 11.3 shows the plan tree we have created so far.

We will simulate a user opening the WebCream demo in a browser, clicking Login Button to go to the Login page, and then clicking OK to go back to the main page. To ensure that there are no memory leaks or multithreading problems on the server, we will simulate the user opening and closing the dialog box several times.

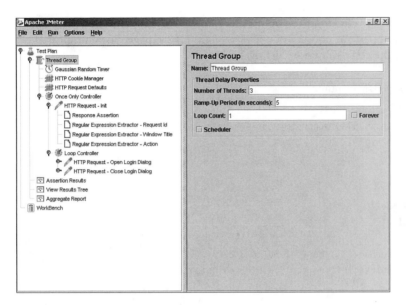

FIGURE 11.3 The JMeter test plan tree, step 1.

To keep the test plan concise, we add `Once Only Controller` to the thread group, enabling us to group the sampling requests into a subtree and separate them from the configuration elements. Next, we add `HTTP Request Sampler` to the controller. We name it `HTTP Request - Init` and, because it is the initial request to the Web application, we specify the `GET` method and leave everything else blank. The information about the Web server (such as the protocol and host) is coming from the request defaults we specified earlier. At this point, we have created a step that is equivalent to a user typing

```
http://localhost:8040/webcream/apps/WebCreamDemo
```

in the browser address bar and pressing Enter. The server should respond with the main page (refer to Figure 11.2). We should verify that we got the right response; we do so by adding a `Response Assertion` to the `HTTP Request - Init` node. An assertion can be as simple as a substring that must be present in the response or as sophisticated as a number of regular expressions that should produce a match. We will keep it simple and just test that the response is the page titled WebCream Demo as we have seen in the browser. While writing the test plan, it helps to keep the browser open with the page you are scripting against. To complete the assertion, we specify that we want the response to contain the pattern `<title>WebCream Demo</title>`. Figure 11.4 shows the plan tree we have created so far.

We are now ready to proceed to the test that opens and closes a page with a dialog box. We want to do it several times, so we first add a `Loop Controller` logic controller to the `Once Only Controller` and specify `5` as the loop count. Our next task is to add an `HTTP Request`

Sampler that simulates the user clicking the Login Dialog button. To see what has to be sent in this request, we need to open the source code for the main HTML page. Searching for Login Dialog takes us to the code shown in Listing 11.4.

LISTING 11.4   Login Button HTML Source

```
<form name="WebCreamForm" method="POST"
    action="http://localhost:8040/webcream/apps/WebCreamDemo"
    onSubmit="onSubmitForm()"
>
...
    <input type=button
        name="JButton31266642"
        value="Login Dialog"
        class=button
        OnClick=javascript:doSubmit('/button/JButton31266642')
        style="position:absolute;left:84;top:5;width:103;height:26"
    >
...
</form>
```

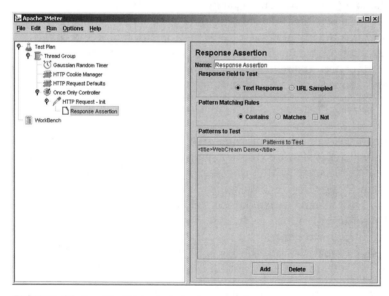

FIGURE 11.4   The JMeter test plan tree, step 2.

With some HTML familiarity, you can determine that when a user clicks the button, it invokes the doSubmit Java script passing '/button/JButton31266642' as a parameter. Searching for doSubmit on the page and the included JavaScript files produces the following snippet found in webcream_misc.js:

```
function doSubmit(action) {
  window.document.WebCreamForm.__Action.value=action;
  onSubmitForm();
  window.document.WebCreamForm.submit();
}
```

Thus, we conclude that when a user clicks the Login Dialog button, it sets the __Action parameter to /button/JButton31266642 and submits the form to the server. Accessing the WebCream demo using the browser several times, we can see that the action string is changing. It always starts with /button/JButton, but the remaining numbers vary from time to time because they are automatically generated. Most Web pages have some form of dynamic content, so the technique we use for WebCream is useful for other applications as well.

To work with dynamically generated content in JMeter, you must rely on variables and regular expressions. The Regular Expression Extractor is a postprocessor that applies a regular expression to the sampling response and places the extracted value into a variable. Regular expressions are a powerful mechanism of working with text input; if you are not familiar with them, I recommend learning about them. There is a plethora of references and tutorials covering regular expressions on the Web, and even a book from O'Reilly called *Mastering Regular Expressions*.

After a variable is initialized by the extractor, its value can be passed to other test elements such as samplers. We will use the extractor to obtain the values for the three parameters we have defined in HTTP Request Defaults (__RequestId, __WindowTitle, and __Action). We right-click the Http Request - Init node and add a post processor called Regular Expression Extractor. Next, we append - Request Id to the name of the extractor because it will be used to retrieve the value of this parameter. In the configuration screen for the extractor, we specify __RequestId as the reference name. Doing so tells JMeter that the result of the extraction should be stored in a variable called __RequestId. Looking at the HTML code in Listing 11.3 that defines the hidden form parameters, we can come up with a regular expression that will match the value of the __RequestId:

```
name="__RequestId" value="(\d+)"
```

This regular expression uses static characters to uniquely identify the __RequestId definition and \d+ mask to specify any number of digits. The parentheses specify which part of the expression should be used as the result. Because we are interested only in the numeric value, the parentheses surround \d+.

The template in the extractor enables the creation of a string out of the matches found by applying the regular expression. The template can include static text and n as a placeholder for the *n*th match of the regular expression. We are expecting only one match, so we specify 1 as the template—and we're done with the __RequestId extraction.

Similarly to __RequestId, we should add two more extractors for the __WindowTitle and __Action variables. This is a good time to exercise your brain and come up with your own regular expressions and template strings. But just in case, I'll make your life easier by saying that the regular expression for __WindowTitle can be

```
name="__WindowTitle" value="(.+)"
```

and the template can be 1. The __Action regular expression can be

```
name="(JButton\d+)" value="Login Dialog"
```

and the template should be /button/1. The key in coming up with the regular expression and template is to produce a string that can be used as a value of a parameter for the next request. Figure 11.5 shows the test plan tree we have created so far.

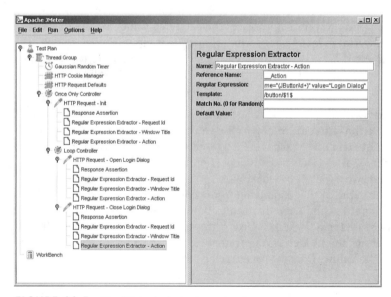

FIGURE 11.5   The JMeter test plan tree, step 3.

We are not ready to use the variables, which contain the extracted values, as parameters to HTTP requests. We have already defined the parameters in the HTTP Request Defaults node, so let's go back to it and specify the values. To obtain a value of a JMeter variable, we must the use the syntax ${*name*}, where *name* is the name of the variable. We specify ${__RequestId} as the value for the __RequestId parameter, ${__WindowTitle} as the value for __WindowTitle, and ${__Action} as the value for __Action.

Hang on, we're almost there. Before running the test, we need to add a few listeners to monitor the test execution. To test the script, the most useful listeners are `View Results Tree` and `Assertion Results`. `View Results Tree` shows each request with the request and response data, whereas `Assertion Results` is a quick and easy way to see which assertions have failed. You should not keep `View Results Tree` in the final version of the test script due to the performance overhead associated with collecting and storing all the data. Finally, we add the Aggregate Report listener to produce a summary of the execution and performance metrics per request.

If you have followed all the steps correctly, your test plan should look as shown in Figure 11.6.

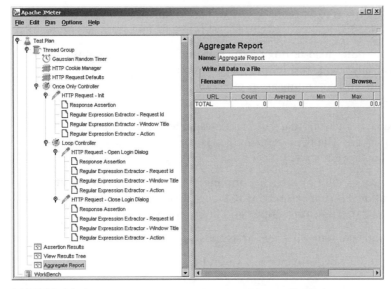

FIGURE 11.6   The JMeter test plan tree for WebCream, finished.

Make sure that WebCream's Tomcat is running, and unleash the fury of JMeter by selecting Start from the Run menu. After a few minutes, the test should finish and you should be able to see the results in the listener nodes.

Quick Quiz

1. What is the purpose of load-testing?

2. What is the difference between simultaneous and concurrent users?

3. Which client protocols can be tested with JUnit?

4. How do JUnit test cases assert the validity of the response?

5. Which client protocols can be tested with JMeter?

6. Which configuration and sampler nodes are used in JMeter test plans?

7. How do you monitor the progress and the results of a running JMeter test plan?

8. What are the benefits and shortcomings of JUnit and JMeter?

In Brief

- The purpose of load-testing is to assess how system performance meets service level requirements under a load.

- Commercial and open-source load-testing products can include the capability to record virtual users automatically, create test scripts programmatically, support multiple programming languages and communication protocols, and generate graphs and reports.

- JUnit is an open-source framework that can be harnessed to conduct simple load tests of RMI or plain Java servers. The JUnit test case is a Java class that is compiled and executed to test the application code.

- JMeter is an open-source tool for load-testing and measuring the performance of Web sites and Java applications. It supports servers that accept HTTP and FTP connections but can be used to test databases, Perl scripts, and Java objects as well.

- JMeter supports dynamic content with regular expression extractors and variables.

- JMeter listeners can produce performance reports and graphs.

Reverse Engineering Applications

"If builders built buildings the way programmers write programs, then the first woodpecker to come along would destroy civilization."

Murphy's Technology Laws

User Interface Elements and Resources

In Chapter 5, "Replacing and Patching Application Classes," we talked about patching classes to alter the application logic. In this chapter we discuss changing the user interface elements such as messages, warnings, prompts, images, icons, menus, and colors. The same principles described in Chapter 5 apply here as well. The first task is to locate a resource that needs to be changed. Then a change can be made and the application updated to ensure that the new resource is used in place of the old one. Table 12.1 shows the association between UI elements and the resources to be patched.

12

IN THIS CHAPTER

TABLE 12.1

Associations Between UI Elements and Resources

ELEMENT TYPE	ELEMENT EXAMPLES	JAVA RESOURCE
Text	Dialog message, warning, exception text	Java string inside a class file or text in a configuration file
Image	Splash screen, icon, background image	JPG or GIF files (or other image formats) in an application directory or inside a JAR file
Visual element	Window layout, menu composition, color	Java class file containing the corresponding element
Configuration setting	Programmatic limits such as a maximum number of connections, an expiration date, the number of threads	A Java class file if the setting is hard coded, .properties files, or .xml files if the setting is configurable
Audio	Background music, sound effect	WAV, AIFF, or AU files representing the clip

Learning by example is one of the easiest ways to digest information, so let's take a hypothetical application and then mutate it according to our whims. You have seen a lot of appearances of the Chat application throughout the previous chapters and in continuation of a good tradition we will hack Chat to illustrate each of the techniques.

Hacking Text

Chat uses the text Send message as the menu item text and the ToolTip hint for the toolbar button. Although it conveys the meaning of the action perfectly, it can be perceived by the younger generation of users as uncool. To satisfy this audience, let's hack Chat to use Unleash the fury instead of Send message. We will be working with the distributed version of the application pretending that we do not have access to the source code.

Because Chat comes packaged in a JAR file, the first thing we must do is unjar CovertJava/distrib/lib/chat.jar into a temporary working directory. We then have to find the classes that define the text strings currently displayed by Chat. Using FAR or a search tool, we do a binary search for Send message in all files located in the working directory and its subdirectories. The result of running the search should be the MainFrame.class file, which we decompile as described in Chapter 2, "Decompiling Classes." Searching the decompiled source code for Send message takes us to the jbInit method, an excerpt of which is shown in Listing 12.1.

LISTING 12.1 jbInit Excerpt Showing the Text Strings

```
private void jbInit()
    throws Exception
{
    ...
    btnSend.setToolTipText("Send message");
    btnHelp.setIcon(imageHelp);

    ...
    menuEditSend.setText("Send message");
    menuEditSend.addActionListener(this);

    ...
}
```

Using the patching technique presented in Chapter 5, we can just replace Send message with Unleash the fury in the decompiled source code and add it as a patch to Chat. That was easy enough, and luckily in most real applications it should be just as easy. Complications can arise if the application code is obfuscated with string encoding, but with the knowledge gained from previous chapters, it should not stop us from finding the class to patch.

Good applications do not hardcode the text strings in the code. Instead, the messages are stored in resource bundles or configuration files, which makes maintenance and localization easy. As long as the strings are not encoded, the binary search performed on the contents of the working directory still yields the desired results. After the file containing the string is located, it can be updated with the new text. After that, the application needs to be repackaged for the change to take effect.

Hacking Images

Working with images is a bit trickier than working with text. Unlike text, you can't just search for an image because you don't know what to use as a search criteria. The first step, therefore, is to find the name of the image and determine how the application is loading it, after which a patch can be applied. There is no direct and easy way of finding the name of the image. Most likely, the application loads it in the UI-related code, but many times developers use a framework or a manager class to help with the groundwork required to load an image in Java. Experience suggests exploring the exploded (that is, not stored in a JAR) application or maybe searching for all .jpg and .gif files. Most of the time, the image name is the best clue to where it is used. For example, a splash screen might be called something like splash.gif and the icon for the New toolbar button might be called new.gif. A typical Java application does not have many images, so you should be able to locate the one you are looking for easily. Obviously, viewing the image is the way to confirm that you found your guy. (I didn't really have to say that, did I?)

What if there are too many images, and the programmer who coded the application used file-names such as img0045.gif? You can still guess which image is yours by looking at the size of it or just going through all of them sequentially. Remember that the application might be storing images in a different JAR file, so you have to open all of them when doing the search.

Now look at a worst-case scenario: You can see that the application is displaying an image and you desperately need to change it, but after going through all the image files packaged with the application, you can't find it. You have several options for determining where is it coming from. Because the easy way didn't work, we'll have to dig deeper and get to the place in the code where the image is loaded. Again, previous chapters covered reverse engineering techniques, and I suggest searching the class files for .gif or .jpg as a starting point. I have never seen an application that stores GIF files with a .txt extension, and I surely hope to never live to see that day. For instance, to change the image in the About dialog box of Chat, we can search for all GIF and JPG files in the working directory. Doing so takes us to the covertjava.chat.images directory that contains several images. Because it contains just a few images, we can simply view them to determine which one is used in the About dialog box. Alternatively, we could have searched for .gif, which would have taken us to the MainFrame class file again. Decompiling it, we would have discovered that Chat uses saturn_small.gif for the About dialog box.

Finally, we can also search for the getImage method of java.awt.Toolkit, which is the most common way to load an image. The following are a couple of examples of Java code that loads an image:

```java
/**
 * Creates an icon from an image contained in "resources/images"
 * directory inside a .jar file
 */
public ImageIcon createImageIcon(String fileName) throws Exception
{
    String path = "/resources/images/" + fileName;
    return new ImageIcon(getClass().getResource(path));
}
/**
 * Loads an image from "images" directory on disk
 */
public Image loadImage(String fileName) throws Exception
{
    return Toolkit.getToolkit().getImage("images/" + filename);
}
```

After you have found the code that is loading the image, you should be able to understand where it is coming from. If the image is not packaged with the application, most likely it is accessed via an external URL similar to `http://mycompany.com/app/images/splash.gif`. At this point, you (the educated hacker) know exactly how to attack the problem. Use your Web browser to download the image from the URL, save it locally, edit it, and package it with the application. Then patch the class that is loading it and, instead of the HTTP URL, use either the `jar:file/` URL to load it from your JAR or `Toolkit.getImage()` to load it from a directory. Voilá—you've done it.

Hacking Configuration Files

Configuration files are just another type of application resource, and the approach to hacking one is the same as for text and images. We are not talking about the configuration files stored in the application directory that can be easily modified; we are talking about the files that can be inside the `.jar` or `.zip` file and that are not necessarily intended for editing. As before, we will unjar the application archive and examine the directory structure looking for suspicious files. If the directory structure is large, we can search for all files with a `.properties` or `.xml` extension. Most likely this simple browsing will yield the results—if not, we can fall back to the reverse engineering techniques described in previous chapters to locate the part of code that is using the setting. Then we can trace our way to the code that is loading the configuration, which will provide enough information to determine the patching strategy.

Quick Quiz

1. Suppose you are using a library that displays an `Unknown error` message if it catches a generic exception. How would you change it to say `Internal error, please contact technical support`?

2. How would you change Chat's About dialog box to have your name on the image?

3. How would you find out whether the maximum number of concurrent connections imposed by the application you are using is configurable?

In Brief

■ Hacking UI elements requires finding and patching the resources that were used to create it.

■ Hacking text requires finding the CLASS file or a configuration file (.properties, .xml, or .resource) that defines it and changing the file.

■ Hacking images requires finding the image file (usually GIF or JPG).

■ Hacking configuration files involves simple text editing after you find the file that defines the properties of interest.

Eavesdropping Techniques

13

IN THIS CHAPTER

▶ Eavesdropping Defined
127

▶ Eavesdropping on HTTP
128

▶ Eavesdropping on the RMI
Protocol   133

▶ Eavesdropping on JDBC
Driver and SQL Statements
135

▶ Quick Quiz   137

▶ In Brief   138

"You can observe a lot by just watching."

Berra's First Law

Eavesdropping Defined

The previous chapters focused mostly on working with the application bytecode and resources. N-tier applications that are dominant on the server side offer additional angles for reverse engineering and hacking. It is common practice to deploy application tiers as separate processes that communicate with each other via network protocols. For instance, a Web browser displaying an HTML front-end on a user workstation uses the Hypertext Transfer Protocol (HTTP) to communicate with the Web server. In turn, the Web server typically uses RMI or IIOP to communicate with the application server. The application server relies on JDBC to communicate with the database. A classic deployment diagram for N-tier distributed Java applications is shown in Figure 13.1.

This chapter presents several techniques that can be employed to eavesdrop on the conversation between the distributed tiers. *Eavesdropping* is intercepting and logging the message exchange between a client and server. It can facilitate the troubleshooting or performance tuning of a complex distributed system, as well as provide insight into the application design and communication principles.

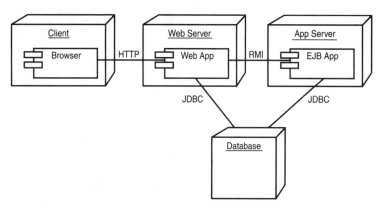

FIGURE 13.1   An N-tier application deployment diagram.

Eavesdropping on HTTP

We will first look at eavesdropping on Web-based applications and Web services that use HTTP as a transport protocol to communicate with their clients. HTTP messages consist of a header and the content that is sent across the network via TCP/IP. For a client to be capable of talking to a server, it must know the server's hostname or IP address and the port on which the server is listening. HTTP messages are sent in plain text, which can be easily read and understood by humans.

To eavesdrop on the client/server communication, you must intercept the message exchange. One way of doing this is by placing an intermediary that traces and tunnels HTTP messages between the client and server. An alternative is to monitor the communication on the network protocol layer, filtering on the messages exchanged by the client and server. We will look at both alternatives in the following sections. Once again, we will use WebCream as the server-side application because it provides static and dynamic HTML content via servlets and JSP pages.

Using a Tunnel to Capture the HTTP Message Exchange

A *tunnel* in this context is a pseudo server placed between the real client and real server to intercept and trace the message exchange. Instead of directly talking to the server, the client is reconfigured to send messages to the tunnel; the tunnel is configured to dispatch requests to the server on behalf of the client and forward the server responses back to the client. The tunnel logs the exchanged messages to the screen or into a file, allowing a hacker or developer to study the details of the conversation. The text-based and stateless nature of HTTP makes it a good choice for tunneling.

We will use the TCPMON utility distributed with Apache AXIS project for tunneling browser requests to WebCream's Tomcat server. Although TCPMON is by far not the most sophisticated tunneling software, it is free and does a good job for most cases. Download AXIS from Apache's Web site and, if you do not have a script to start TCPMON, copy the CovertJava\bin\axis subdirectory to the directory where you have installed AXIS. TCPMON takes in three command-line parameters, which are the port to listen on, the host, and the port number of the server to tunnel the requests to. Because WebCream runs Tomcat on port 8040, we will run TCPMON on port 8000 and tell it to forward to port 8040 of localhost.

We need to make a few simple configuration changes in WebCream to support tunneling through AXIS. WebCream generates page forms with fully qualified URLs for submission, which include the host and the port number. We want all traffic to go through the TCPMON, so we need WebCream to always submit forms to port 8000 rather than 8040 as it does by default. We can achieve this by adding the following two lines to WebCreamconf\ WebCreamDemo.properties (see the WebCream documentation for more information):

```
html.docsURL=http://localhost:8040/webcream
html.submitURL=http://localhost:8000/webcream/apps/WebCreamDemo
```

Start WebCream's Tomcat using WebCream\bin\startServer.bat. Open your favorite Web browser and type the following in the address line:

```
http://localhost:8000/webcream/apps/WebCreamDemo
```

Notice that we are using port 8000, which is the port on which TCPMON is running, rather than pointing the browser directly to Tomcat, which is running on port 8040.

The browser should display the WebCream demo main page. Switch to TCPMON and make sure that you see the intercepted request in the top (or left) panel. TCPMON can be rather slow at detecting that the request is fully transmitted, so be sure to wait until the status of the request in the top panel changes to Done. Go back to the browser and click the Login Dialog button to open the next page; then enter **Neo** as the username and **Wakeup** as the password and click OK. (You are free to pick your own username and password, however.) If you switch to the TCPMON screen, it should look similar to Figure 13.2.

We can now examine the requests and the data intercepted by TCPMON. The top panel shows three messages, which corresponds to the number of pages requested by the browser. The most interesting piece of information is shown in the bottom-left and bottom-right panels. The left panel shows the request header and data, whereas the right panel shows the response header and content. Looking at the various attributes and content elements gives us an insight into the data exchange between the browser and server. For example, selecting the third request in the top panel and looking at the request data, we can see the actual values of the login name (Neo) and password (Wakeup). In the header, we can see a cookie, JSESSIONID, that can be exploited to hijack the user session.

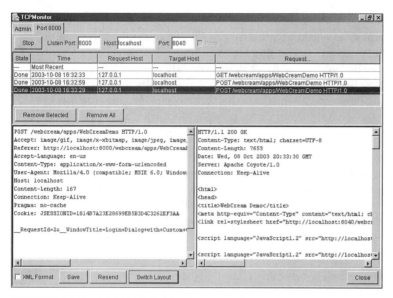

FIGURE 13.2 TCPMON showing intercepted requests.

Using a Network Sniffer to Capture the HTTP Message Exchange

Tunneling is a simple and effective way to see what is actually transmitted between the client and server. It is good for debugging and studying Web-based applications, but it has the drawback of requiring a reconfiguration of the client (and possibly even the server, as we had to do with WebCream) to send requests to the tunneling agent instead of directly to the server. The second technique you will learn allows eavesdropping on the network protocol level, which does not have the limitations of tunneling.

All distributed communications go through a layer of protocols supported by the JVM, operating system, and network driver. Protocols are stacked on top of each other, meaning that higher-level protocols rely on lower-level protocols to perform more basic tasks. Thus, HTTP relies on TCP, which in turn relies on IP. A single HTTP message can be represented by several low-level IP packets, and it's the job of the networking layers to disassemble and then reassemble the packets. Most of the physical networks are composed of interconnected Ethernet segments of workstations. Within a segment, packets from one node are transmitted to all nodes regardless of the target node address. To communicate with a computer outside the segment, routers redirect the packets to other segments. The bottom line of this crude summary is that, when an application on one host communicates with a remote application on a different host, the protocol packets have to traverse a number of other network hosts before reaching the target. Network sniffing and monitoring takes advantage of this principle to spy on the communications. Normally, a network node accepts only the packets that are targeted to it, ignoring all other packets. However, a node can be running in *promiscuous* mode in which it accepts all packets regardless of the destination address. Then an engineer or a hacker can examine the packets and their contents to gain insight into the application communications.

Working on the protocol level can be hard and time-consuming. Because HTTP is a very common protocol, products are available that simplify eavesdropping on HTTP communications. We are going to look at HTTP Sniffer from EffeTech, which is a Windows-based shareware application. We will try to perform the same task of intercepting the communication between the browser and WebCream's Tomcat and see whether we get a different result than with TCPMON. One of the drawbacks of using a network sniffer is that it does not work when the client and server are running on the same host. No packets are passed to the network driver, so the sniffer is incapable of capturing the protocol requests and responses. Thus, for this and the next section you need to make sure that the Tomcat server is running on a different network host from the browser. If you do not have access to another machine, you can use any Web site instead of WebCream.

Download and install EffeTech's HTTP Sniffer. It installs WinPcap, a packet capture library that is added as a device driver to Windows to capture raw data from the network card. Because WebCream is running Tomcat on port 8040, we need to add that port to the sniffer filter using the Filter item of the Sniffer menu. You might have to switch the current network adapter in the sniffer if the recording will not produce any results, but for now leave it as the default. Start WebCream's Tomcat on the remote server and then bring up the Web browser. Note that the sniffer can run on the same machine as the browser, on the same machine as the Web server, or on any machine connected to the same Ethernet segment as the browser or the server hosts. Start the recording using the Sniffer menu or the toolbar and type the server URL in the browser. If testing with WebCream, open the main screen, click the Login Dialog button to go to the next page, enter **Neo** as the username and **Wakeup** as the password; then click OK. After stopping the recording in HTTP Sniffer, its screen should look as shown in Figure 13.3.

The way the information is presented and the type of information intercepted is almost the same as in TCPMON. Besides sporting a cleaner user interface, HTTP Sniffer shows other resources that were obtained by the browser from the server, such as GIF and JavaScript files. Once again, looking at the request data we can obtain values of form parameters such as the username and password. The beauty of this approach is that we didn't have to do anything to the target application, yet we have captured a complete log of the communication between the client and server.

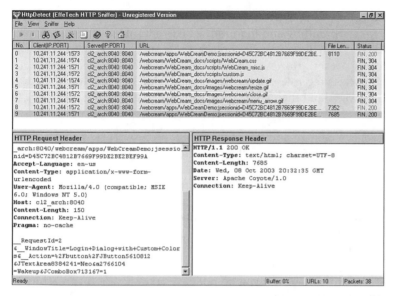

FIGURE 13.3   HTTP Sniffer showing intercepted requests.

Protecting Web Applications from Eavesdropping

In a short amount of time, you have learned how to eavesdrop on browser-based user interfaces. The ease with which you can obtain the values of potentially sensitive parameters is rather alarming. A few precautions can make the job of hacking a Web application much harder. The simplest and most effective way to protect the data integrity and secure the client/server communication is via the use of Hypertext Transfer Protocol Secure (HTTPS). This protocol mandates that a client establish a secure channel to the server using Secure Sockets Layer (SSL) before sending any HTTP data. After the channel is established, the message exchange occurs just as with HTTP. The benefit of HTTPS is that all data is encrypted, so even if someone intercepts a network packet, decrypting it is virtually impossible. SSL does have an overhead that can slow down the server, so for high-performance applications doing all communications via HTTPS, this might not be feasible. A good compromise is to use HTTPS selectively or to continue using HTTP but encrypt the sensitive content on the application tier. If the user interface is a Web browser, JavaScript functions can be used to perform encryption and decryption on the client side.

Eavesdropping on the RMI Protocol

Java Remote Method Invocation (JRMI) uses either Java-specific Java Remote Method Protocol (JRMP) or Internet Inter-Orb Protocol (IIOP) to send binary messages to remote hosts. JRMP and IIOP rely on the Transmission Control Protocol/Internet Protocol (TCP/IP) to transport the messages across the network, which makes the communication channel subject to network sniffing. Theoretically, you can write a tunnel that would receive and log the messages before passing them on to the intended receiver, but this would be a very tedious task. We will therefore rely on network sniffing to eavesdrop on RMI. Unfortunately, no tool has native support for higher-level Java protocols, similar to how HTTP Sniffer supports HTTP. This means we must work at a lower level, studying TCP and IP packets that represent all or parts of RMI calls. We will practice spying on the conversation between two users of Chat applications.

The RMI Transport Protocol

RMI uses a concept of a stream to represent the wire format. Internally, the communication has two associated streams—an out stream and an in stream. The streams are mapped to the corresponding socket streams and used to send and acknowledge messages. The output stream consists of a header followed by a sequence of messages. If HTTP is used, the output stream is embedded in an HTTP message. The header contains the protocol identification and attributes describing the type of protocol used. The essence of an RMI call is contained in the message section. Output messages consist of method calls, remote ping, or garbage collection traffic; input messages can be the return result of a call or an acknowledgement of a ping.

To execute a remote call, RMI uses the Java Object Serialization protocol to format the method name and parameter values into a binary structure that is sent across the wire. Therefore, all remote calls follow the same format on the binary level. Knowledge of the transport specifics is not required for eavesdropping on RMI, but if you would like to get more information on it, go to http://java.sun.com/j2se/1.4.2/docs/guide/ rmi/spec/rmiTOC.html. For our purpose, it is sufficient to know that when two Java applications use RMI to exchange messages, a low-level TCP/IP connection with input and output streams is created and used.

Using a Network Sniffer to Intercept RMI Messages

One of the most popular network sniffing tools is Ethereal. It is free and has ports to Unix and Windows. It can analyze just about any conceivable protocol (save for RMI) and, even though its user interface is somewhat crude, it will do in the absence of a better tool. Ethereal relies on WinPcap, the same library HTTP Sniffer uses to capture network packets. Download, install, and run Ethereal. Start recording the network traffic just to get an idea about the type of information it can capture. Open a browser and visit a couple of Web sites; then stop recording and look at the items displayed in the top panel. You'll see several packets. Our first task is to configure the tool to show only the information we are interested in seeing.

We start by opening the Capture Options dialog box, which is displayed when you select Start from the Capture menu. Deselect the Capture Packets in Promiscuous Mode button, select Update List of Packets in Real Time, and make sure that all the Stop Capture After buttons are deselected. Because network sniffing requires the client and server run on different hosts, run Chat on two machines. Click OK to confirm the capture options and start recording. Then switch to Chat and send a Hi Alex message to the other host. (I won't be offended if you use your own name instead of mine.) Send one more message and remember the text (my second message is IT jobs are becoming boring); you will need it later. Then switch back to Ethereal and stop the capture.

We have captured a lot of packets and, to see the Chat conversation, we need a way of filtering the packets that carry the pieces of the text messages users sent. We can start by searching for a packet that carries the string we know was sent during the recording. Select Find Frame from the Edit menu to bring up the Search dialog box. Enter a part of the message you sent (I would enter Alex), and be sure to select the String option for the Find Syntax button group. This tells Ethereal to search for the string in any part of the packet. Click OK and the packet that contained the string should become selected. In the lower panels you should see the contents of the packet, which should include your search string among the binary content. Because one RMI call can be broken down into multiple TCP/IP messages, it generally helps to use the Follow TCP Stream feature that reassembles the stream and shows it in a separate window. Right-click the selected packet frame and select Follow TCP Stream.

At this point, we are looking at the binary version of an RMI packet. It is somewhat cryptic, but with a little bit of patience we can gain some knowledge out of it. It starts with the header JRMI, indicating that the JRMI protocol is used for RMI transport. Next is the IP address of the originating host, the object ID of the server, and miscellaneous distributed garbage collection (DGC) information. The message content is at the very end. In my case, I can see the string Hi Alex followed by covertjava.chat.MessageInfo, which we guess is the message class name. It is followed by other parameters of the message, such as the hostname and username.

After examining the TCP/IP stream representing the RMI message sent by Chat, we can make an assumption that subsequent messages will have the same format. In other words, even though the message text might change, the header and the format of the message will remain the same. If this assumption is correct, we should be able to search for Chat messages based on a substring from the message header or format. To test this theory, let's try searching all frames for covertjava.chat.MessageInfo using the Find Frame dialog box. If the filter string is set at the bottom of the screen, reset the filter. Then go to the first frame and execute the search. The first frame I found has the Hi Alex string and, after searching for the next frame, I found a message with IT jobs are becoming boring in the content. This supports our assumption about Chat and allows us to follow the conversation between the users.

A similar approach can be used for other applications. Ethereal works at a very low level, but with due diligence and a little bit of analysis, you can eavesdrop on network communication between any applications.

Protecting RMI Applications from Eavesdropping

Based on what we have learned about network sniffing, we can conclude that you cannot really prevent eavesdropping on network communications. At the end of the day, the data has to travel over the wire and go through several network nodes, which makes it susceptible to interception. The only way to protect the data is to encrypt it. SSL offers industry-standard features for securing network channels, and it can be used for RMI communication. Java Secure Sockets Extension (JSSE) is a set of APIs that enable Java applications to take advantage of SSL for data encryption, authentication, and message integrity. RMI enables applications to provide custom socket factories for exported objects that are used instead of the default TCP/IP sockets. Using JSSE SSL factories as custom socket factories for both the client and server effectively secures the channel. An example of an RMI and SSL marriage is provided on JavaSoft's Web site at the following URL:

```
http://java.sun.com/j2se/1.4.1/docs/guide/rmi/socketfactory/SSLInfo.html
```

SSL communication does introduce an overhead, which might be unnecessary for all possible client/server data exchange. It might be a better option to keep using the default socket factories, but to encrypt the sensitive parts of the data using JSSE. An example of using Java encryption is shown in Chapter 19, "Protecting Commercial Applications from Hacking."

Eavesdropping on JDBC Driver and SQL Statements

Most of the server applications use a database to store and retrieve data. Knowing how the application interacts with the database and which SQL statements it employs can be of great help in performance tuning or reverse engineering. The overwhelming technology of choice for persistence is JDBC, and it is not going to change any time soon. To use JDBC, an application must identify and load a driver, obtain a connection, and then execute statements to perform updates and queries. The most interesting logic from the performance tuning and reverse engineering perspective is the structure and the parameters of SQL statements. It is common knowledge that database performance depends immensely on how effective the application SQL statements are. Analyzing the SQL and the execution times can lead to improvements on the application side, database side, or both.

Theoretically, you can go through the application source or bytecode and collect all the SQL statements that are stored as strings. This can, of course, be problematic for applications that have a large number of statements or form the SQL dynamically. You also can rely on the database itself to provide the logging of the SQL statements. Although this is definitely a better option than the application code, it requires administrative privileges to the database and might not be very easy if multiple applications share the same database.

JDBC API provides a method of logging the database operations at the driver level via the `DriverManager`'s `setLogWriter` method. It outputs information such as the registration of drivers, URLs used to create database connections, and connection class names. The problem with driver manager logging is that it does not provide the most important information, such as the SQL statements and values passed to the database. I have redirected the JDBC driver logging to System.out and tested it with a simple program that registers a driver, obtains a database connection, and executes a few `SELECT` statements with parameters. Examining the output of driver logging in Listing 13.1 shows no traces of the `SELECT` statements the program executed.

LISTING 13.1   JDBC Driver Logging Output

```
DriverManager.initialize: jdbc.drivers = null
JDBC DriverManager initialized
registerDriver: driver[className=com.sybase.jdbc2.jdbc.SybDriver...]
registerDriver: driver[className=com.sybase.jdbc2.jdbc.SybDriver...]
DriverManager.deregisterDriver: com.sybase.jdbc2.jdbc.SybDriver@1d4c61c
registerDriver: driver[className=com.sybase.jdbc2.jdbc.SybDriver...]
DriverManager.getConnection("jdbc:sybase:Tds:he1unx142:2075/pslwrkdb1")
    trying driver[className=com.sybase.jdbc2.jdbc.SybDriver...]
getConnection returning driver[className=
com.sybase.jdbc2.jdbc.SybDriver...]
```

STORIES FROM THE TRENCHES

At Riggs Bank we have started using Wily Introscope for performance monitoring of a cluster of servers. Introscope is a Java application that collects performance metrics at runtime and allows storing them in a relational database for later analysis. Built around good ideas, Introscope was lacking polishing and, with the amount of performance data we had, it was simply failing to work with the historical data. The tables used by Introscope grew to millions of records, and we suspected that inefficient database design and SQL statements were the cause of the problem. The technical support did not have a lot of suggestions other than, "Keep less data or upgrade the machine." To revive the product, we decided to spy on the SQL used to execute the queries. After we logged and analyzed the SQL statements, we were able to add indexes to tables, optimize the database design, and reconfigure the persistence within the product. This resulted in a tenfold increase in query performance and a great win for the development team.

To provide a reliable way of eavesdropping on database calls, you must replace the JDBC driver with a wrapper that logs the statement and then delegates to the "real" driver. There is a very good old maxim that states that a good technology/product makes "simple things easy and complex things possible." P6Spy, which we'll use for JDBC logging, demonstrates just that. In less than 10 minutes and with minimal configuration changes, it enables the logging of database calls from existing applications without any code changes. P6Spy is a free, open source application that can be downloaded from SourceForge.

After downloading and installing P6Spy, the `p6spy.jar` and `spy.properties` files must be placed on the `CLASSPATH` of the target application. To activate the spy, the real driver class used by the application should be replaced with the spy driver class. The name of the real driver should be configured in `spy.properties` so the spy can delegate to it. The rest of the database-related configuration for the application does not need to change. For example, if the application is connecting to an Oracle database using the standard driver, the name of the real driver class is `oracle.jdbc.driver.OracleDriver`. To activate the spy, this name should be replaced with `com.p6spy.engine.spy.P6SpyDriver` in the application configuration file and in `spy.properties` the real driver must be configured as follows:

```
realdriver=oracle.jdbc.driver.OracleDriver
```

Restarting the application produces a log that contains the intercepted database calls. For example, after configuring P6Spy with the standard JDK demo application `TableExample` and typing a few `SELECT` statements in the table, I got the following log:

```
1066073757578|16|0|statement||SELECT * FROM TAB
1066073780718|0|0|statement||SELECT * FROM TAB where tname='Alex'
```

P6Spy uses Log4J and is very customizable. Refer to the product documentation for further details.

Quick Quiz

1. What are the general approaches to eavesdropping?

2. Why is it easy to eavesdrop on HTTP communication?

3. How can HTTP communication be protected?

4. What makes network sniffing possible?

5. How can you eavesdrop on RMI communication?

6. What is the most reliable way of intercepting JDBC SQL statements?

In Brief

- *Eavesdropping* is intercepting and logging the message exchange between a client and server. It is possible because the communication has to traverse the process or machine boundaries.

- *Tunneling* is a technique that is based on placing an intermediary between a client and server and reconfiguring the client to send messages to the intermediary. The intermediary dispatches the requests to the server and forwards the response back to the client, logging the communication in the process.

- Eavesdropping on HTTP is easy due to the simple text-based nature of the protocol and a wide variety of tools.

- Network sniffing is possible because the networking protocol packets have to travel between nodes. A promiscuous network node chooses to receive all packets regardless of the destination address, which enables the sniffer to intercept the messages traversing the network.

- RMI eavesdropping is possible using a network sniffer such as Ethereal. It requires analysis of lower-level network packets that carry the binary contents of RMI messages.

- JDBC eavesdropping can be easily achieved with the help of wrappers around the real driver and the connection objects. The wrappers log every statement before forwarding it to the real driver classes.

Controlling Class Loading

14

"Nobody notices when things go well."
Zimmerman's Law of Complaints

Class loaders load and initialize classes and interfaces in the Java virtual machine (JVM). This chapter provides an overview of this process and shows you how to develop a custom class loader that allows decoration of loaded bytecode.

JVM Internals from a Class Loading Perspective

The Java virtual machine running on top of the operating system (OS) provides a level of abstraction to the applications written in Java. Language specification and standardized Application Programming Interfaces (APIs) enable cross-platform development and deployment because the applications do not make platform-specific calls directly to the OS. Most of the core Java APIs are themselves written in Java, with only a small portion of native code accessed via JNI. Java applications can contain bytecode and native dynamic libraries. The native libraries are distributed as dynamically linked libraries (.dll) for Windows and shared libraries (.so) for Unix. To execute a Java application, the JVM uses a class loader to load and initialize the system and application classes, which can result in loading of the application native libraries. The JVM from a class loading perspective is shown in Figure 14.1.

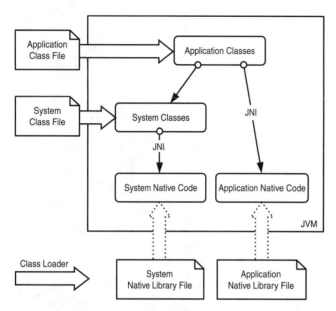

FIGURE 14.1   The JVM from a class loading perspective.

Although a typical application need not be concerned with the loading and initialization, the capability to control this process is exploited in techniques such as runtime bytecode instrumentation and bytecode integrity protection.

The application loading process begins with the initial class that was provided to the Java launcher (typically a command-line parameter to the Java runtime). All parent classes and any classes referenced by the main() method of the initial class are lazily loaded and initialized as the references are made. Unless explicitly specified, the class loader of the referring class is used to load the referred class. If class loaders load Java classes, what is used to load class loaders, you might ask? The answer is the *bootstrap* class loader, which is implemented in native code and is used to load Java core classes such as java.lang.Object and java.lang.ClassLoader. The *extensions* class loader is used to load the extension libraries typically from the lib/ext directory of JRE, and the JAR files placed in that directory are automatically available to Java applications. The *application* class loader is created internally by the JVM launcher to load classes from the standard CLASSPATH. Finally, a class loader called the *system* class loader is generally the same as the application class loader.

Class loaders are organized in a chain, in which a child lets the parent find the class before attempting to find it itself. Generally, a class loader first checks whether it has already loaded and initialized the class. If the class is not loaded yet, the class loader attempts to create or load it and, if found, initialize it in the JVM. The bootstrap class loader is the root of the class loaders hierarchy and corresponds to the value of null, whereas the system class loader is the default delegation parent for new class loaders. Table 14.1 lists the class loaders and the information about their sources of class data.

TABLE 14.1

Class Loaders and Their CLASS File Sources

CLASS LOADER	SOURCE OF CLASS DATA
Bootstrap	Directories and JAR files listed in the system property sun.boot.class.path, which by default includes the core runtime classes in rt.jar and a few other standard JARs. It can be manipulated using the -Xbootclasspath command-line parameter to the Java launcher.
Extensions	Directories listed in the system property java.ext.dirs, which by default points to the lib/ext directory of the JRE. However, it can be explicitly specified at the command line using -Djava.ext.dirs=<path>.
Application	Directories and JARs listed in the system property java.class.path, which by default is set from the CLASSPATH environment variable.

To peek at the hierarchy of class loaders at runtime, we will write a simple class that prints the class loader used to load it and the chain of its parents. The code for the class is shown in Listing 14.1.

LISTING 14.1   PrintClassLoaders Source Code

```
public class PrintClassLoaders {

    public static void main(String[] args) {
        System.out.println("System class loader = " +
            ClassLoader.getSystemClassLoader());
        System.out.println("Thread context class loader = " +
            Thread.currentThread().getContextClassLoader());

        System.out.println("Class loader hierarchy for this class:");
        String padding = "";
        ClassLoader cl = PrintClassLoaders.class.getClassLoader();
        while (cl != null) {
            System.out.println(padding + cl);
            cl = cl.getParent();
            padding += "    ";
        }
        System.out.println(padding + "null (bootstrap class loader)");
    }

}
```

The PrintClassLoaders class is located in the covertjava.classloader package. Running the class produces the following output:

```
System class loader = sun.misc.Launcher$AppClassLoader@12f6684
Thread context class loader = sun.misc.Launcher$AppClassLoader@12f6684
Class loader hierarchy for this class:
sun.misc.Launcher$AppClassLoader@12f6684
    sun.misc.Launcher$ExtClassLoader@f38798
        null (bootstrap class loader)
```

We can conclude from the output that the class loaders hierarchy corresponds to the order in which the runtime attempts to find and load a class. The AppClassLoader instance returned by the getClassLoader() call from the initial class is the class loader that is associated with PrintClassLoaders. The same class loader instance is used as the system class loader returned by ClassLoader.getSystemClassLoader(), and its immediate parent is the extension class loader ExtClassLoader. The extension class loader has null as its parent, which implies the bootstrap class loader. As a result of class loaders delegating to the parent before trying to load a class themselves, the classes found on the boot class path are always loaded by the bootstrap class loader. If the class is not found on the boot class path, the extensions class path is checked next. Only if a class is not found on either path is the application class path checked. If the class is not found by the application class loader as well, the notorious ClassNotFound exception is thrown.

Several important points about class loading require a clear understanding:

- The class loader that has loaded and defined a class process is associated with it and referred to as the *defining class loader*.

- The loaded class is identified not just by its name, but by a pair of the name and the defining class loader. Two classes that share the same name but have different class loaders are deemed to be different.

- If class A makes a reference to class B that is not loaded yet, A's defining class loader is used to load B.

Thus, if a class was loaded from the boot class path by the bootstrap class loader, it is incapable of referring to the classes from the application class path, unless it explicitly goes through the system class loader or a custom class loader. A thread has an associated class loader that can be obtained using getContextClassLoader(). It is typically set to be the class loader of the class that started the thread. Sometimes you need to use the thread context class loader rather than the defining class loader to access classes from a different source. This can be the case for servlets loaded using a custom class loader of the Web container. The container's class loader might be configured to load only the classes from the Web application, which means the classes on the system class path are inaccessible.

Writing a Custom Class Loader

Java gives applications control over how the classes are created or loaded through custom or user-defined class loaders. For example, Web and application servers provide each deployed application with its own class loader to better isolate the logical applications running inside the same JVM. Recall that, even if two classes were loaded from the same class file, they are deemed to be different if they were defined by different class loaders. With each application having its own class loader, static variables used so often to implement singleton patterns and store global data become applicationwide rather than JVM-wide. Custom class loaders also allow Web and application servers to reload classes without restarting the JVM. Another powerful technique is using a custom class loader to either create classes on-the-fly or alter the binary structure of the class data before defining it in the Java runtime.

In this section we are going to create a custom class loader called `DecoratingClassLoader` in package `covertjava.classloader` that allows modification of loaded binary class data on-the-fly. After it's coded, this class can be used to support encrypted class files or bytecode decoration, which are discussed later in this book. For now, we will focus on loading the classes from a user-defined class path and invoking a callback method that will have an opportunity to examine and modify the binary data. The code will be loosely based on JUnit's implementation of a class loader. All class loaders must extend the abstract class `java.lang.ClassLoader` and, at minimum, override the `findClass` method to load or create the class for a given name. `DecoratingClassLoader`'s implementation of `findClass` is shown in Listing 14.2.

LISTING 14.2   `findClass` Implementation

```
protected Class findClass(String name) throws ClassNotFoundException {
    System.out.println("DecoratingClassLoader loading class " + name);
    byte[] bytes = getClassBytes(name);

    if (getDecorator() != null)
```

STORIES FROM THE TRENCHES

WebCream converts Java applications to HTML Web sites on-the-fly. One of the critical features of this product is the capability to execute multiple virtual clients within the same JVM. Multithreading makes running several instances of a Java application in a JVM easy, but the applications end up sharing the classes. This leads to errors because the static initializers run only for the first client and the static members are common to all clients. To provide clean separation between the virtual clients, WebCream uses a custom class loader. Each virtual client is given its own class loader instance that loads all the application classes. Because the JVM uses the class loader together with the class name to identify the class, each virtual client receives its own class and static data.

LISTING 14.2   Continued

```
        bytes = getDecorator().decorateClass(name, bytes);

    return defineClass(name, bytes, 0, bytes.length);
}
```

The findClass method is called only if the class is not found by any parent class loader in the hierarchy. This way, the loading of core classes such as java.lang.Object is done by the bootstrap class loader. After the binary class data is loaded, the decorator is given a chance to augment the bytecode. Then the class bytes are passed to the defineClass method of java.lang.ClassLoader, which converts the binary class representation to an internal Class object. The reading of binary class data is performed in method getClassBytes(), shown in Listing 14.3.

LISTING 14.3   getClassBytes Implementation

```
protected byte[] getClassBytes(String className)
    throws ClassNotFoundException
{
    byte[] bytes = null;
    for (int i = 0; i < classPathItems.size(); i++) {
        String path = (String)classPathItems.get(i);
        String fileName = className.replace('.', '/') + ".class";
        if (isJar(path) == true) {
            bytes = loadJarBytes(path, fileName);
        }
        else {
            bytes = loadFileBytes(path, fileName);
        }
        if (bytes != null)
            break;
    }

    if (bytes == null)
        throw new ClassNotFoundException(className);

    return bytes;
}
```

The method iterates the items of the configured class path and attempts to locate and load the data from a .class file in the corresponding directory. If the class data is not found, ClassNotFoundException is thrown. DecoratingClassLoader takes the class path as a parameter to its constructor, and the default constructor uses the value of the decorate.class.path system property to initialize its class path. The full source code for the DecoratingClassLoader can be found in the CovertJava/src/covertjava/classloader directory.

To use the custom class loader, it must be explicitly specified for the loading of a class that is inaccessible to the parent class loaders. This can be done by passing a class loader instance to the Class.forName() method or by directly calling the loadClass() method of the custom class loader. Remember that class loaders delegate the loading to the parent chain and, if a parent class loader can locate the class, the child class loader's findClass() method is not called. This means that the cleanest way of allowing a custom class loader to load a class is to ensure that the class is not found on the system class path, boot class path, or extension class path. This is a common choice for Web server and application server implementations that caution against placing application classes on the system CLASSPATH. If full control of the class loading is required, the loadClass(String name, boolean resolve) method can be overridden. This method is called to initiate the class loading, and the default implementation lets the parent attempt to load the class first. By overriding this method, the custom class loader is called for every class in the system, regardless of where the class data is found. An alternative is to use the bootstrap class loader as a parent by passing a null value to the ClassLoader constructor. However, taking the jars and directories with classes that are supposed to be loaded using a custom class loader off the system CLASSPATH is the best alternative because it achieves the separation of system and custom classes.

To test the delegation of DecoratingClassLoader, we will add a decorator called PrintingClassDecorator that simply prints the name of the class on which it is invoked (see Listing 14.4).

LISTING 14.4 PrintingClassDecorator Implementation

```
public class PrintingClassDecorator implements ClassDecorator {

    public byte[] decorateClass(String name, byte[] bytes) {
        System.out.println("Processed bytes for class " + name);
        return bytes;
    }
}
```

To see our DecoratingClassLoader in action, let's try it on the PrintClassLoaders class we looked at earlier. We'll need a launcher class that instantiates our custom class loader and then loads the test class using it. DecoratingLauncher in package covertjava.classloader takes the name of the test class to launch and uses DecoratingClassLoader to load it. It then invokes the main() function of the test class via the reflection API. The main() method of DecoratingLauncher is shown in Listing 14.5.

LISTING 14.5   DecoratingLauncher main() Method

```
public static void main(String[] args) throws Exception {
    if (args.length < 1) {
        System.out.println("Missing command line parameter <main class>");
        System.out.println("Syntax: DecoratingLauncher " +
          "[-Ddecorate.class.path=<path>] <main class> [<arg1>, [<arg2>]..]");
        System.exit(1);
    }

    DecoratingClassLoader decoratingClassLoader = new DecoratingClassLoader();
    decoratingClassLoader.setDecorator(new PrintingClassDecorator());
    Class mainClass = Class.forName(args[0], true, decoratingClassLoader);

    String[] mainArgs = new String[args.length - 1];
    System.arraycopy(args, 1, mainArgs, 0, args.length - 1);
    invokeMain(mainClass, mainArgs);
}
```

Notice that we are passing the instance of our class loader to the forName() method. Before running the test, we need to ensure that the PrintClassLoaders class is removed from CLASSPATH and placed in a directory that will be pointed to by the decorate.class.path system property. We'll have to modify the release target in our build.xml to move covertjava.classloaders.PrintClassLoaders to the CovertJava/lib/classes directory before we create a JAR. We also need to create a new batch file in the bin directory that will invoke the launcher and pass it PrintClassLoaders as a parameter. The batch file content is shown in Listing 14.6.

LISTING 14.6   classLoaderTest.bat Code

```
@echo off
rem Demonstration of using custom class loader on PrintClassLoaders class

call setEnv.bat
set JAVA_OPTS=-Ddecorate.class.path=..\lib\classes %JAVA_OPTS%

java %JAVA_OPTS% covertjava.classloader.DecoratingLauncher
covertjava.classloader.PrintClassLoaders
```

Running `classLoaderTest.bat` produces the following output:

```
Processed bytes for class covertjava.classloader.PrintClassLoaders
System class loader = sun.misc.Launcher$AppClassLoader@12f6684
Thread context class loader = sun.misc.Launcher$AppClassLoader@12f6684
Class loader hierarchy for this class:
covertjava.classloader.DecoratingClassLoader@ad3ba4
    sun.misc.Launcher$AppClassLoader@12f6684
        sun.misc.Launcher$ExtClassLoader@f38798
            null (bootstrap class loader)
```

From the output, we can see that the class loader associated with the `PrintClassLoaders` class is an instance of `DecoratingClassLoader`. `DecoratingClassLoader` got the system class loader as its parent and the rest of the hierarchy is the same.

Quick Quiz

1. What is the purpose of a class loader?

2. What is the bootstrap class loader, and which classes does it load?

3. What is the extensions class loader, and which classes does it load?

4. Which classes are considered to be the same inside JVM?

5. What can a custom class loader be used for?

6. Can a custom class loader be used to load *all* classes (including core Java classes)?

7. Why does `DecoratingClassLoader` use its own class path?

In Brief

■ Class loaders load and initialize classes and interfaces in the JVM.

■ The application loading process begins with the initial class passed to the launcher. All parent classes and any classes referenced by the `main()` method of the initial class are lazily loaded and initialized as the references are made.

■ The bootstrap class loader is implemented in native code and used to load Java core classes, such as `java.lang.Object` and `java.lang.ClassLoader`.

■ The class loaders are organized in a chain, in which a child lets the parent find a class before attempting to find the class itself.

■ A loaded class is identified not just by its name, but by a pair of the name and the defining class loader.

■ Custom class loaders enable Java applications to take control of class loading. They are used to implement the reloading of classes, the separation of logical applications inside the same JVM, and the decoration or creation of the bytecode on-the-fly.

Replacing and Patching Core Java Classes

"A path without obstacles probably leads nowhere."

Defalque

Why Bother?

In Chapter 5, "Replacing and Patching Application Classes," we talked about the patching of Java classes to change or extend the underlying logic. The techniques presented in that chapter work for application and library classes loaded by the system or a custom class loader. However, attempting to apply the techniques to patch the core classes in a package whose name starts with `java` yields no results because the original version of the class continues to be used. Chapter 14, "Controlling Class Loading," provided a detailed discussion of how the classes are loaded, and with a little bit of reckoning, we can see why the system classes require a different approach. Recall that the system classes are loaded by the native bootstrap class loader, which does not use the `CLASSPATH` environment variable. Although the overall approach to system class patching is similar to application class patching, there are a few subtle differences, and they're the subject of this chapter.

Is there really a need to patch the core classes? In my career I have had to patch the application classes a lot more often than the system classes. One of the reasons might be that the core classes have been well designed and by now have matured into a form that suits most developers. However, every once in a while you can bump into a deficiency in a core class with no good workaround.

It is definitely not advisable to patch core Java classes as a permanent solution. This has legal consequences (the JDK license prohibits modifications to core classes) and can require additional work to migrate to a new version of JDK. However, this technique provides a lot more control to the developer. It can be used to insert traces into the JDK code and temporarily change the implementation of the core logic to suit the application needs. Last, but not least, it is just plain cool and being armed with this powerful technique would not hurt. Just be sure to read the license agreement before embarking on this path.

Patching Core Java Classes Using the Boot Class Path

As I have already mentioned, the approach to patching core classes is similar to the approach used to patch application classes. A source file needs to be obtained for a class that requires patching. JDK is conveniently distributed with the source code (thank you, Sun!), so most of the time you can just obtain the code from `src.jar`. Note that some of the system classes are shipped without the source code; this is true for the classes inside the sun package and other nonpublic packages. You can decompile the class files as described in Chapter 2, "Decompiling Classes," although the license agreement must be observed.

STORIES FROM THE TRENCHES

I worked on a product called WebCream that is capable of running multiple virtual Swing clients inside the same JVM. While testing, it was observed that after running for a certain time the JVM would become locked and no new clients would be able to initialize themselves. Using the JVM thread dumps as described in Chapter 10, "Using Profilers for Application Runtime Analysis," the examination revealed that the locking was occurring in a call to the `java.awt.Component`'s method `getTreeLock()`. The implementation of `getTreeLock()` simply returns a variable that is declared in `Component` as follows:

```
static final Object LOCK = new AWTTreeLock();
```

Thus, AWT uses a global lock that is shared by *all* components and, if one thread fails to release the lock monitor in a timely fashion, no other thread can perform AWT and Swing operations. This was done by Java designers to prevent races when redoing a layout, but it is an absolute killer of scalability for a product such as WebCream. An immediate solution at that time was to patch the `java.awt.Component` class so that it uses a virtual client-specific lock instead of a global lock. With the patch in place, the locking of virtual clients was no longer reported.

After you get your hands on the source code, you can insert the new logic. Compile the class just like you would compile any other class, and please be sure to not add bugs. Now that you have a new version of the bytecode, the remaining task is to tell the JVM to use it instead of the original bytecode. This can be achieved by manipulating the boot class path, as was explained in Chapter 14. The bootstrap class loader uses the boot class path to locate the core classes. By default, it is set to include only `rt.jar` and possibly a few other system libraries. `rt.jar`, located in `JRE_HOME\lib`, contains most of the core classes, so if there is no source code for a class and you want to find its bytecode, check `rt.jar` first. The boot class path can be set using the `-Xbootclasspath` parameter to the Java launcher command line. Running `java -X` displays the following help:

```
C:\CovertJava\java -X
    -Xbootclasspath:<directories and zip/jar files separated by ;>
                      set search path for bootstrap classes and resources
    -Xbootclasspath/a:<directories and zip/jar files separated by ;>
                      append to end of bootstrap class path
    -Xbootclasspath/p:<directories and zip/jar files separated by ;>
                      prepend in front of bootstrap class path
    . . .
```

Using the command-line parameter, we can set or augment the boot class path. Because we are interested in replacing an existing class, we use `-Xbootclasspath/p:` to prepend the directory that contains the patches in front of the default path. Running the JVM with this parameter results in the patched class being used instead of the original class.

Example of Patching `java.lang.Integer`

To put the theory in practice, let's write a simple patch to `java.lang.Integer`. For reasons unknown to the Java community, the `Integer` object is immutable. After the value is set, it cannot be changed. The idea was probably to make `Integer` objects behave like `String` objects, in that if you need to change a value that is represented by an `Integer` object, you should create a new instance and use it instead of the old value. The problem with this approach is that it results in inefficient memory usage for applications that need dynamic collections of integers. Java does not provide collection classes for primitive types, so the only way to get a dynamic array of integers is to use a `java.util.Array` of `Integer` instances. If the value of the stored integer needs to change, you must create a new instance of `Integer` and place it in the array where the old value used to be. Of course, the allocations and subsequent garbage collections produce significant overhead. A much better approach is to change the internal value of the `Integer` object. However, because `java.lang.Integer` is immutable, the only legitimate workaround is to create and use your own class that mimics the `Integer` and give it a `setValue()` method.

We, nevertheless, are going to patch the existing java.lang.Integer class and grant it a
setValue() method. We will do this from a purely academic interest and to practice what we
preach because we do not want to commit violations to the Java license agreement.
Examining the source code for java.lang.Integer reveals that the value of the object is
stored in a private field, value. Thus we must copy the source file to the CovertJava\src\
java\lang directory and insert a method called setValue (see Listing 15.1).

LISTING 15.1   setValue() Method Source Code

```
public void setValue(int value) {
    this.value = value;
}
```

The next step is to create a test class, CorePatchTest, that accesses the newly inserted
setValue() method. The code for the test class is shown in Listing 15.2.

LISTING 15.2   Using the Patched java.lang.Integer

```
package covertjava.patching;

public class CoreClassTest {
    public static void main(String[] args) {
        Integer i = new Integer(10);
        System.out.println("Old value = " + i);
        i.setValue(100);
        System.out.println("New value = " + i);
    }
}
```

Compiling the classes that use the patched versions of the core classes can be a little bit
tricky if the public interface of the core class has changed. Trying to run javac on our test
class results in an error because the JDK implementation of Integer does not have the
setValue() method. Because of this, we cannot use Ant to compile the patched
java.lang.Integer. The easiest workaround is to compile our patched Integer manually
using javac and then copy the class file to the CovertJava/distrib/patches directory. We
can now configure the compiler to use our patched version of Integer for our project, which
we can do by placing the patched class on the boot class path before the original version.
javac takes a -bootclasspath parameter that enables overriding the default boot class path,
as does Ant's javac task. However, if we try to override the boot class path for javac, we must
specify the location of rt.jar and all the other system libraries. That makes the build scripts
dependent on the path to the JDK installation or environment variables. A simpler way is to
pass -Xbootclasspath/p: to the JVM that runs Ant, so that instead of overriding the default
path we just add an item in front of it. The ant.bat script uses the ANT_OPTS environment

variable for passing command-line options to the Java invocation line. We will take advantage of this by adding the following line to `CovertJava\bin\build.bat`:

```
ANT_OPTS=-Xbootclasspath/p:..\distrib\patches
```

Now we can use Ant to build the project and the distribution libraries (the release target). Our final task after building the project is to create a batch file called `corePatchTest.bat` in the `CovertJava\bin` directory that executes `CorePatchTest`. Once again, to ensure that the patched version of `Integer` is used, we pass the `-Xbootclasspath` parameter to `java`. The relevant source code for `corePatchTest.bat` is shown in Listing 15.3.

LISTING 15.3   Executing a Test of a Core Class Patch

```
set JAVA_OPTS=-Xbootclasspath/p:..\distrib\patches
java %JAVA_OPTS% covertjava.patching.CoreClassTest
```

`corePatchTest.bat` produces the following output:

```
Old value: 10
New value: 100
```

Voilá! One more technique is added to our bag of tricks.

Quick Quiz

1. Can you think of a case in which you would want to patch a core class?

2. How is the process of patching core classes different from patching application classes?

3. Why do we need to alter the boot class path?

In Brief

- Patching core Java classes can help in debugging and understanding the JVM.

- Core classes are always loaded by the bootstrap class loader, which uses the boot class path to locate the bytecode.

- To patch a core class, the new version must be placed in the boot class path in front of the old version.

- To compile a class that uses the patched version of the core class that has changed its public interface, the patched version must be specified on the boot class path of the Java compiler.

Intercepting
Control Flow

"Nothing is so simple it cannot be misunderstood."

Freeman's Law

Control Flow Defined

Control flow is a sequence of execution of methods and instructions by a thread. The Java virtual machine (JVM) executes Java bytecode instructions in the order in which they are found in the class file. The control flow can be programmed using conditional statements such as `if`, `else`, and `for` or by invoking a method. Intercepting control flow includes the awareness of the executing instruction or method and the ability to alter the execution flow at runtime. For example, you might want to intercept a call to `System.exit()` to prevent the JVM from shutting down. Before you get too excited about the possibilities, let me set the expectations straight. There is no direct way of intercepting any instruction or method call in a running JVM unless it was started in profiling mode. The executing of methods is done by the JIT, and there is no standard Java API that can be used to add a listener, or *hook*, to the method calls. However, we will look at several indirect approaches to intercepting the control of common scenarios. We will also examine the JVM profiler interface that can be harnessed to intercept any call in debug mode.

Intercepting System Errors

System errors are reported by the JVM on abnormal conditions that are presumably outside the application control. They are thrown as subclasses of `java.lang.Error` and therefore are undeclared, meaning they can be thrown by any method even if its signature does not explicitly declare them. System errors include virtual machine errors such as OutOfMemoryError and StackOverflowError, linkage errors such as ClassFormatError and NoSuchMethodError, and other failures. Conventionally, application programmers are supposed to catch only instances of java.lang.Exception, which means that a condition such as out of memory goes undetected through the application error handling logic. For most real-life applications, this is not desirable because, even if nothing can be done when an error occurs, the application should generally log the error to a log file and attempt releasing held resources. A good design solution is to have a try-catch block at the top of the call stack on main application threads, catching java.lang.Error or java.lang.Throwable and delegating to a method that analyzes the error condition, logs it, and attempts a clean shutdown. Here's an example:

```
public static void main(String[] args) {
    try {
        // Execute application logic
        runApplication();
    }
    catch (Throwable x) {
        // Log error and attempt clean shutdown
        onFatalError(x);
    }
}
```

In situations where the JVM is out of memory or a class is not found, the application can attempt to mend it by freeing the contents of caches or disabling a feature affected by the missing classes. Anything is better than a disgraceful vanishing without a trace.

Intercepting System Streams

Before logging had become a de facto requirement for Java applications it was common to use System.out.println to output the debug traces. The disadvantages of this approach are abundant and obvious. Once written, such traces cannot be turned on or off without changing the code. Even though the application output stream can be redirected to a file for persistence, there is no rollover and because the file is kept open, it cannot be deleted until the application is shut down (hence, the file size can get exorbitant). When dealing with legacy Java code riddled with System.out.println() calls, a common problem is converting them to calls to a logging framework (see Chapter 6, "Using Effective Tracing," for a discussion of logging and tracing). It is also important to capture the standard error stream, which receives output of methods such as Exception's printStackTrace(). One of the neat solutions to this is intercepting the output to System.out and System.err and sending it to the log file instead. The technique relies on the fact that the system output stream can be redirected to a custom `PrintStream` using the `setOut` method of `java.lang.System`. `PrintStream` is a decorator class around an instance of `OutputStream`, which is responsible for the actual output. The task at hand is therefore to develop a redirecting `OutputStream` that writes to a log file instead of the process standard output and to then assign the `System.out` to it.

We are going to develop a class called `LogOutputStream` that extends `java.io.OutputStream` and writes its output to a log file using Apache Log4J. The Java input/output framework is very well designed, and all methods of `OutputStream` eventually delegate to a single method—`write()`—that takes an integer parameter. `LogOutputStream` uses a `StringBuffer` to accumulate characters that it gets in the `write(int)` method and, when a line separator is detected, the whole buffer is written to disk using Log4J. The only tricky part about the implementation is detecting the end of a line. As you are undoubtedly aware, on Unix the end of a line is marked by a single character: \n (new line). On Windows, the end of a line is marked by a combination of two characters: \r and \n (carriage return and new line). To write truly cross-platform code in Java, you must rely on a system property called `line.separator`. Because the property is a string, the implementation has to rely on a substring search rather than character comparison. Our implementation is optimized to first use the character comparison to check for the *possible* end of a line and then use a substring search to ensure that it is the end of a line indeed. The overridden `write()` method is shown in Listing 16.1.

LISTING 16.1   The `write()` Method of `LogOutputStream`

```
public void write(int b) throws IOException {
    char ch = (char)b;
    this.buffer.append(ch);
    if (ch == this.lineSeparatorEnd) {
        // Check on a char by char basis for speed
        String s = buffer.toString();
        if (s.indexOf(lineSeparator) != -1) {
            // The whole separator string is written
            logger.info(s.substring(0, s.length() - lineSeparator.length()));
            buffer.setLength(0);
        }
    }
}
```

The logger here is a reference to a static variable of type `org.apache.log4j.Logger` declared in `LogOutputStream` as follows:

```
static Logger logger = Logger.getLogger(LogOutputStream.class.getName());
```

Thus, the entire output to `System.out` is redirected to the Log4J framework as INFO-level messages from the `LogOutputStream` class. To see our class in action, we have to configure a file appender in `log4j.properties` and install the interceptor as shown in Listing 16.2.

LISTING 16.2   Installing `System.out` Interception

```
public static void main(String[] args) {
    System.out.println("Installing the interceptor...");
    PrintStream out = new PrintStream(new LogOutputStream(), true);
    System.setOut(out);
    System.out.println("Hello, world");
    System.out.println("Done");
}
```

Running the `main()` method of `LogOutputStream` displays an `Installing the interceptor...` message on the console but writes `Hello, world` and `Done` messages to the log file. The same interceptor can be installed for the `System.err` stream. To make it flexible, it can be parameterized to take in the logging level and a stream name in the constructor. In a similar fashion, `System.In` stream can be programmatically set using `System.setIn()` to feed a desired input into an application.

Intercepting a Call to `System.exit`

The JVM process normally terminates when no active threads exist. Threads running as *daemons* (`Thread.isDaemon() == true`) do not prevent the JVM from being shut down. In multithreaded applications, which include Swing GUIs and RMI servers, it is not easy to achieve a clean shutdown by letting all threads end gracefully. Frequently, a call to `System.exit()` is made to forcefully shut down the JVM and terminate the process. Relying on `System.exit()` has become a common practice even in programs that are not very sophisticated; even though it makes the life of the application developer easier, it can present a problem for middle-tier products such as Web and application servers. An inadvertent call to `System.exit()` by a Web application, for example, can bring down the Web server process and possibly prevent users from accessing other Web applications and static HTML pages. This is no way to make friends with the system administrators, and every good developer knows the value of a healthy relationship with that team.

This section examines a simple way to intercept a call to `System.exit()` and prevent the shutdown of the JVM. This technique can be discovered by examining the source code of the `exit()` method in `java.lang.System`. The first thing the method does is check whether a security manager is installed. If it is, the method verifies that the caller has a permission to exit the JVM. Our task, therefore, is to install a custom security manager (or modify the security policy if a security manager is already installed) that disallows the exit until it is explicitly allowed. The InterceptingSecurityManager class located in the covertjava.intercept package extends the SecurityManager class and overrides the isExitAllowed() method to control the JVM shutdown. It uses an internal flag that can be set via the setExitAllowed() method to determine whether to allow the JVM to shut down. If the exit is not allowed, an unchecked SecurityException is thrown to alter the control flow. The main() method shown in Listing 16.3 shows how to install the intercepting security manager and how it affects the execution flow.

LISTING 16.3   Intercepting System.exit()

```
public static void main(String[] args) {
    InterceptingSecurityManager secManager = new InterceptingSecurityManager();
    System.setSecurityManager(secManager);
    try {
        System.out.println("Run some logic...");
        System.exit(1);
    }
    catch (Throwable x) {
        if (x instanceof SecurityException)
            System.out.println("Intercepted System.exit()");
        else
            x.printStackTrace();
    }
    System.out.println("Run more logic...");
    secManager.setExitAllowed(true);
    System.out.println("Finished");
}
```

To keep the example simple, the actual business logic that would normally be invoked inside the try block was replaced with a Run some logic... message. The key is to catch the Throwable class rather than the usual Exception because the intercepted System.exit() is reported as an unchecked exception. Running the main() method shown in Listing 16.3 produces the following output:

```
Run some logic...
Intercepted System.exit()
Run more logic...
Finished
Process terminated with exit code 0
```

Instead of terminating the JVM after a call to System.exit() inside the try block, the program continues to run until the exit is allowed.

Reacting to a JVM Shutdown Using Hooks

The previous section has shown how to intercept a programmatic attempt to shut down the JVM by calling `System.exit()`. Sometimes the JVM shutdown is initiated by a user through a `kill` command on Unix or a Ctrl+C signal on Windows. The JVM can also be shut down because the user is logging off or the OS is being shut down. Can a Java program intercept the shutdown signal? The answer is no; it cannot intercept this signal, but it can react to it. Since JDK 1.3, an application can install a shutdown hook using the `addShutdownHook()` method of `java.lang.Runtime`. *Shutdown hooks* are instances of `java.lang.Thread` that are initialized but not started. When the JVM is being shut down, all shutdown hook threads are started to run concurrently with the other threads in the JVM. The hooks have access to the entire Java API, but they should be sensitive to the delicate JVM state. The hook threads should not perform any time-consuming operations and should be thread safe. No expectations should be made about the availability of the system services because they might be in the process of shutting down themselves. A good use for a shutdown hook is to write an entry into a log file before closing it and to release all other resources, such as open database connections and files. An example of installing a shutdown hook is shown in Listing 16.4.

LISTING 16.4   Installing a Shutdown Hook

```
public static void main(String[] args) {
    Runtime.getRuntime().addShutdownHook(new Thread() {
        public void run() {
            handleJVMShutdown();
        }
    });
}


public static void handleJVMShutdown() {
    // Record the shutdown and close all resources
}
```

Intercepting Methods with a Dynamic Proxy

Sometimes you need to do some preprocessing and post-processing for a method call. This can include tracing the method name and its parameter values, measuring the execution time, or even providing an alternative implementation. Assume you are developing a drawing editor application that uses interfaces such as Line, Circle, Rectangle, and Curve to represent the basic shapes. If you want to add tracing for all methods in those interfaces, you have several options. You can go through each function and meticulously insert tracing calls. Or you can code a proxy class, implementing every interface that prints the trace and then delegates to the original implementation. This is a cleaner approach because it keeps the debugging code separate from the implementation, but it requires a lot of mundane coding. An interesting and a somewhat unknown alternative is a dynamic proxy that uses reflection to intercept method calls. The java.lang.reflection package offers the interface InvocationHandler and a class (proxy) that together can be used to dynamically create an instance implementing multiple interfaces specified at runtime. This approach does not require compile-type definition of the interfaces that proxy implements. Once instantiated, the proxy can be cast to any of the interfaces that were specified during creation, and any call to a method defined by those interfaces is dispatched to a single method (invoke) of the proxy. The only requirement for the dynamic proxy class is that it implements the InvocationHandler interface that defines the invoke method.

Let's develop a dynamic proxy for Chat that traces out the invocations of the message listener. Recall that Chat relies on the MessageListener interface to associate the main frame with the RMI server. Even though MessageListener has only one method, it is good enough to illustrate the concept. We will place the dynamic proxy between the MainFrame instance and ChatServer instance to add tracing of the method calls. We'll create a TracingProxy class in the covertjava.intercept package and have it implement the InvocationHandler interface. The proxy will delegate the method invocations to the actual object, so we'll code the constructor to take the target object as a parameter. The TracingProxy class declaration and its constructor are shown in Listing 16.5.

LISTING 16.5   TracingProxy Declaration

```
public class TracingProxy  implements InvocationHandler {

    protected Object target;

    public TracingProxy(Object target) {
        this.target = target;
    }
    ...
}
```

Notice that the tracing proxy takes the target as a java.lang.Object type. This is the key point because the proxy class is not tied to MessageListener and therefore can be used on *any* interface.

We now have to code the invoke() method from the InvocationTarget interface. It takes three parameters—the proxy object itself, the method, and the array of method parameters. Our implementation prints the method name and then delegates the invocation to the target that was passed to the proxy constructor. Listing 16.6 shows that code.

LISTING 16.6   Implementation of the `invoke()` Method

```java
public Object invoke(Object proxy, Method method, Object[] args) throws Throwable {
    Object result;
    try {
        System.out.println("Entering " + method.getName());
        result = method.invoke(target, args);
    }
    catch (InvocationTargetException e) {
        throw e.getTargetException();
    }
    finally {
        System.out.println("Leaving " + method.getName());
    }
    return result;
}
```

The proxy is now ready for a test drive. To see it in action, let's create an instance of
`TracingProxy` initialized with an instance of Chat's `MainFrame` as the target. Then we'll create
a `java.lang.reflect.Proxy` object that implements the `MessageListener` interface dynamically and delegates calls to the instance of the tracing proxy. Finally, we'll pass the reflection
proxy to the Chat server, casting it to the `MessageListener` interface. Listing 16.7 shows the
corresponding Java code.

LISTING 16.7   Using a Dynamic Proxy

```java
public static void main(String[] args) throws Exception {
    ChatServer chatServer = ChatServer.getInstance();
    chatServer.setMessageListener(new MainFrame(false));

    TracingProxy listener = new TracingProxy(chatServer.getMessageListener());
    Object proxy = Proxy.newProxyInstance(
        chatServer.getClass().getClassLoader(),
        new Class[] {MessageListener.class},
        listener
        );
    chatServer.setMessageListener((MessageListener)proxy);
    MessageInfo messageInfo = new MessageInfo("localhost", "alex");
    chatServer.receiveMessage("Test message", messageInfo);
    System.exit(0);
}
```

Running the `main()` method of `TracingProxy` produces the output shown here:

```
C:\Projects\CovertJava\classes>java covertjava.intercept.TracingProxy
Received message from host localhost
Entering messageReceived
Leaving messageReceived
```

Thus, we were able to intercept a call to the `messageReceived` method without having to implement the `MessageInfo` interface. Dynamic proxies can also come in handy for framework and tool development when you need to interface with classes whose types are unknown at compile time. Rather than having to generate and compile static Java proxy classes, the frameworks can rely on dynamic proxies as the glue between the components.

The Java Virtual Machine Profiler Interface

A promising development is the introduction of the Java Virtual Machine Profiler Interface (JVMPI), which standardizes the interaction between a profiler and the JVM. It was first exposed in JDK 1.2.2 and further extended in JDK 1.4. The API is a two-way interface specifying how a virtual machine should notify a profiler agent about the events inside the VM, such as thread starts, method calls, and memory allocations. It also specifies the means for a profiler to obtain the information about the state of the JVM and to configure which events it is interested in. The profiler agent runs inside the JVM and all API methods are C-style functions invoked via JNI. To access the API, the JVM has to be started with the `-Xrun`*ProfilerLibrary* parameter, where *ProfilerLibrary* is the name of the native library to be loaded. It is somewhat unfortunate that there is no Java-based interface to JVMPI, and going into the details of C implementations and JNI is outside the scope of this book. However, I have included a list of the most interesting events that can be intercepted:

- `JVMPI_EVENT_CLASS_LOAD`—Sent when a class is loaded.

- `JVMPI_EVENT_CLASS_LOAD_HOOK`—Sent after the class data is loaded by the class loader, but before the internal representation of the class is created. This gives the profiler the ability to decorate or instrument the bytecode.

- `JVMPI_EVENT_METHOD_ENTRY`—Sent when a method is entered.

- `JVMPI_EVENT_METHOD_EXIT`—Sent when a method is exited.

- `JVMPI_EVENT_THREAD_START`—Sent when a thread is started.

- `JVMPI_EVENT_THREAD_END`—Sent when a thread has ended.

The complete reference on JVMPI can be found at

`http://java.sun.com/j2se/1.4.2/docs/guide/jvmpi/jvmpi.html`

Quick Quiz

1. Why and where in the application is it important to use `java.lang.Throwable`?

2. How can the output to the system error stream be redirected to a database?

3. How can a call to `System.exit()` be intercepted?

4. How can a Java application running as a service close all database connections when the machine is shutting down?

5. Which events can be received through the JVMPI?

In Brief

- There is no good way to intercept control flow in Java. JVMPI gives the most power to interfere with the execution, but it requires JNI programming.

- System errors are reported as undeclared errors and can be caught as instances of `java.lang.Throwable`.

- Standard system output and error streams can be redirected programmatically to a custom `PrintStream`.

- A call to `System.exit()` can be intercepted by installing a custom `SecurityManager` that disallows the exit until explicitly permitted.

- Applications can execute code on a JVM shutdown using shutdown hooks. The hooks are threads started by the JVM when a shutdown signal is received.

- The JVMPI provides tremendous control over the runtime environment, class loading, and method execution.

Understanding and Tweaking Bytecode

"Every solution breeds new problems."

Murphy's Fifth Corollary

Bytecode Fundamentals

Chapter 2, "Decompiling Classes," presented a brief overview of bytecode and the purpose it serves in Java. As you undoubtedly know, the bytecode is the intermediate step between the source code and the machine code, which enables cross-platform execution of the Java programs. The bytecode is defined by the Java Virtual Machine Specification (`http://java.sun.com/docs/books/vmspec/2nd-edition/html/VMSpecTOC.doc.html`), which also describes the language concepts, the class file format, the Java Virtual Machine (JVM) requirements, and other important aspects of the Java programming language. Strict adherence to the specification ensures the portability and ubiquitous execution of applications compiled into bytecode. The JVM running on top of the operating system is responsible for providing the execution environment and converting the Java bytecode instructions into native machine instructions.

Most of the hacking techniques presented earlier in this book required obtaining and manipulating the source code to alter an application behavior. In this chapter we will work at the bytecode level rather than the source code level. We will discover how to view the class file data structures, instrument (enhance) the existing bytecode, and programmatically generate new classes. Here are some of the benefits of making changes at the bytecode level:

- You don't need to obtain the source code or decompile the bytecode and then recompile the source later.

- Bytecode can be generated or instrumented by a class loader on-the-fly as the classes are loaded into a JVM.

- It is easier and faster to automate bytecode generation than source code generation because fewer steps are involved and the compiler doesn't need to be executed. For example, Hibernate generates the persistence code for Java classes at runtime.

- Tools can rely on bytecode instrumentation to introduce additional logic that does not need to be present in the source files. Some implementations of Aspect Oriented Programming (AOP), for instance, insert custom attributes into the bytecode and instrument the methods to support AOP.

The next two sections present a brief introduction to the aspects of the JVM specification that are related to bytecode. Although it is useful to familiarize yourself with how the JVM operates and the format of the class file, it is not strictly necessary for implementing the techniques presented in this chapter. If you are not known to be patient and reading specification-like material is comparable to writing end user documentation for your code, feel free to skip the next two sections and go directly to the section titled "Instrumenting and Generating Bytecode."

Viewing Class Files Using the jClassLib Bytecode Viewer

The Bytecode Viewer shipped with the free jClassLib library is an excellent GUI utility that enables browsing the content of the class file. It shows a hierarchical view of the file structure in the left pane and the content of the selected element in the right pane. Figure 17.1 shows jClassLib displaying the content of `SimpleClass` from the `covertjava.bytecode` package.

The jClassLib Bytecode Viewer does not allow modifications of the class file, but it is great for visualizing the structures that are presented in the next sections. A useful way of learning about the bytecode is by comparing the instructions in the bytecode with the statements and operators in the source code. The viewer can also be used to debug the generation and instrumentation of the bytecode that we will perform at the end of this chapter.

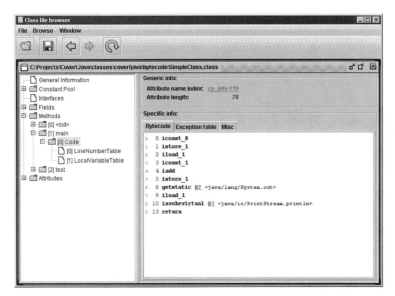

FIGURE 17.1 The jClassLib Bytecode Viewer.

The JVM Instruction Set

Java source files are compiled into the binary class files, which follow a specific format. The logic of each Java method is represented with a set of primitive JVM instructions defined in the JVM specification. JVM instructions are basic commands that are similar to the machine code. Each JVM instruction consists of an operation code (*opcode*) followed by zero or more operands representing the parameters of the operation. In the class file, the instructions are stored as a binary stream representing the Code attribute of a method. The opcode is stored as 1 byte, which can be followed by the bytes representing the operands data. For example, the source code shown in Listing 17.1 is represented by the set of instructions shown in Listing 17.2.

STORIES FROM THE TRENCHES

Hibernate is a free high-performance object/relational persistence and query service for Java. One of the biggest selling points for Hibernate is its capability to transparently persist Java objects. Instead of coding tedious JDBC calls, developers write an XML file of object mapping to a database schema and Hibernate provides all the plumbing. The persistent service draws on reflection and runtime bytecode generation to ensure that it does not impact upon IDE debugging and incremental compile. Hibernate touts how using Apache's Byte Code Engineering Library—and later the CGLIB bytecode generation library—to manipulate the bytecode allows it to avoid the overhead of Java reflection API.

LISTING 17.1   Sample Java Source Code

```
int i = 0;
i = i + 1;
System.out.println(i);
```

LISTING 17.2   Bytecode Representation of Sample Source Code

```
0 iconst_0
1 istore_1
2 iinc 1 by 1
5 getstatic #21 <java/lang/System.out>
8 iload_1
9 invokevirtual #27 <java/io/PrintStream.println>
12 return
```

Most of the instructions are very simple, and tracing the instructions back to the source code they represent is easy. For instance, iconst_0 defines an integer constant with a value of 0, and istore_1 stores a value from the top of the stack (0 in our case) into a local variable specified by an index (i in our case). A more interesting scenario is a method call. As you can see from the listings, the name of the static class field (System.out) and the value of the parameter (i) are first pushed onto the operand stack before the method println is invoked. The detailed information on the instructions can be obtained from the JVM specification, but that is beyond the scope of this book. It is useful to familiarize yourself with the instructions and their operands, even though we are going to use a framework that provides a layer of abstraction for the bytecode. The instrumentation and generation of bytecode require constructing instruction sets programmatically, so at least a basic understanding of the instruction set and how it maps to Java is essential.

Class File Format

The format of the binary class file is mandated by the JVM specification. It is described by a series of data structures that represent the class itself, its methods, its fields, and its attributes. To manipulate the bytecode, you need to learn about the naming conventions used for various elements and the format of the key data structures.

Field and Method Descriptors

Java supports overloaded methods by coupling the method with the descriptor, created based on the parameters the method takes. That way, internally print(int i) and print(char ch) are stored as two separate methods. Name mangling follows a convention mandated by the

JVM specification, and because the bytecode stores the mangled names, you can get a glimpse of it here.

The fields and method descriptors are encoded based on their types. Table 17.1 shows the Java declared type and the corresponding field descriptor type that is used in the bytecode.

TABLE 17.1

Field Type Codes

DECLARED TYPE	DESCRIPTOR TYPE
byte	B
char	C
double	D
float	F
int	I
long	J
short	S
boolean	Z
Classname instace	L<Classname>;
[] (one dimension of array)	[

Table 17.2 shows some examples of Java declarations and their descriptors in the bytecode.

TABLE 17.2 Examples of Descriptor Types

TYPE DECLARATION	DESCRIPTOR TYPE
int number;	I
int[][] numbers;	[[I
Object reference;	Ljava.lang.Object;

Method descriptors are created using the following format:

([<param1>[...<paramN>]])<return>

where

■ <param1> ... <paramN> are optional parameter type descriptors.

■ <return> is the return type descriptor, or V if the method is void.

For example, a method that is declared as

Integer getIntProperty(String propertyName, int defaultValue) would have the method descriptor

`(Ljava.lang.String;I)Ljava.lang.Integer;`

Certain special methods have predefined names. Static initializers are named `<clinit>`, and instance initializers and constructors are named `<init>`.

Class File Structure

Each Java class is defined by a binary stream, typically stored in a class file, consisting of 8-bit bytes. The stream content is described by a pseudo structure given in the JVM specification and quoted here in Listing 17.3. Although this might look like too much information, the structures presented in this and the following sections will help in understanding the generation and instrumentation of bytecode later.

LISTING 17.3   ClassFile Structure

```
ClassFile {
    u4 magic;
    u2 minor_version;
    u2 major_version;
    u2 constant_pool_count;
    cp_info constant_pool[constant_pool_count-1];
    u2 access_flags;
    u2 this_class;
    u2 super_class;
    u2 interfaces_count;
    u2 interfaces[interfaces_count];
    u2 fields_count;
    field_info fields[fields_count];
    u2 methods_count;
    method_info methods[methods_count];
    u2 attributes_count;
    attribute_info attributes[attributes_count];
}
```

For clarity, the JVM specification defines pseudo-types u1, u2, and u4 representing unsigned 1-, 2-, and 4-byte types, respectively. Table 17.3 lists each field of the `ClassFile` structure and its meaning.

TABLE 17.3

ClassFile **Fields**

FIELD	DESCRIPTION
Magic	Class file format marker. It always has the value of 0xCAFEBABE.
Minor_version, major_version	Version of JVM for which the class file was compiled. JVMs might support lower major versions but do not run higher major versions.
constant_pool_count	Number of items in the constant pool array. The first item of the constant pool is reserved for internal JVM use, so the valid values of constant_pool_count are 1 and higher.
constant_pool[]	An array of variable-length structures representing string constants, class and field names, and other constants.
access_flags	A mask of modifiers used in class or interface declarations. The valid modifiers are ACC_PUBLIC, ACC_FINAL, ACC_SUPER, ACC_INTERFACE, and ACC_ABSTRACT.
this_class	An index of the constant_pool array item that describes this class.
super_class	A zero or an index of the constant_pool array item describing the super class for this class. For a class, a value of 0 indicates that the super class is java.lang.Object.
interfaces_count	Number of super interfaces of this class or interface.
interfaces[]	An array of indexes of constant_pool items describing the super interfaces of this class.
fields_count	Number of items in the fields array.
fields[]	An array of variable-length structures describing the fields declared in this class.
Methods_count	Number of items in the methods array.
Methods[]	An array of variable-length structures describing the methods declared in this class, including the method bytecode.
attributes_count	Number of items in the attributes array.
Attributes[]	An array of variable-length structures declaring attributes of this class file. The standard attributes include SourceFile, LineNumberTable, and others. The JVM is required to ignore the attributes that are not known to it.

The constant pool deserves a little more attention because it is used frequently by other structures. Any text string found in a Java class, regardless of its nature, is stored in the same pool of constants. This includes the class name, names of fields and methods, names of classes and methods the class invokes, and literal strings used inside the Java code. Anytime a name or string needs to be used, it is referred to by an index into the constant pool. The constant pool is an array of cp_info structures, the general format of which is shown in Listing 17.4.

LISTING 17.4   Constant Pool Item Structure

```
cp_info {
    u1 tag;
    u1 info[];
}
```

The actual items stored in the pool follow the structure that corresponds to the tag. For example, a string is defined using a CONSTANT_String structure and a reference to a field using CONSTANT_Fieldref. The list of structures and their contents can be found in the JVM specification.

The ClassFile structure uses three other structures: field_info, method_info, and attribute_info. field_info is similar to method_info, so we'll show only the method_info structure in Listing 17.5.

LISTING 17.5   method_info Structure

```
method_info {
    u2 access_flags;
    u2 name_index;
    u2 descriptor_index;
    u2 attributes_count;
    attribute_info attributes[attributes_count];
}
```

The meanings of the method_info fields are given in Table 17.4.

TABLE 17.4

method_info **Fields**

FIELD	DESCRIPTION
access_flags	A mask of modifiers describing the method accessibility and properties, including static, final, synchronized, native, and abstract.
name_index	An index into the constant_pool array item representing the method name.
descriptor_index	An index into the constant_pool array item representing the method descriptor.
attributes_count	The number of items in the attributes array.
attributes[]	An array of method attributes. The attributes defined by the JVM specification include Code and Exceptions. The attributes not recognized by the JVM are ignored.

Attributes

The attributes are used in the ClassFile, field_info, method_info, and Code_attribute structures to provide additional information that depends on the structure type. For example, class attributes include the source filename and debugging information, whereas method attributes include the bytecode and exceptions. Listing 17.6 shows the structure of attribute_info, and Table 17.5 lists its fields.

LISTING 17.6   attribute_info Structure

```
attribute_info {
    u2 attribute_name_index;
    u4 attribute_length;
    u1 info[attribute_length];
}
```

TABLE 17.5

attribute_info **Fields**

FIELD	DESCRIPTION
attribute_name_index	An index of the constant_pool item representing the attribute name
attribute_length	The length of the attribute_info array in bytes
attribute_info	The binary content of the attribute

The compilers and post processors are allowed to define and name new attributes, as long as they do not affect the semantics of the class. For instance, AOP implementations can use bytecode attributes to store the aspects defined for a class.

Bytecode Verification

When a compiler compiles Java source into bytecode, it performs extensive checks on syntax, keyword, operator usage, and other possible errors. This ensures that the generated bytecode is valid and safe to run. As the class is loaded into a JVM, a simplified subset of verifications is performed to ensure that the class file has the correct format and has not been tampered with. For instance, the bytecode verifier checks that the first 4 bytes contain the magic number and the attributes are of the proper length. It checks that the final classes are not subclassed and that the fields and methods have correct references into the constants pool; it also performs a number of other checks.

Instrumenting and Generating Bytecode

We have reached the point where you can finally get your hands on the keyboard and do some nifty stuff. Now that you know enough about the bytecode, you can implement the two most common methods of bytecode manipulation. Obviously, working directly with the binary content of the class file is a tedious task. To make our job easier, we will use an open source library from Apache called the Byte Code Engineering Library (BCEL).

BCEL Overview

The home page for BCEL is located at http://jakarta.apache.org/bcel, where you can download the binary distribution, source code, and manual. The library provides an object-oriented API to work with the structures and fields that compose a class. It can be used to read an existing class file and represent it with a hierarchy of objects; transform the class representation by adding fields, methods, and binary code; and programmatically generate new classes from scratch. The class representation can be saved to a file or passed to the JVM as an array of bytes to support instrumentation and generation on-the-fly. BCEL even comes with a class loader that can be used to dynamically instrument or create classes at runtime. The class diagram of BCEL's main classes is shown in Figure 17.2.

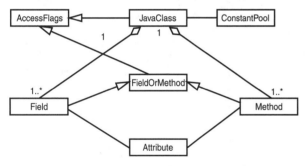

FIGURE 17.2 Class diagram of BCEL's main classes.

Table 17.6 provides brief descriptions of the main classes we will use. The detailed information is available from BCEL JavaDoc.

TABLE 17.6

Main BCEL Classes

BCEL CLASS	DESCRIPTION
JavaClass	Represents an existing Java class. It contains fields, methods, attributes, the constant pool, and other class data structures.
Field	Represents the field_info structure.
Method	Represents the method_info structure.

BCEL CLASS	DESCRIPTION
ConstantPool	Represents a pool of constants contained in the class.
ClassGen	Dynamically creates a new class. It can be initialized with an existing class.
FieldGen	Dynamically creates a new field. It can be initialized with an existing field.
MethodGen	Dynamically creates a new method. It can be initialized with an existing method.
ConstantPoolGen	Dynamically creates a new pool of constants. It can be initialized with an existing constant pool.
InstructionFactory	Creates instructions to be inserted into bytecode.
InstructionList	Stores a list of bytecode instructions.
Instruction	Represents an instruction, such as iconst_0 or invokevirtual.

As you can see, most of the classes are a direct mapping to the terms and data structures defined in the JVM specification.

Instrumenting Methods

Instrumenting is inserting new bytecode or augmenting the existing bytecode of a class. Products that produce runtime performance metrics of executing Java applications rely on instrumentation to collect the data. To get some practical experience, let's develop a framework that produces a log of method invocations at runtime. Omniscient Debugger, covered in Chapter 9, "Cracking Code with Unorthodox Debuggers," uses a similar technique to record the program execution so it can be viewed later. Recording the method invocations at runtime provides the benefit of having a detailed log of the code, executed by the JVM.

To test the implementation, we'll use a class called SimpleClass defined in package covertjava.bytecode, with a main method that is shown in Listing 17.7.

LISTING 17.7   SimpleClass's main() Method

```java
public static void main(String[] args) {
    int i = 0;
    i = i + 1;
    System.out.println(i);
}
```

To keep the example simple, we are not going to write the entire invocation logging framework. Instead, we'll limit the implementation to the InvocationRegistry class with a static method, as shown in Listing 17.8.

LISTING 17.8   Entry Point into the Method Logging Framework

```
public static void methodInvoked(String methodName) {
    System.out.println("*** method invoked " + methodName);
}
```

methodInvoked() is the entry point into the method logging framework, and it is used to log a method invocation. For each thread, it can store a call stack of methods, which can be saved or printed at the end of the application run. For now, the implementation just prints the method name to indicate that the framework was called for that method.

With the foundation laid, we can embark on implementing the class that will do the method bytecode instrumentation. We'll call it MethodInstrumentor and have its main() method take in the name of the class and the methods we want to instrument from the command line. When executed, MethodInstrumentor will load the given class, instrument the methods whose names match the given regular expression pattern by adding a call to InvocationRegistry.methodInvoked(), and then save the class under a new name. Running the new version of the class should log its method invocations in the Registry. MethodInstrumentor is located in the covertjava.bytecode package, and we are going to use a top-down approach to develop it. The main() method of MethodInstumentor is shown in Listing 17.9.

LISTING 17.9   MethodInstrumentor's main() Method

```
public static void main(String[] args) throws IOException {
    if (args.length != 2) {
        System.out.println("Syntax: MethodInstrumentor " +
                           "<full class name> <method name pattern>");
        System.exit(1);
    }
    JavaClass cls = Repository.lookupClass(args[0]);
    MethodInstrumentor instrumentor = new MethodInstrumentor();
    instrumentor.instrumentWithInvocationRegistry(cls, args[1]);
    cls.dump("new_" + cls.getClassName() + ".class");
}
```

After checking the command-line syntax, the MethodInstrumentor attempts to load the given class using BCEL's Repository class. The Repository uses the application class path to locate and load the class, which is just one of many alternatives to loading a class with BCEL. For some inexplicable reason, BCEL returns null on error conditions instead of throwing an exception, but for the sake of code clarity we won't check for it. After the class is loaded, an instance of MethodInstrumentor is created and its instrumentWithInvocationRegistry()

method is called to perform the transformations. When finished, the class is saved to a file with a new name. Let's look at the implementation of instrumentWithInvocationRegistry shown in Listing 17.10.

LISTING 17.10   instrumentWithInvocationRegistry Implementation

```
public void instrumentWithInvocationRegistry(JavaClass cls,
                                            String methodPattern) {
    ConstantPoolGen constants = new ConstantPoolGen(cls.getConstantPool());
    Method[] methods = cls.getMethods();

    for (int i = 0; i < methods.length; i++) {
        // Instrument all methods that match the given criteria
        if (Pattern.matches(methodPattern, methods[i].getName())) {
            methods[i] = instrumentMethod(cls, constants, methods[i]);
        }
    }
    cls.setMethods(methods);
    cls.setConstantPool(constants.getFinalConstantPool());
}
```

Because we are going to be adding invocation of a method from a different class, we must refer to it by name. Recall that all names are stored in the constants pool, which means we'll have to add new constants to the existing pool. To add new elements to structures in BCEL, we must rely on the generator classes, which have a suffix Gen in their names. The code creates an instance of ConstantPoolGen that is initially populated with constants from the existing pool; then it iterates all the methods, harnessing the power of regular expressions to test which methods must be instrumented. When all the methods are processed, the class is updated with the new methods and the new pool of constants. The actual job of instrumenting is done in instrumentMethod(), as shown in Listing 17.11.

LISTING 17.11   instrumentMethod() Implementation

```
public Method instrumentMethod(JavaClass cls, ConstantPoolGen constants,
                               Method oldMethod) {
    System.out.println("Instrumenting method " + oldMethod.getName());
    MethodGen method = new MethodGen(oldMethod, cls.getClassName(), constants);
    InstructionFactory factory = new InstructionFactory(constants);
    InstructionList instructions = new InstructionList();

    // Append two instructions representing a method call
    instructions.append(new PUSH(constants, method.getName()));
    Instruction invoke = factory.createInvoke(
```

LISTING 17.11   Continued

```
            "covertjava.bytecode.InvocationRegistry",
            "methodInvoked",
            Type.VOID,
            new Type[] {new ObjectType("java.lang.String")},
            Constants.INVOKESTATIC
            );
    instructions.append(invoke);

    method.getInstructionList().insert(instructions);
    instructions.dispose();
    return method.getMethod();
}
```

As you can see, instrumentMethod() programmatically creates bytecode instructions that correspond to a method call. The easiest way to select the correct JVM instructions and their parameters is to write the code in Java first, compile it, and then use something like the jClassLib viewer to see how it is translated to the bytecode. Then the corresponding bytecode can be constructed using BCEL objects.

The first thing instrumentMethod() does is instantiate a MethodGen object that is used to store the new bytecode. Then a factory to create and a list in which to store the instructions are created. If you have paid attention to this chapter and played with the jClassLib Bytecode Viewer, you might recall that a Java method call is represented by several bytecode instructions. First, the method parameters must be pushed onto the operands stack, and then the invokevirtual instruction is issued to transfer the control to the method (refer to Listing 17.2 for an example of method call bytecode). This is precisely what we have to insert into the method code before its existing bytecode. If we were working with the bytecode directly, we'd have to insert two constants into the constants pool: covertjava.bytecode. InvocationRegistry for the class name and methodInvoked for the method name. Luckily, BCEL does this for us because we are using the high-level classes such as InstructionFactory and PUSH, which automatically add constants to the pool. After the instructions are created, they are appended to the instruction list. When the code generation part is finished, the list is inserted into the generated method instructions and the method structure is returned.

To test that the instrumentation works, compile the classes and run MethodInstrumentor on SimpleClass.class using the following command line:

```
java covertjava.bytecode.MethodInstrumentor covertjava.bytecode.SimpleClass .*
```

A new class file called new_covertjava.bytecode.SimpleClass.class should be created in the current directory. Copy this class to the classes directory, overriding the existing

SimpleClass.class file; then run the SimpleClass main() method. If all works well, you should see the following on the console:

```
C:\Projects\CovertJava\classes>java covertjava.bytecode.SimpleClass
*** method invoked main
1
```

As you can see, the instrumented class starts by calling InvocationRegistry, which outputs the first line; then it executes its own body, which outputs 1.

Generating Classes

Our second task is to learn how to generate a new class programmatically. As was mentioned earlier, this comes in handy for middleware products and frameworks that want to avoid source code generation. In our example, we'll create a generator of a value object that contains all the fields of the given class but no methods. The value object is a common design pattern used in distributed applications to pass data across the network. Admittedly, our generator will produce a very crude version of the value objects, but we'll make it a little interesting by ensuring that it generates only the fields whose values are meant to be retained.

Once again, we will use SimpleClass as a guinea pig in our experiment. SimpleClass defines five fields, as shown in Listing 17.12.

LISTING 17.12   SimpleClass Fields

```
public int number;
protected String name;
private Thread myThread;
static String className;
transient String transientName;
```

We will write a ClassGenerator class in package covertjava.bytecode that takes two command-line parameters—a fully qualified class name and a regular expression pattern for field names to copy. The main() method of ClassGenerator is shown in Listing 17.13.

LISTING 17.13   ClassGenerator's main() Method

```
public static void main(String[] args) throws IOException {
    if (args.length != 2) {
        System.out.println("Syntax: ClassGenerator " +
                            "<full class name> <field name pattern>");
        System.exit(1);
    }
```

LISTING 17.13   Continued

```
    JavaClass sourceClass = Repository.lookupClass(args[0]);
    ClassGenerator generator = new ClassGenerator();
    JavaClass valueClass = generator.generateValueObject(sourceClass, args[1]);
    valueClass.dump(valueClass.getClassName() + ".class");
}
```

Just as in MethodInstrumentor, the implementation checks the command-line syntax, loads the class, and then calls the generateValueObject() method that is shown in Listing 17.14.

LISTING 17.14   ClassGenerator's generateValueObject() Method

```
public JavaClass generateValueObject(
    JavaClass sourceClass,
    String fieldPattern)
{
    String newName = sourceClass.getClassName() + "Value";
    ClassGen classGen = new ClassGen(
            newName,
            "java.lang.Object",
            newName,
            Constants.ACC_PUBLIC | Constants.ACC_SUPER,
            new String[] { "java.io.Serializable" });
    Field[] fields = sourceClass.getFields();
    for (int i = 0; i < fields.length; i++) {
        if (Pattern.matches(fieldPattern, fields[i].getName())) {
            int skipFlags = Constants.ACC_STATIC | Constants.ACC_TRANSIENT;
            if ((fields[i].getAccessFlags() & skipFlags) == 0) {
                fields[i].setAccessFlags(Constants.ACC_PUBLIC);
                addField(classGen, fields[i]);
            }
        }
    }
    return classGen.getJavaClass();
}
```

The implementation first creates an instance of ClassGen to represent the class being generated. The class has the same name as the parameter class, but with a Value suffix. It extends java.lang.Object and implements java.io.Serializable. Next, the implementation iterates the fields of the parameter class looking for names that match the given criteria. Using a bitmask, the implementation filters out the static and transient fields and copies the qualifying fields to the class being generated. The access modifier of the generated field is set as public for simplicity. After the generation is complete, the class representation is returned to the caller, which persists it to disk.

Running `ClassGenerator` on `SimpleClass` produces a file called `covertjava.bytecode.SimpleClassValue.class` in the current directory. Listing 17.15 shows the decompiled version of the class.

LISTING 17.15 Decompiled Version of the `SimpleClassValue` Class

```
package covertjava.bytecode;
import java.io.Serializable;

public class SimpleClassValue
    implements Serializable
{
    public int number;
    public String name;
    public Thread myThread;
}
```

Voilá! All the appropriate fields of `SimpleClass` have been generated for `SimpleClassValue`.

ASM Library

A new open source project that is gaining momentum is the ASM bytecode manipulation library, hosted at `http://asm.objectweb.org/`. It is designed to achieve the same goals as the BCEL library but claims a significantly better performance because of a different implementation approach. BCEL creates a complete object tree representing a binary class file, down to the individual bytecode instructions. Therefore, it can potentially have hundreds of objects created for one class file, which can lead to performance degradation. Although having an object for every class file attribute is convenient, this approach can become costly for runtime bytecode manipulation if thousands of classes are instrumented.

ASM uses a visitor design pattern to avoid instantiating objects when not required. A class analyzer provided by the framework invokes a user-defined visitor class passing method and field data as parameters. For most of the parameters, the visitor implementation simply passes them to the next visitor, keeping the data in binary form. For those fields or methods that need to be changed, the visitor implementation obtains object representation from the framework and then manipulates the object. This way, most of the bytecode remains in binary form and the performance overhead is minimal.

If having minimal performance overhead of instrumentation is important, ASM is a better choice than BCEL. If clarity and simplicity of implementation are of a higher priority, I recommend BCEL.

Bytecode Tweaking Compared with AOP and Dynamic Proxies

Now that you have learned how to tweak the bytecode, you can compare this technique with other approaches of augmenting the functionality at runtime. Chapter 16, "Intercepting Control Flow," presented dynamic proxies that enable intercepting methods of any interface without a static implementation of that interface. Although dynamic proxies are simple to write and easy to use, their main drawback is the fact that they work only with interfaces (not with classes) and require explicit instantiation in the calling code. Thus, to use a dynamic proxy with Chat, we had to call the `setMessageListener()` method of `ChatServer` to install the proxy. If we didn't have the source code for Chat, this wouldn't have been possible without decompiling. Changing the application code is acceptable during the development, but it is not a suitable solution for third-party code or runtime integration. Unlike the dynamic proxy, bytecode tweaking does not require any compile-time changes in the code being tweaked.

AOP, an emerging technology for adding cross-sectional properties to objects and methods, is a clean and well-structured enhancement for traditional programming. Using aspects, you can easily add functionality such as the tracing of method calls or preprocessing and post-processing. AOP cleanly separates the implementation of the program logic from the infra-structure tasks, such as tracing, profiling, security, and others. The aspects are defined in separate files that are compiled and processed together with the application code. Implementations of AOP rely on bytecode instrumentation to insert the additional behavior. In that, they are more similar to the bytecode tweaking we've looked at in this chapter than to the dynamic proxies. AOP is a high-level approach that lacks the flexibility offered by direct bytecode engineering. When appropriate, aspects can be the easiest way of adding the covert logic to an existing application.

Quick Quiz

1. What are the reasons to manipulate the bytecode?

2. What is opcode, and how are the operands passed to a bytecode instruction?

3. What would a method descriptor look like for a Java method named `getCount()` declared as `public Object[] getObjects(String name, char type)`?

4. What structures is class file composed of?

5. Which main classes of BCEL are used to instrument or generate a class?

6. Which attribute of a method needs to be altered to instrument its bytecode?

In Brief

■ Bytecode manipulation is useful for code generation, instrumentation of existing classes, and enhancement of the behavior of classes without altering their source code.

■ The format of the Java class file and the possible instructions are defined in the JVM specification.

■ The logic of each Java method is represented with a set of primitive JVM instructions that are basic commands bearing a close resemblance to the machine code.

■ The binary format of the class file is represented by pseudo structures defined in the JVM specification, which include data on the class, fields, methods, attributes, and other properties.

■ The Apache Byte Code Engineering Library (BCEL) provides an object-oriented API for working with the structures and fields that compose a class.

■ Instrumenting is inserting new bytecode or augmenting the existing bytecode of a class.

Total Control with Native Code Patching

18

"Every man has a scheme that will not work."

Howe's Law

Why and When to Patch Native Code

We have looked at various techniques for replacing, patching, and reverse engineering Java classes. All the techniques require working at the source code or bytecode level, and that has confined our capabilities to the high-level Java world. The Java Virtual Machine (JVM) interacts with the operating system (OS) via native libraries, which means that all low-level operations are not coded in Java and therefore cannot be manipulated by the presented techniques. For instance, System.currentTimeMillis() is a native method, and all methods of ClassLoader delegate the actual class definition to its native method, called defineClass0. Although patching the Java class is typically easier and cleaner, in some cases you have no other option but to patch the native code. This chapter presents several low-level techniques of native code patching that, together with the earlier techniques, give you total control over the JVM.

I would like to bring up two important points before we get our hands dirty with native patching. The first one has to do with the legality of the work we are about to perform. As discussed earlier in this book, it is your responsibility to check that reverse engineering and patching is not prohibited by a license agreement of the product with which you are working. Besides being illegal, stealing intellectual property from other people is unethical, so I highly encourage you to use the presented techniques only for a good cause. The second point is that working with native code requires a solid knowledge of the C language, some basic understanding of machine instructions, and familiarity with binary file formats. Binary files have different formats on different platforms, and even two different compilers can produce different executable files for the same platform. For instance, object files compiled by a Microsoft C compiler differ from files created by a Borland C compiler. Patching binary code requires insertion of machine instructions into the existing machine code and manipulation of the binary file. This is like venturing into uncharted waters, so be prepared to deal with challenges and do not expect that everything will work from the start. The absence of a common, well-defined format and the complexity of dealing with raw machine instructions result in a lack of the good tools that have helped us so much previously. For instance, no decompiler can produce C code from a binary executable.

The following is a list of prerequisites for this chapter:

- An understanding of C language

- An ability to write and compile native libraries for the target platform

- A basic knowledge of machine instructions and assembly language

- Some familiarity with the Java Native Interface (JNI)

Native Code Usage in the Java Virtual Machine

Most of the code executing inside the JVM, including the core classes, is written in Java. This makes perfect sense because Java is clean, safe, and platform independent. However, at some point the JVM needs to interact with the hardware; to do that it relies on the OS. The low-level operations, such as reading a block of bytes from a hard disk or creating a network socket, are delegated to the native libraries that make OS-specific calls. Figure 14.1 in Chapter 14, "Controlling Class Loading," showed a primitive diagram of class and native code loading by the JVM. Most of the time the native libraries simply delegate the call to the operating system in a platform-dependent manner. The native libraries for Java can be written only in the C language and accessed via the JNI.

JNI Overview

To be cross platform, Java has to use a layer of abstraction between itself and the operating system. This level of abstraction is implemented in a set of native libraries that are accessed through the JNI. JNI is a specification describing how to define native methods in Java and how to provide the implementation of those methods in C libraries. In other words, JNI provides a contract between Java classes and native libraries.

The Java side of the contract is simple: To declare a native method, you simply add a keyword (native) to the method declaration and end the declaration with a semicolon. Let's assume that a Java program needs to find out memory parameters such as the total amount of physical and virtual memory and the amount of available physical and virtual memory on the local machine. The java.lang.Runtime class can provide only information about the memory parameters for the JVM, not the total memory properties, so we have to resort to making a native call to the OS. To achieve that, we write a Java class called OSMemoryInfo having a set of native methods. This is the declaration of the method returning the total physical memory:

```
public native static long getPhysicalTotal();
```

After the method is declared, it can be compiled and used by other Java classes. An attempt to execute the method results in java.lang.UnsatisfiedLinkError because no implementation is provided for getPhysicalTotal() yet. To execute the native methods, the Java class that declares it must load a native library that provides the method implementation. The native libraries are OS dependent, which means a different version of the library must be written for every platform the application is required to run. The library is loaded only by name because the extension is platform dependent. On Windows, the library file names end with .dll; on Unix they end with .so. Listing 18.1 shows how to load a library called OSMemoryInfo.

LISTING 18.1   Loading a Native Library from a Java Class

```
public class OSMemoryInfo {
    static {
        try {
            System.loadLibrary("OSMemoryInfo");
        } catch (Exception x) {
            System.err.println("Error while loading native library");
            x.printStackTrace(System.err);
            System.exit(1);
        }
    }
    ...
}
```

The library is loaded by a static initializer that is executed when the class is first loaded into a JVM. This step completes the contract on the Java side and brings us to the native code side.

To execute the OSMemoryInfo class, the JVM has to be provided with a library containing implementations of all the native methods. The location of the library is determined by a platform-specific search path. On Windows, the search path includes the current directory and the directories specified by the PATH environment variable. On Unix, the search path is determined by an environment variable, whose name depends on the Unix flavor. For instance, on Solaris its name is LS_LIBRARY_PATH and on HP UX it is SH_LIB_PATH. The name of the native library is also OS specific. On Windows, our native library would be named OSMemoryInfo.dll, whereas on Unix it would be OSMemoryInfo.so. The requirement for the library is to export the functions that match the name and the declaration syntax of the native methods defined in the Java class. JNI specifies the type mapping between C types and Java types and provides extensive mechanisms for accessing Java objects, throwing exceptions, and manipulating the data types. For instance, a C function that implements the Java method getPhysicalTotal(), shown earlier, should be declared as follows:

```
JNIEXPORT jlong JNICALL
    Java_covertjava_nativecode_OSMemoryInfo_getPhysicalAvail(JNIEnv *, jclass);
```

JNI Implementation Example

Learning by example is the most effective way to learn, so let's work with the OSMemoryInfo class presented in the previous section. Recall that the class was designed to use JNI to obtain memory information from the operating system. It has four native methods, returning the total and available amount of physical and virtual memory. All methods have the syntax shown in Listing 18.1, and the entire class source can be found in CovertJava/src/covertjava/nativecode/OSMemoryInfo.java.

The easiest way to find the right syntax for the C functions that correspond to Java native methods is to use the javah utility. javah generates a C header file based on the provided Java class file. For every native method found in the Java class, javah creates a function signature in the output C header file. Running javah on the covertjava.bytecode. OSMemoryInfo class produces a file, covertjava_nativecode_OSMemoryInfo.h, that can also be found in the CovertJava/src/covertjava/nativecode directory. Take a moment to examine the function declarations and how Java data types are mapped to C types.

The next step is to code the bodies of the four functions declared in covertjava_ nativecode_OSMemoryInfo.h. To keep the example concise, we will look at only the Windows implementation because the Unix implementation differs only in the function call that is made to the OS. All four functions use the same Win32 API function— GlobalMemoryStatusEx—that returns a slew of information about the OS memory. The function bodies are coded in OSMemoryInfo.c, which can be found in the CovertJava/src/ covertjava/nativecode directory. Listing 18.2 shows the implementation of Java_covertjava_nativecode_OSMemoryInfo_getPhysicalTotal().

LISTING 18.2 Native Implementation of getPhysicalTotal()

```
JNIEXPORT jlong JNICALL
  Java_covertjava_nativecode_OSMemoryInfo_getPhysicalTotal
    (JNIEnv *env, jclass cls)
{
    MEMORYSTATUSEX memStat;
    memStat.dwLength = sizeof (memStat);
    if (GlobalMemoryStatusEx(&memStat) == 0 && (*env) != 0) {
        jclass exceptionCls = (*env)->FindClass(env, "java/lang/Exception");
        char msg[100];
        sprintf(msg,
                "Failed to get memory information from the OS, error code %li",
                (long)GetLastError());
        if (exceptionCls != 0)   /* Raise Java exception */
            (*env)->ThrowNew(env, exceptionCls, msg);
        return -1;
    }
    return (jlong) (int) memStat.ullTotalPhys;
}
```

There's nothing complicated here—just a call to a Win32 function, a check for an error, and a return of the result. In the spirit of Java ideology, the C function we have created throws a java.lang.Exception if the Win32 API call fails.

With the function bodies coded, we can build a Windows Dynamically Linked Library (DLL). I am going to use the MSVC compiler, which is actually shipped free when you download Windows SDK and .Net SDK. The makefile that builds the DLL can be found in the CovertJava/build directory, and the batch file CovertJava/bin/build_native.bat can be used to run nmake.exe. You are free to choose the compiler and the build method of your choice, but I recommend using the Microsoft compiler for reasons explained later. If you want to rebuild the native libraries, be sure to update all the paths inside build_native.bat.

We can now run the OSMemoryInfo class's main() method, which outputs the values received from the native methods. Executing the CovertJava/bin/OsMemoryInfo.bat file that invokes the main() method produced the following output on my machine:

```
C:\Projects\CovertJava\bin>OsMemoryInfo.bat
Total     Physical Memory: 535121920
Available Physical Memory: 199958528
Total     Virtual  Memory: 2147352576
Available Virtual  Memory: 1960931328
```

We now have a working JNI implementation that we can experiment with.

Generic Approaches to Patching Native Methods

Knowing the basic principle of how Java code interacts with native code and the architecture of JNI, we can now look at the methods of overriding the native functions. Just as with byte-code patching, the goal is to intercept a native method invocation and provide our own implementation of it. The patch should be transparent to the caller, requiring no changes in the Java client code. Let's examine three approaches, each with its own pros and cons.

Patching a Java Method Declaration

The easiest solution is to patch the Java class that declares the method, removing the `native` keyword and replacing it with a Java implementation. The implementation can delegate to a helper class that provides the actual method logic. Even though it's simple, this method is the most effective and should be your first choice. Because all the changes are done at the Java level, you don't need to delve into C programming and binary file manipulations. A complication to this approach is a situation in which you actually want to make a native call but need to change some of its logic. Assume you have a new requirement to have the OS user created in the Users group instead of the Administrators. Here you won't avoid calling a native method that interacts with the OS. Even in this case, however, you can patch the original Java method to be non-native and then have it call a native method. The native method is then implemented in a custom native library with an alternative name that creates a user at the OS level. The only time when declaration patching cannot be used is when a license agreement prohibits reverse engineering of Java classes but does not restrict the modifications of native libraries.

Substituting Native Libraries

The second approach is to replace the original native library with a substitute that exports the same functions that are exported by the original library. The substitute functions delegate to the original functions unless an alternative implementation is required. The substitute library acts like a smart proxy to the original library, capable of preprocessing, post-processing, and completely overriding the method calls. This approach works well if the library has few functions, or if patching is needed for most of the methods exported by the library. Because all the work can be done in C, this is a relatively simple approach requiring no changes to either the Java classes or the binary machine code. If the number of exported functions is high, coding the substitute library can become tiresome. Just as with patching the Java method declaration, a potential problem can occur with trying to keep some of the logic from the original native method. It is pretty much an all-or-nothing approach—you either delegate to the original method or you don't.

Patching Native Code

Do you remember one of the questions we contemplated in Chapter 15, "Replacing and Patching Core Java Classes"? It was, "What do we do when we have tried every road but failed?" I don't expect this to be quoted on the Internet, but in a way this is what this book is all about. The previous two approaches provide clean and relatively simple solutions to native code patching, but they do not live up to the promise of "total control." To get total control, we must be able to hack the native libraries and patch the code similarly to how we have done it with the bytecode. The third approach does exactly that: It relies on exploring the binary format of the library, finding the machine code to be changed, and patching it with the new logic. It is not an easy path, which is why I recommend using the first two approaches before attempting this one. Patching native code is platform specific, requiring a thorough understanding of the executable file format and knowledge of assembly language and processor addressing. But the payoff is great, too. The technique we will study here can be used on any executable, not just JNI libraries. It also gives you an insight into the executable file formats and how the operating system loads and runs programs. The following sections explore patching of native code on the Windows and Unix platforms.

Patching Native Code on the Windows Platform

Understanding this section requires a basic knowledge of assembly language and some familiarity with the Portable Executable format. Hacking and patching is a rather popular subject among gamers and college students, which results in an abundance of utilities that greatly simplify the task on the Windows platform. Instead of having to manually edit the binary code and insert new machine instructions, we can rely on the utilities and libraries to do the low-level patching.

Portable Executable Format

Windows Portable Executable (PE) format is loosely based on Unix's Common Object File Format (COFF). It describes the binary structure of an executable file that can run on any Win32-compatible OS. Executable files include EXE, DLL, SCR, VxD, and other types. Structurally, a PE file is much like a JAR or Zip archive that contains other files or sections. A PE file has a DOS header; a PE header; and a section table followed by a number of sections representing various resources such as text, data, and UI resources. Table 18.1 shows the structure of a PE file.

TABLE 18.1

PE File Structure

ELEMENT	DESCRIPTION
DOS MZ header	Provided for backward compatibility to ensure that the file is recognized as a valid executable when run under MS-DOS.
DOS stub	A small built-in program that usually just outputs a line saying that the file must be run on Win32.
PE header	Contains various information about the PE portion of the file, such as the number of sections and the entry point addresses.
Section table	An array of structures describing each section. The structures contain information such as the section attribute, file offset, and virtual offset.
.text section	Contains the program binary code.
.data section	Contains the initialized data.
.idata section	Contains the import table.
.edata section	Contains the export table.
Debug symbols	Various debugging information such as line numbers.

A great way to explore the internal structure of a portable executable is to open it in the PE Explorer utility. It is a well-written shareware program that displays the headers, sections, and contents of the known PE sections in a GUI window. PE Explorer also includes a disassembler that can be used to study the machine code inside the file. PE Explorer can be downloaded for free evaluation from http://www.heaventools.com. For instance, loading the OSMemoryInfo.dll file we created earlier into PE Explorer enables us to see the sections and exports of that DLL. Viewing exports reveals that the DLL exposes four functions with mangled names. We can see that Java_covertjava_nativecode_OSMemoryInfo_getPhysicalTotal is exported as Java_covertjava_nativecode_OSMemoryInfo_getPhysicalTotal@8. The C compiler automatically appended an @ followed by the number of bytes the parameters take on the stack to all the functions, following the __stdcall convention.

Because we are interested in patching the function logic, we need to be able to view its corresponding machine code. C language source code is compiled directly into the binary machine code. Unlike Java bytecode, which needs to be further compiled or interpreted by the JIT, the machine code is directly executed by the processor. The direct implication of this is that the compiled executable can run only on the processor architecture for which it is built. The indirect implication is that there is no easy way to decompile the machine code back into the source code. The two are very different; there is no standard as to how to represent C language constructs with machine instructions; and every compiler makes different optimizations that further complicate the decompiling. Therefore, the only way to reverse engineer the binary executables is to work at the assembly language level. The assembly language is a human-readable representation of the machine instructions. It is very primitive, but its code corresponds directly to the way in which the processor will execute it. We are not going to write any code in assembly language, but if you want to learn more about it, pick up a book from Amazon.com or just read the online documentation. For Intel architectures, I recommend *Assembly Language for Intel-Based Computers* by Kip R. Irvine (Prentice Hall, ISBN: 0130910139).

Let's try to locate the code of the Java_covertjava_nativecode_OSMemoryInfo_ getPhysicalTotal function inside the binary file using PE Explorer. If you haven't done it yet, download, install, and run PE Explorer; then load OSMemoryInfo.dll into it. Take a look at the exports to see the names of the functions exposed by the DLL. Then run the Disassembler from the Tools menu with the default settings. You will see a blue screen showing panels with various information. The main panel shows the disassembled code for the entry point into the DLL. Because we are interested in the getPhysicalTotal() code, we will use the search feature to locate it quickly. Select Find from the Search menu and in the Find dialog box, type **getPhysicalTotal** in the text field. The Name List panel should highlight an item called Java_covertjava_nativecode_OSMemoryInfo_getPhysicalTotal, and its disassembled code should be displayed in the main panel, as shown in Figure 18.1.

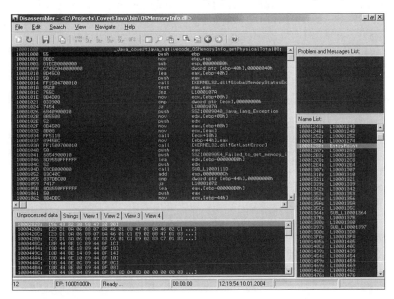

FIGURE 18.1 PE Explorer showing the disassembled code of getPhysicalTotal().

With a basic understanding of assembly language, you should be able to discern that the function starts by saving the stack pointer and allocating space on the stack for the local variables. It then calls GlobalMemoryStatusEx from the KERNEL32.dll module and checks

whether the return value is 0. If the result is 0, it checks whether the env parameter to
getPhysicalTotal() is 0; if it's not, it formats an error message and calls a subroutine to
throw an exception. Otherwise, it uses the value from a local structure populated by
GlobalMemoryStatusEx as the return value. It then restores the stack pointer and returns.
What we see is a virtually one-to-one match to the C code of the function body because
getPhysicalTotal uses only primitive operations such as comparison and function calls. We
are now ready to patch that code with a new logic.

Patching a Native Function Using the Function Replacer Utility

As I stated earlier, the process of patching a native function involves locating the binary code
of the function and replacing a portion of it with new code or a diversion to the new code.
The diversion can be a simple JMP assembly instruction to the address where the new
instructions begin or a piece of code that loads a dynamic library and calls a procedure from
it. The patch must be applied carefully to avoid unsettling the state of the registers and the
call stack. Another delicate issue is the fate of the code that was overridden with the diversion code. If you don't need to execute the original code, the patch code can be written over
the original instructions. However, if the patch adds logic on top of the original logic by
doing pre- or post-processing, the original code must be relocated to a different space before
being replaced with the diversion. As you can see, binary patching is a rather complex and
fragile process requiring a thorough analysis of the state of the caller and the code being
called. That is why I recommend that you patch the Java method declaration or substitute
the entire library as the first choice.

No reliable tools can safely do the binary patching. The only decent utility that I was able to
find and use with marginal success (it didn't work under JDK 1.4) is a Function Replacer
written by a member of the Execution coding group with the flamboyant name of Death. It
can be downloaded from the Execution group's Web site, which is currently hosted at
http://execution.cjb.net. The idea behind the utility fits our requirements perfectly.
Function Replacer replaces an exported function from one Win32 DLL with an exported
function from another DLL. The replacement function has to have the same number of parameters and the same calling style to preserve the state of the stack. We'll use this utility to
patch the getPhysicalTotal() method of OSMemoryInfo.dll with a stub from another DLL
that is hardcoded to always return a value of 10. Listing 18.3 shows the source code for the
patch.

LISTING 18.3   getPhysicalTotal() Patch Source Code

```
JNIEXPORT jlong JNICALL Java_covertjava_nativecode_OSMemoryInfo_getPhysicalTotal
    (JNIEnv *env, jclass cls)
{
    return (jlong) (int) 10;
}
```

The DLL containing the patch is called `OSMemoryInfoPatch.dll` and is prebuilt for this book. It can be rebuilt using the `CovertJava/bin/build_native.bat` script, provided you have installed a C compiler and updated the build script for it. Make a backup copy of the `OSMemoryInfo.dll` and run Function Replacer. In the Function Replacer UI, specify `OSMemoryInfo.dll` as the To-Be-Patched DLL and select `Java_covertjava_nativecode_OSMemoryInfo_getPhysicalTotal@8` (the second item in the list box) as the function to replace. Specify `OSMemoryInfoPatch.dll` as the Replacer DLL and select `Java_covertjava_nativecode_OSMemoryInfo_getPhysicalTotal@8` as the function to replace with. Click the Replace Function button and be sure that the utility does not report any errors. Now try to run the Java application and see whether the patch has worked. Make sure that the current JDK is 1.2 or 1.3 and run `CovertJava/bin/OSMemoryInfo.bat`. On my machine I got the following output:

```
C:\Projects\CovertJava\bin>OsMemoryInfo.bat
Total     Physical Memory: 10
Available Physical Memory: 318607360
Total     Virtual  Memory: 2147352576
Available Virtual  Memory: 1992871936
```

Instead of printing 535121920, which is the real value of the total physical memory on my machine, the Java native method now returns 10. The patch has worked, so let's investigate the magic behind it. Function Replacer works by writing bootstrap code over the original code of the method and inserting a call to the replacement procedure. The bootstrap code, written at the start of the original function code, loads the patch DLL using a `LoadLibrary()` API call and locates the replacement function using `GetProcAddress()`. This is a standard way of dynamically loading a DLL on the Win32 platform. After the replacement function is located, the control is transferred to it via a JMP instruction. The assembly code of the bootstrap is shown in Listing 18.4.

LISTING 18.4   Patched Assembly Code of `getPhysicalTotal()`

```
push    esi
call    osmemory.10001006
pop     esi
sub     esi,401005
lea     eax,dword ptr ds:[esi+40102c]
push    eax
call    dword ptr ds:[<&kernel32.LoadLibraryA>]
push    ebx
lea     ebx,dword ptr ds:[esi+401042]
push    ebx
push    eax
call    dword ptr ds:[<&kernel32.GetProcAddress>]
pop     ebx
```

LISTING 18.4   Continued

```
pop     esi
; OSMemoryInfoPatch._java_covertjava_nativecode_osmemoryinfo_GetPhysicalTotal@8
jmp     eax
; Define strings for library and patch function name
db      ...
```

Because the control is transferred via a JMP instruction, the replacement procedure returns directly to the caller instead of going back to the bootstrap code. The analysis of the code enables us to understand the limitations of the Function Replacer design. The size of the bootstrap code depends on the length of the patch DLL and function name, so the approach does not work for very small native functions. Because the bootstrap code overrides the original code, the original function cannot be called.

Another problem with Function Replacer is that it crashes the JVM when the patch is running under JDK 1.4.2. Even though the assembly code is valid and the patched DLL can be loaded by C programs without any problems, it seems to interfere with the internal state of the JVM. Function Replacer makes patching easy, but the utility is unreliable. We will therefore look at an alternative approach of using a powerful library to implement and install the patch manually.

Manual Patching Using Microsoft Detours Library

Detours is a Microsoft library for working with PE files at the binary level and for intercepting functions at runtime. It is a solid and well-written framework that can be used in C programs. Following are the main features of the Detours library:

- **Function interception at execution time**—Functions are intercepted in memory at runtime, not on disk. This is a cleaner approach that also can help to overcome certain license agreement restrictions.

- **Original function invocation**—Detours preserves the code of the patched function. Unlike Function Replacer, the Detours library saves the machine instructions from the original function code to an entity called *trampoline* before overriding them with the detour code. This allows for pre- and post-processing logic around the original function.

- **Small footprint of the detour**—The detour is implemented as a JMP to the patching logic, which requires only 4 bytes and therefore works for very short functions, as well.

- **Import table editing for DLL insertion**—Detours provides functions for editing the import table of a PE executable. This is useful for inserting a DLL that implements and installs a patch as a detour for a target function. Import modifications are saved to a file on the disk.

■ **Clean high-level C API**—The library is well designed and fairly easy to use. It still requires an understanding of Win32 architecture, but it makes assembly coding unnecessary. The patch and the detour are coded as C functions, and the interception is installed with just a few lines of code.

The Detours library can be downloaded free from http://research.microsoft.com/ sn/detours. It comes with good documentation and many examples, and because this book is Java centric, we are not going to spend time writing C code. Listing 18.5 shows a few key excerpts from an example that patches a Win32 Sleep function and measures the total time a program spends sleeping.

LISTING 18.5   Key Steps in Using the Detours Library

```
/* Declare a Sleep() trampoline using Detours macro */
DETOUR_TRAMPOLINE(VOID WINAPI UntimedSleep(DWORD dwMilliseconds), Sleep);

/* DLL entry point that installs and removes a detour for Sleep */
BOOL WINAPI DllMain(HINSTANCE hinst, DWORD dwReason, LPVOID reserved)
{
    if (dwReason == DLL_PROCESS_ATTACH) {
        printf("slept.dll: Starting.\n");
        Verify((PBYTE)Sleep);
        printf("\n");
        fflush(stdout);
        DetourFunctionWithTrampoline((PBYTE)UntimedSleep, (PBYTE)TimedSleep);
    }
    else if (dwReason == DLL_PROCESS_DETACH) {
        DetourRemove((PBYTE)UntimedSleep, (PBYTE)TimedSleep);
        printf("slept.dll: Removed trampoline, slept %d ticks.\n", dwSlept);
        fflush(stdout);
    }
    return TRUE;
}

/* This is a patch for Sleep() that measures the total time spent sleeping */
VOID WINAPI TimedSleep(DWORD dwMilliseconds)
{
    DWORD dwBeg = GetTickCount();
    UntimedSleep(dwMilliseconds);
    DWORD dwEnd = GetTickCount();

    InterlockedExchangeAdd(&dwSlept, dwEnd - dwBeg);
}
```

The code in Listing 18.5 installs a detour (patch) called `TimedSleep()` for the `Sleep()` function. The original `Sleep()` function can still be invoked via the trampoline called `UntimedSleep()`. To use Detours for a JNI function, a replacement function having the same signature as the target function needs to be written and placed inside a DLL. The `DllMain()` function of that DLL should install a detour using `DetourFunctionWithTrampoline()`; then the DLL needs to be inserted as the first import to the DLL or EXE that contains the JNI function being patched.

Patching Native Code on Unix Platforms

Patching binaries in the Unix world is a much harder task compared to on a Windows platform. Because Unix is a diverse platform with multiple hardware architectures and software standards, the low-level undertaking such as disassembling an executable file and editing the machine code requires different implementations for different architectures. For instance, the common Unix processor architectures include SPARC used by Sun Solaris, PA-RISC or Itanium used by HP UX, RS/6000 or PPC used by IBM AIX, and Intel used by Linux. Each processor has a different instruction set, so the binary files are not portable across the architectures. This means no common disassembler can convert the machine code into assembly on all platforms. Free and commercial disassemblers are available for each platform, but the quality and the ease of use vary greatly. One of the best utilities is IDA Pro (`http://datarescue.com`), which supports a plethora of processor types. It can run only on Windows, but it claims to be capable of disassembling the binaries for most of the common hardware architectures.

The situation with the software standards is not much better. Many standards exist for executable file formats, with the Common Object File Format (COFF) and Executable and Linking Format (ELF) being the two most prominent choices today. COFF was traditionally used on Unix systems. It has certain limitations and lacks flexibility, which is why a more modern ELF has been gradually replacing it. Both COFF and ELF are similar to Microsoft's PE format. Table 18.2 shows a high-level structure of the ELF format from the linking view.

TABLE 18.2

ELF File Structure

ELEMENT	DESCRIPTION
ELF header	Contains various information about the file such as the number of sections and the entry point addresses.
Program header table (optional)	Provides the location and description of segments.
Section 1	Data specific to section 1. It can be machine instructions, data, a symbol table, and so on.
Section N	Data specific to section N.
Section header table	An array of structures describing the attributes of each section such as the name, the type, the section starting address, and how the information should be interpreted.

Patching binaries requires reading and writing. Working with ELF files can be simplified by using the `libelf` library. `libelf` provides a set of high-level C functions that manipulate executable files, shared libraries, object files, and other files that follow the ELF format. `libelf` is available for Solaris, HP-UX, AIX, and Linux; it can most likely be found for other Unix flavors, as well. Because `libelf` is a general-purpose library, it does not provide the functions for patching that we have found in Microsoft's Detours library. `libelf` offers a convenient way of locating the code to be patched and updating the executable file with the changes, but the actual task of inserting assembly instructions and possibly implementing a trampoline has to be done manually.

The approach to patching Unix shared libraries that contain native code is identical to the work we have done on Windows. The native code for the target function has to be located and disassembled. Then it can be overwritten with the new code or a JMP instruction to the new code. The new logic can also be implemented in a shared library that is dynamically loaded by the patch. As long as the function signature and the calling convention are the same, the passing of the parameters and the return occurs correctly. To design the specific assembly code, refer to the target processor documentation.

Quick Quiz

1. What role does JNI play in Java architecture?

2. What steps need to be executed to implement and execute a native method?

3. For each of the three approaches to patching native methods, list their pros and cons.

4. Which section of the PE file needs to be accessed to get the machine code?

5. Why does the Function Replacer utility not work for native functions with just a few machine code instructions?

6. When implementing a detour in assembly code, can the control to the patch be transferred via a CALL instead of JMP? Explain why.

7. What advantages does the Detours library offer over the Function Replacer?

8. What are the dominant formats for executable files on Unix?

9. How would you patch a native function in Unix?

In Brief

- Native code patching provides the ultimate control over the JVM because it allows altering the behavior on the lowest level. It relies on exploring the binary format of the library, finding the machine code to be changed, and patching it with the new logic.

- JNI is a specification describing how to define native methods in Java and how to provide the implementation of those methods in native libraries.

- Java native methods require development of a dynamic (shared) library in the C language that is loaded by JVM at runtime.

- The easiest approach to native patching is patching the Java class that declares the method, removing the `native` keyword, and providing a new Java method implementation.

- Substituting a native library with a delegating proxy offers a second alternative to native code patching. The substitute library is implemented in the C language with no changes made to the Java classes. The original library is renamed to a different name, and the new library is given the name of the original library.

- On the Windows platform a utility such as Function Replacer can be used to patch an exported function from one DLL with an exported function from another DLL. Function Replacer is easy to use, but it has limitations and reliability problems.

- Microsoft Detours is a library for working with PE files at the binary level and for intercepting functions at runtime. It is a solid and well-written framework that can be used in C programs for manual patching.

- Unix-executable files typically adhere to the COFF or ELF format. The general approach to patching Unix libraries is similar to the Windows approach.

- `libelf` is a commonly used library for the manipulation of executable files in the ELF format on Unix.

Protecting Commercial Applications from Hacking

"Murphy was an optimist."

Beck's Postulate

Setting Goals for Application Protection

Throughout the chapters of this book, we have looked at a variety of techniques for reverse engineering, hacking, eavesdropping, and cracking. In many of the chapters I was calling on the reader's conscience and good ethics to not abuse the intellectual rights of the software authors. Even though most users have fair moral values, it is the other few who can cause a lot of damage. This chapter offers practical advice on how to protect Java applications from hacking and implement a distribution model for commercial software products.

A typical Java application is delivered as a bundle (most of the time as a JAR or Zip file but sometimes as an executable installer) that contains Java and native libraries, configuration files, documentation, and various resource files. Today it is a common practice to offer a no-frills version of the software for free public use, with the full set of features available only in licensed versions. Another strategy to attract potential buyers is to allow a limited-time evaluation period during which the entire functionality is available. After the evaluation period, the commercial features of the application are disabled until a license is purchased. Borland uses such a strategy to distribute JBuilder X. It initially runs as a 30-day Enterprise Edition trial and then becomes the limited-functionality JBuilder X Foundation. Many enterprise software vendors offer their products free for development or rely on users' honesty and the fear of prosecution to encourage the purchase of the correct license. Regardless of the choice of the licensing and distribution model, each vendor is vitally interested in collecting the license fees to generate revenues. The simple techniques demonstrated in this chapter provide good insurance that the licensing model is followed.

It is important to understand that there is virtually no way to achieve absolute protection from hackers, especially when the application can be downloaded from the Internet. Even if the strongest security algorithm is used to produce and encrypt the sensitive data, such as a serial number, a good hacker with access to the application can patch the verification code to altogether bypass the checking. Previous chapters of this book have shown how easy it is to find and hack Java classes, and even the native code can be cracked if the stakes are high. Therefore, a key to a successful protection mechanism is to make it too difficult to crack for 95% of the typical users and to force the remaining 5% of experienced hackers into spending a significant amount of time on cracking. In other words, the goal is to make it cheaper to buy a license than to spend the time hacking the protection. Another vital aspect is to prevent the easy redistribution of hacked versions on the Net and to preclude hackers from being able to issue their own licenses for the product.

We will start by looking at key aspects of security and cryptography. Using Java Cryptography APIs, you will learn by example how to encrypt and decrypt information with ciphers, protect data integrity with a message digest, and implement a robust licensing mechanism with asymmetric key pairs. In addition to these measures, we will examine several techniques that protect the application core files from hacking and patching.

Securing Data with Java Cryptography Architecture

The word *cryptography* is based on the ancient Greek words *kryptos* (meaning hidden) and *graphein* (meaning writing). *Cryptography* provides a means of converting readable information into incomprehensible code that can be transmitted openly and then transformed back to its original form. *Encryption* is the process of encoding readable information into the code, and *decryption* is the process of extracting the readable information from the code. Another commonly used service of cryptography is producing a *hash*, or a message digest, to verify that a message has not been modified since it left the sender. Various mathematical algorithms are used to implement the cryptographic services. The algorithms can be grouped into three main categories by the type of service they provide: message digest, encryption/decryption, and signing.

Message digest algorithms do not modify the content of the message; rather, they produce a unique hash based on the message content and a secret key. The key can be anything—a number that is passed as a parameter to a computational algorithm, a string of characters used as a password, or a sequence of bytes. The sender of a sensitive message computes the digest using a secret key and sends it along with the message. The receiver uses the same secret key to compute the digest of the received message and, if it does not match the sender's digest message, the content is considered compromised. A third party who intercepts the message can view its content and modify it, but in the absence of the secret key, cannot recalculate the digest. Thus, the integrity of the communication is preserved.

Encryption/decryption algorithms serve the purpose of protecting sensitive information that can be intercepted by a third party. The message content is modified using a secret key, producing output that is virtually impossible to convert back to the original content. A third party who intercepts the message cannot decipher its content without the key.

There are two categories of encryption/decryption algorithms: the ones using symmetric keys and the ones using asymmetric keys. *Symmetric* algorithms require the sender and receiver to have the same exact key to perform encryption and decryption. Symmetric algorithms are sometimes referred to as *two-way* algorithms because the same key is used for encryption and decryption. The strength of protection obviously depends on how well the keys are protected from third-party access. *Asymmetric* algorithms use key pairs for transformations. A key pair consists of a public key and a private key. This type of algorithm is referred to as *one-way* because the information encrypted with a public key can only be decrypted with a private key and the information encrypted with the private key requires the public key. Generally, the *public* key is freely available to the world, whereas the *private* key is kept in secrecy by the owner. For client/server and server-side applications, this provides better security than symmetric algorithms because only the public key needs to be included in the client application distribution.

A typical example of asymmetric algorithm usage is a browser that needs to establish a secure communication with a Web server. The browser is given the public key to encode the information sent to the Web server. The Web server decrypts the information using its secretly held private key, but if a third party intercepts the message, it cannot decrypt it with the public key. The server uses the private key to encrypt the information sent to the browser so the entire communication is secure. Symmetric algorithms are much faster than asymmetric ones, which is why the two are often used in conjunction. For instance, SSL implementation establishes a session using an asymmetric algorithm. When the secure channel is created, symmetric keys are generated and exchanged for encryption of the transmitted data.

Signing refers to generating a relatively short digital signature based on arbitrarily sized data using a private key of an asymmetric algorithm. The signature is produced by the sender and is transmitted with the message. The receiver uses the public key and the signature to verify the integrity of the message. Just like a message digest, the signature is mathematically unique for the given data, so if the data has been modified, the signature does not match the content. Authenticity is ensured through the use of an asymmetric algorithm, in which only the sender has the private key. To prevent a third party from forging a public key and claiming it to be the sender's key, digital certificates are commonly used. A *digital certificate* contains the public key of the sender that is signed by a public key of a trusted certificate authority (CA). For instance, browsers are preconfigured to trust Verisign (`http://www.verisign.com`) as a CA. A company that wants to allow users to establish a secure communication channel with its Web server must send its public key to Verisign to obtain a digital certificate. When the certificate is obtained, it is installed on the Web server to be handed to the browser at the communication initiation. The browser verifies the authenticity of the certificate using Verisign's public key and establishes a secure connection only if the verification succeeds.

Java Cryptography Architecture Overview

Java Cryptography Architecture (JCA) provides a complete and robust implementation of cryptography services and algorithms. Like most of the Java APIs, JCA provides interfaces that define how an application can interact with the services in a vendor-neutral way. Java Cryptography Extensions (JCE), which was once a separate module, is now a part of J2SE starting from JDK 1.4. JCE comes with a Sun provider that implements the most commonly used algorithms, such as HmacSHA1 for secure hashing and DES for key pair generation and signing. Because of U.S. government export restrictions, some algorithms such as RSA are not included in the JDK. In addition to Sun JCE, other excellent open-source packages implement a rich set of algorithms. Bouncy Castle (`http://www.bouncycastle.org`) and Cryptix (`http://www.cryptix.org`) provide Java implementations and can be downloaded and used free.

The core JCA classes are in the javax.crypto package, although the classes and interfaces for working with message digests are found in the java.security package. The Java Security home page (located at `http://java.sun.com/j2se/1.4.2/docs/guide/security`) is a good starting point for getting the Java-centric details on various security topics. The JCE home page at `http://java.sun.com/products/jce/index-14.html` provides a high-level overview of JCE and links to JCE-related pages such as the reference guide. If you like to dig deep, I recommend buying a book on Java security because the subject is vast and interesting. *Java Security Handbook* by Jamie Jaworsky and Paul Perrone (Sams Publishing, ISBN: 0672316021) offers comprehensive coverage of various security topics. The focus of the following sections of this chapter is on the practical use of security to protect Java applications from hacking.

Securing Chat Messages with JCA

Once again, I will use the notorious Chat application to illustrate the most useful methods of safeguarding user privacy and the author's intellectual property. Because Chat sends messages across the network, the user conversation is prone to interception and eavesdropping by a third party. The most obvious starting point to secure Chat is therefore the protection of transmitted message content.

Recall that Chat uses RMI over TCP/IP to exchange messages between instances running on different hosts. This is not as bad as HTML over HTTP because the binary TCP/IP streams are much harder to eavesdrop on than the text-based HTTP. Still, as you saw in Chapter 13, "Eavesdropping Techniques," with the right tools a hacker can listen to the conversation and read the message content. The main reason eavesdropping is possible is that the strings inside the serialized Java objects remain as text. Securing the Chat messages therefore requires encrypting the strings. Just about any kind of encryption will work for Chat because the messages are binary and, as long as the strings are not human recognizable, they do not stand out in the body of the message (see Chapter 13). Even simple XORing of characters works. In theory, the most secure way to protect the RMI communication channel is to use custom socket factories that create SSL sockets. However, because we are interested in learning a generic method for data protection, we will code with the Java Cryptography API.

The first design decision is which algorithm to use. Asymmetrical algorithms generally offer better protection because the private key is not available to the general public. However, in the case of Chat, an asymmetric algorithm is not the right solution for message encryption. The Chat application installed on a desktop should be capable of both encrypting the messages it sends and decrypting the messages it receives. Using an asymmetric algorithm would mean shipping both private and public keys with the Chat distribution. This effectively negates the extra protection you would get from the asymmetric algorithm, so you should use symmetric encryption because it performs better and is easier to write.

The second design decision is which security provider to use. The provider gives a concrete implementation of a particular algorithm. To avoid having to redistribute additional libraries with Chat, let's first check on the algorithms implemented by Sun JCE because it is bundled with the JRE. Sun JCE supports the following cipher algorithms: Data Encryption Standard (DES), DESede, and PBEWithMD5AndDES. DES is a widely used standard that has been adopted by the U.S. government. Even though there are known ways to crack it with a lot of computing power, it provides adequate protection for most applications. DESede, also known as *multiple DES*, uses multiple DES keys for extra strength. PBEWithMD5AndDES uses a combination of algorithms that includes a password-based encryption defined in the PKCS#5 standard and a message digest from the MD5 and DES algorithms. Because of the standardization specified by JCA, the client code that draws on these algorithms is virtually independent of the algorithm used. We'll select PBEWithMD5AndDES because it offers the strongest protection of the three.

A picture is worth a thousand words, and in the world of programming, the source code is worth a thousand pictures. All the source code we will be working with in this chapter is located in the covertjava.protect package. We will begin by looking at a class that provides the encryption services for the Chat application. Listing 19.1 shows the constructor of `covertjava.protect.Encryptor`.

LISTING 19.1   Preparing Ciphers for Encryption and Decryption

```java
import javax.crypto.*;
import javax.crypto.spec.*;

public Encryptor(char[] password) throws Exception {
    PBEKeySpec keySpec = new PBEKeySpec(password);
    SecretKeyFactory keyFactory =
            SecretKeyFactory.getInstance("PBEWithMD5AndDES");
    secretKey = keyFactory.generateSecret(keySpec);

    PBEParameterSpec paramSpec = new PBEParameterSpec(this.keyParams, this.iter_count);
    this.encCipher = Cipher.getInstance("PBEWithMD5AndDES");
    this.encCipher.init(Cipher.ENCRYPT_MODE, secretKey, paramSpec);
    this.decCipher = Cipher.getInstance("PBEWithMD5AndDES");
    this.decCipher.init(Cipher.DECRYPT_MODE, secretKey, paramSpec);
}
```

Let's dissect the source code and understand what is being done. The `Encryptor` constructor takes in a password as a character array. The PBEWithMD5AndDES algorithm uses three parameters: It passes the salt and the iteration count to initialize the DES algorithm and passes the password used for encryption with PKCS#5. The JCE class that represents an encrypting algorithm is `javax.crypto.Cipher`. A program obtains an instance of a cipher by calling the `Cipher.getInstance()` method, which takes the algorithm name (there is an overloaded method that can also take the provider name).

Security algorithms often require parameters to be supplied by the client code. The parameters are used in mathematical calculations performed during the encryption, and they represent a secret *seed* or a password that is required to decrypt the data later. Even though most of the algorithms that require parameters can use the default values supplied by the provider, it is highly recommended to initialize them with custom values.

There are two ways to initialize our cipher. One is to provide algorithm parameters such as the salt and the iteration count. Another is to provide an already generated key. If we were to choose to provide a key, we would have to ship the key with the distribution of Chat, which makes it easier for hackers to extract the key. The algorithm parameters, which are regular numbers, can be hardcoded into the Java code and placed in different classes. Obfuscation makes the code very difficult to read, so we will opt for providing the parameters instead of the key. Listing 19.2 shows the declaration of the algorithm parameters inside the `Encryptor` class.

LISTING 19.2   PBEWithMD5AndDES Parameters Used by Encryptor

```
public class Encryptor {
    private static byte[] keyParams = {
        (byte)0x10, (byte)0x15, (byte)0x01, (byte)0x04,
        (byte)0x55, (byte)0x06, (byte)0x72, (byte)0x01
    };
    private static int iter_count = 20;


    ...
}
```

In a real-life application, it would be better to place the parameters in a different class or generate them on-the-fly using a random number generator with the hardcoded seed. That would make hacking the application harder, but we'll keep things simple. Looking back at Listing 19.1, we can see that the first block of code creates a key specification based on the provided password. Key specification is an intermediate form of key data, which is used by the factory to generate a secret key. Because all instances of Chat use the same algorithm parameters and the password, the generated keys are identical. This means that messages encrypted by one Chat instance can be decrypted by another instance. After the secret key is generated, two instances of the cipher are obtained. One of them is initialized for encryption, and the other is initialized for decryption.

After an instance of Encryptor is constructed, it is ready to perform encryption and decryption. Most cryptography algorithms deal with raw bytes. The cipher class has two methods—update() and doFinal()—that can be used to encrypt an array of bytes. For instance, if we have an initialized cipher named cipher and an array of bytes named data, the data can be encrypted as follows:

```
byte[] ecryptedData = cipher.doFinal(data);
```

JCE has a utility class called SealedObject that wraps around any serializable object and uses a provided cipher to encrypt or decrypt the wrapped object during the serialization. Because Chat sends messages as objects, SealedObject is a better choice than raw byte data because it provides a higher-level API to encryption. The two methods provided by Encryptor for encrypting and decrypting instances of java.io.Serializable are shown in Listing 19.3.

LISTING 19.3   Methods That Implement Encryption and Decryption

```
public Serializable encryptObject(Serializable object) throws Exception {
    return new SealedObject(object, this.encCipher);
}

public Object decryptObject(Serializable object) throws Exception {
    return ((SealedObject)object).getObject(this.decCipher);
}
```

As you can see, `SealedObject` makes the implementation trivial. The `Encryptor` class we have discussed can now be used in the Chat application. Rather than passing instances of `covertjava.chat.MessageInfo` to each other, Chat would call `Encryptor` to obtain the encrypted version of the message before sending it. When a new message is received, Chat would use `Encryptor` to extract the `MessageInfo` object from the received sealed object. This code would have to be placed in ChatServer's `sendMessage()` and `receiveMessage()` methods, but we are not going to do this because we want to save time and space. The `main()` method in the `Encryptor` class shows a self test that writes and reads a text string to a file.

Protecting Application Distribution from Hacking

Encrypting the transmitted data protects the information from eavesdropping at the protocol level. This safeguards the user's information, but not the intellectual property in the software such as the algorithms, design patterns, and code. Many reverse-engineering techniques presented in this book can be easily used to crack a commercial product and unlock the functionality that would otherwise require a purchase of a license. For licenses that are issued based on the number of hosts where the software is installed, another potential threat can come from an unethical organization buying the cheapest license for one host and then rolling it out to a large number of hosts. This section discusses several techniques that protect the application distribution from hacking and ensure that the fees are paid according to the licensing model.

Protecting Bytecode from Decompiling

Chapter 2, "Decompiling Classes," has shown how easily you can obtain the source code from Java bytecode and that, in most cases, the decompiled code is virtually a one-to-one match to the original source code. Chapter 3, "Obfuscating Classes," provided details on how bytecode can be protected from decompiling. It should be obvious that the strength of the overall protection is as strong as the code that implements it. You can use the strongest algorithm to encrypt the data, but if the code can be decompiled and patched in 30 minutes, the encryption can be simply commented out.

Obfuscation, obfuscation, obfuscation. That is the only reliable way to protect the bytecode and therefore the intellectual property of an application. Control flow obfuscation, which was covered in Chapter 3, is crucial to achieve the best results. The ultimate countermeasure against decompiling bytecode is to compile the Java application into a native executable. We have looked at the complexity of reverse engineering and patching the native code and, no matter how good the bytecode obfuscator is, the native code is much harder to crack. Unfortunately, by now most vendors that were offering Java to native code compilers have either gone out of business or stopped actively supporting their products. The JIT improvements and the increasing processor speeds provide enough performance for Java applications, eliminating the need to compile into the native code. TowerJ and Excelsior probably have the best implementations for Windows, but I advise caution and thorough testing of the compiled application to ensure that all the features are properly functioning. For most Java applications, using an aggressive obfuscator such as Zelix KlassMaster is probably a better choice than compiling the code into the native binaries.

Protecting Bytecode from Hacking

No matter how good of a job is done by the obfuscator, the bytecode can still be decompiled. And if it can be decompiled, it can be modified and the application can be patched. To strengthen the protection, we will review a few ideas on safety checks that can safeguard classes from patching.

Throughout the book, we've developed various techniques for hacking and patching. We have discussed how to decompile and then patch entire classes, access protected and private methods, and work with the system boot class path. Used for the wrong reasons, those techniques can harm the intellectual property inside a Java application. Here we look at the techniques that make hacking much harder and the countermeasures for each.

Hacking Non-Public Methods and Variables of a Class (Chapter 4)

The easiest solution to this is to seal the application JAR. Sealing a JAR guarantees that all the classes in a package come from the same code source. This means that a hacker cannot place custom classes in the packages supplied by the JAR. JAR sealing is achieved by adding the following line to the manifest file:

```
Sealed: true
```

The JAR itself needs to be protected from modifications. Just as you can easily seal it, a hacker can easily unseal it. All the hacker would have to do is unjar the contents of the JAR file to a temporary directory, remove the `Sealed` attribute, and then rejar it back. Java supports the notion of signed JARs that can protect its contents from modifications by signing every class in it with a digital signature. This works well for signed applets that are downloaded and verified by the browser. The problem is that the signed JAR itself is not protected, so once again a hacker can unjar the file, remove the manifest with the digital signatures, and rejar the file. Even though the JAR would no longer be considered authentic and originating from its true vendor, it could be executed and used just fine. Thus, you need a way to ensure that the application distribution contents are not modified; we look at this in the following section.

Replacing and Patching Application Classes (Chapter 5)

Sealing a JAR provides a remedy for this hacking technique as well. For extra protection, you can add a check asserting that a class is indeed loaded from the application distribution JAR and not from a third-party JAR. The implementation of this simple method is provided in `covertjava.protect.IntegrityProtector`. Listing 19.4 shows the source code for `assertClassSource()`.

LISTING 19.4   Asserting Class Source JAR

```
public void assertClassSource(Class cls, String jarName) {
    // Class loader should not be null
    if (cls.getClassLoader() == null)
        throw new InternalError(BOOT_CLASSLOADER);

    String name = cls.getName();
    int lastDot = name.lastIndexOf('.');
    if (lastDot != -1)
        name = name.substring(lastDot + 1);
    URL url = cls.getResource(name + ".class");
    if (url == null)
        throw new InternalError(FAILED_TO_GET_URL);

    name = url.toString();
    if (name.startsWith("jar:") == false || name.indexOf(jarName + "!") == -1)
        throw new InternalError(UNEXPECTED_JAR);
}
```

The first `if` statement ensures that the class loader of the given class is not the boot class loader by comparing it with a `null`. This assertion can be made because you know that none of the Chat classes are placed on the boot class path, which means they should be loaded using the default application launcher's class loader.

The rest of the method code obtains a URL for the source of the CLASS file that was used to create the given class. This is the URL returned by `Class.getResource()` for the `MessageInfo` class:

`jar:file:/C:/Projects/CovertJava/distrib/lib/chat.jar!/covertjava/chat/MessageInfo.class`

The URL indicates that the class was loaded from the `chat.jar` file located in the `C:/Projects/CovertJava/distrib/lib` directory. After obtaining the URL, `assertClassSource()` ensures that it starts with `jar:` and contains the name of the JAR file that was passed as a method parameter. An unchecked `InternalError` is thrown to abort the execution if the asserting fails. This might not be a completely foolproof verification, but it should be good enough to thwart most attempts at patching. To take advantage of this protection, the Chat application must invoke `assertClassSource()` on the key classes that are prime candidates for patching. We will add a new class, `ProtectedChatApplication`, as an alternative entry point for the Chat application. `ProtectedChat` will extend `covertjava.chat.ChatApplication` and use various protection mechanisms developed in this chapter. The code in Listing 19.5 shows a portion of `ProtectedChatApplication`'s `main()` method that asserts the origin of the `LicenseManager` class.

LISTING 19.5   Asserting the Origin of `LicenseManager`

```
public static void main(String[] args) throws Exception {
    LicenseManager licenseManager = new LicenseManager("conf/chat.license");
    IntegrityProtector protector = new IntegrityProtector();
    protector.assertClassSource(licenseManager.getClass(), "/lib/chat.jar");
    ...
}
```

The `main()` method ensures that the `LicenseManager` class is loaded from the `chat.jar` file located in the `lib` subdirectory. We should insert checks like that in other classes of Chat. The more checks we use, the more work a hacker must put in to crack the application.

Manipulating Java Security (Chapter 7)

Manipulating Java security enables hackers to gain access to protected, package, and private members of a class and to bypass other security checks normally enforced by a security manager. If an application installs a security manager or uses a custom policy file, you should insert checks that assert that the security manager is installed and that the correct policy file is used. The security manager can be obtained using `System.getSecurityManager()`, and to verify the original policy file you can check the value of the `java.security.policy` system property. The policy file itself can be protected from modifications using the application content protection technique described later in this chapter.

Reverse Engineering Applications (Chapter 12)

Depending on the type of the resource, the protection requires either bytecode protection or application content protection. Resources such as menu item strings and error messages are often hardcoded in the bytecode, whereas resources such as images and media files are typically stored in a separate directory or inside a JAR file. The bytecode protection was reviewed earlier, and the application content protection is presented in the next section.

Controlling Class Loading (Chapter 14)

Custom class loaders provide a lot of power because they can manipulate the bytecode on-the-fly. It is certainly not a common technique to hack applications, but if you want to protect an application class from runtime bytecode manipulations, you can install and use a predefined custom class loader instead of the system class loader. Then, in various places of the application code, a check can be made to see whether a class was loaded with the expected class loader.

Understanding and Tweaking Bytecode (Chapter 17)

Bytecode tweaking requires either a custom class loader that performs the tweaking on-the-fly or static modifications to the application CLASS files. We have discussed how to prevent the use of a third-party class loader in the previous paragraph, and the next section describes how to protect the application distribution files.

Protecting Application Content from Hacking

Application content here refers to the files distributed with the application. This includes the libraries as JAR and Zip files, images, configuration files, and other content. Ensuring that the key application files are not modified is critical for application integrity protection because most hacking techniques require changing some file. The most important type of file that needs integrity protection is the JAR archive. We have already looked at a trick that can ensure that the class is loaded from the expected JAR. Now we will develop a class allowing an application to assert that none of its files have been tampered with.

The most straightforward way of verifying the integrity of the application content is to iterate the distribution files and check the attributes, such as size and modification time. For ultimate protection, the application can produce a checksum of the file content and verify it against the checksum of the original files taken at the distribution preparation time. We are going to develop a class called `IntegrityProtector` in the `covertjava.protect` package and use it to protect the infamous Chat application. To keep the example concise, we will limit the verification to file lengths, although it can easily be extended to include other file attributes and the content hash. `IntegrityProtector` iterates a list of key application files, produces a total size of files in bytes, and then calculates a checksum using the message digest algorithm. We will then add a configuration file to Chat that stores the version and the digest of the application distribution. Storing the digest instead of the total length of files makes hacking much harder. Finally, at Chat application startup we will use `IntegrityProtector` to assert that the current checksum of the distribution files matches the original checksum provided in the configuration file.

Our first task is to decide which files in Chat should be protected from modifications. We cannot simply include all the files because certain files are meant to be changed by the end user. For instance, `bin/setenv.bat` can be modified to provide a specific home directory for Chat or to run it on a different port. `conf/log4j.properties` can change if a user adjusts the logging levels. However, files such as `lib/chat.jar` and `conf/java.policy` should never differ from the original versions (unless we want to send the customer patches, in which case the new checksums can be provided with the patch). In this example, we will protect only the core files of the Chat distribution:

```
conf\java.policy
lib\chat.jar
lib\log4j-1.2.8.jar
```

For flexibility of design, we will read the list of core files from a configuration file called `ChatFileList.class`. To confuse hackers, we gave the list file a `.class` extension, although its content is text. During the development, this file will be kept in the `CovertJava/conf` directory, but we will modify the `build.xml` file to copy `ChatFileList.class` into the `covertjava/protect` directory together with the classes from the `covertjava.protect` package. Listing 19.6 shows the `<copy>` task that has been added to `build.xml`.

LISTING 19.6   Copying the File List into the Distribution Directory

```
<copy todir="classes/covertjava/protect">
    <fileset dir="conf">
        <include name="ChatFileList.class"/>
    </fileset>
</copy>
```

Spending an extra 15 minutes to disguise the file list as a regular class file is worth the effort because it makes a trivial protection method less obvious to a hacker. We can now proceed with the development of the IntegrityProtector class in the covertjava.protect package. We first must write a few helper methods that read the contents of a text file (such as ChatFileList.class for Chat) and parse it to produce an array of strings. If you open the IntegrityProtector.java file in the src/covertjava/protect directory, you can see the implementations of the helper methods: readFilePathsFromResource(), readFilePathsFromFile(), and readFilePathsFromString(). Now we can code a method that produces a checksum for a given list of file paths. We then add the getFilesCheckSum() method to IntegrityProtector and implement it as shown in Listing 19.7.

LISTING 19.7   Calculating a Checksum for a List of Files

```
public String getFilesCheckSum(String[] paths, char separator,
        String installPath) throws Exception {
    long totalSize = 0;
    for (int i = 0; i < paths.length; i++) {
        String path = paths[i];
        if (separator != File.separatorChar)
            path = path.replace(separator, File.separatorChar);
        path = installPath + File.separatorChar + path;
        totalSize += new File(path).length();
    }

    byte[] checkSum = toByteArray(totalSize);
    MessageDigest sha = MessageDigest.getInstance("SHA-1");
    checkSum = sha.digest(checkSum);
    BASE64Encoder encoder = new BASE64Encoder();
    return encoder.encode(checkSum);
}
```

The method iterates the array of filenames, adding the size of each file in bytes to the total size. After the total size is calculated, it is converted to an array of bytes using a helper method called toByteArray(). getFilesCheckSum() then obtains an instance of a message digest algorithm SHA-1 (Secure Hash Algorithm provided by Sun JCE) and gets a hash of the total size. Because the checksum has to be stored in a text file, we need to convert the bytes into human-recognizable ASCII characters. We cannot simply cast `byte` variables to `char` type because it produces nonprintable characters (for instance, the byte value of 7 would produce a beep, and the byte value of 8 would produce a backspace). The standard solution to this problem is *base64 encoding*. Base64 encoding uses a subset of ASCII code that contains only 64 printable characters. The subset includes characters A–Z and a–z, numerals 0–9, and a few other safe characters such as punctuation marks. Because fewer characters are used, base64 allocates 6 bits per character instead of the 8 bits used for ASCII characters. Consequently, 3 bytes of input data are encoded into 4 bytes of output data. `IntegrityProtector` uses the `Base64Encoder` class, found in the `sun.misc` package, to obtain a printable representation of a file's checksum.

Now that we are able to obtain the file's checksum, we will use it to verify the integrity of the Chat installation. We will code `IntegrityProtector`'s `main()` method to output the checksum for a given file list. Listing 19.8 shows the body of the `main()` method.

LISTING 19.8   Outputting a File's Checksum

```
public static void main(String[] args) throws Exception {
    if (args.length != 1) {
        System.out.println("Syntax: IntegrityProtector " +
                "[-Dhome=<path to home>] <file list path>");
        System.exit(1);
    }

    IntegrityProtector protector = new IntegrityProtector();
    String[] paths = protector.readFilePathsFromFile(args[0]);

    String homePath = System.getProperty("home", "..");
    String checksum = protector.getFilesCheckSum(paths, '\\', homePath);
    System.out.println("Checksum = [" + checksum + "]");
}
```

The `main()` method takes in one parameter that specifies the list file (`conf/ChatFileList.class` in our case) and an optional parameter giving the home directory for files (`distrib` in our case). For convenience, we have included a batch file `getChatChecksum.bat` in the `CovertJava/bin` directory that uses `IntegrityProtecor` to output the Chat checksum. Running `getChatChecksum.bat` after building the Chat distributing with the Ant release task produces the following output:

```
Checksum = [gLmBOKQe88gLrC9vaSjBarf2Rfw=]
```

Every time a core file of Chat changes (for instance, when you rebuild `lib/chat.jar`) the checksum is different. But if the file sizes do not change, the checksum remains the same, which potentially opens a hole in protection. This is why getting a checksum based on the actual file content is more secure; however, most hackers will not bother to keep the file size unchanged, so even our simple mechanism would work for Chat.

We can now add a configuration file called `chat.properties` to the Chat `conf` directory. Inside the file, we will store the checksum of the Chat distribution as the value of the `chat.versionInfo` property. Once again, we avoid using an intuitive name for the property to make hacking harder. Our final task is to ensure that, at the start, the Chat application verifies the current checksum for its files against the checksum read from the configuration file. The portion of `ProtectedChatApplication`'s `main()` method that does it is shown in Listing 19.9.

LISTING 19.9   Verifying the Current Checksum Against the Distribution Checksum

```
public static void main(String[] args) throws Exception {
    String homePath = System.getProperty("chat.home");
    String propPath = homePath + File.separator + "conf" +
                      File.separator + "chat.properties";
    AppProperties props = new AppProperties(propPath);
    String checkSum = props.getProperty("chat.versionInfo");
    IntegrityProtector protector = new IntegrityProtector();
    String[] paths = protector.readFilePathsFromResource("ChatFileList.class");
    protector.assertFilesIntegrity(paths, '\\', homePath, checkSum);
}
```

After reading the original checksum and the list of protected files, the method uses `IntegrityProtector`'s `assertFilesIntegrity()` method to ensure the integrity of the content. `assertFilesIntegrity()`, shown in Listing 19.10, simply invokes `getFilesChecksum()` for the given list of files and throws an `InternalError` if the calculated checksum does not match the original checksum.

LISTING 19.10   `IntegrityProtector.assertFilesIntegrity()` Implementation

```
public void assertFilesIntegrity(String[] paths, char separator,
                 String installPath, String checkSum) throws Exception {
    String installCheckSum = getFilesCheckSum(paths, separator, installPath);
    if (installCheckSum.equals(checkSum) == false)
        throw new InternalError("Some of the installation files are corrupt");
}
```

With all the coding done, we can test our protection. The Chat files provided for this book are shipped with the correct checksum. You should be able to run Chat using `chat_protected.bat` from the `distrib/bin` directory. Verify that you can bring up the main Chat window on your machine. Now let's pretend we are hacking Chat by modifying `java.policy` in the `distrib/conf` directory. Open that file, add a new line, and save it. Be sure that the file length has changed, and try running `chat_protected.bat` again. You should see the following exception:

```
Exception in thread "main" java.lang.InternalError:
Some of the installation files are corrupt
     at covertjava.protect.IntegrityProtector.assertFilesIntegrity(...)
     at covertjava.protect.ProtectedChatApplication.main(...)
```

Because the file length has changed, the calculated checksum no longer matches the original checksum and `IntegrityProtector` throws an error. If we were to distribute the protected implementation of Chat, we would of course not ship the `getChatChecksum.bat` file and would remove `distrib/bin/chat.bat` along with the `main()` method of `ChatApplication`. This would ensure that the only way to launch Chat is through the `ProtectedChatApplication` class. To enable the protected Chat to run with the new version of files, we would have to obtain the new checksum and set it as the value of the `chat.versionInfo` property in the `chat.properties` file.

Implementing Licensing to Unlock Application Features

This section examines the way in which the applications are licensed today and then discusses how to develop a licensing framework for a commercially distributed application.

Modern Software Licensing Models

Several dominant license models govern the distribution of modern software. The terms of distribution and use are typically written in the end user license agreement (EULA) that is shipped with the product. Although each vendor has a choice of writing out the licensing terms, the license models can be grouped in the following three categories.

Closed Source Commercial Software

This is the traditional model for distributing for-profit software. It includes proprietary products such as Microsoft Windows; software that can be downloaded for a free evaluation, such as ItelliJ IDEA; and products that have a limited-functionality free edition, such as Borland JBuilder and BEA WebLogic. Offering a limited-functionality free edition is becoming more and more popular with Java vendors because developers like to get a good feel for a product before they make their purchase decision. When a product is well written, the users get accustomed to it and in the end often decide to buy the fully functional version.

Open Source Commercial Software

This emerging licensing model is gaining popularity and enables end users to not only download and use the software, but to also obtain the source code. The terms of use typically allow free development and deployment but might require fees for documentation, technical support, or advanced features. The most prominent examples in this category are the JBoss application server and MySQL database.

Open Source Free Software

Software in this category is made available to the public free without any restrictions. The most common license used for open source free software is the General Public License (GPL) that allows the use of the software and its source code for commercial and noncommercial use. There are variations of GPL and other open source licenses, such as Apache, that might impose certain restrictions on the software use, but they all strive for the basic idea of free-for-all.

Implementing Licensing to Unlock Commercial Features

When the source code is provided with a product, it is obvious that having programmatic restrictions to enforce the licensing model is pointless. Any user can easily remove restrictions on the functionality by modifying the source code and rebuilding the product. However, the majority of products today are not shipped with the source code, so programmatic enforcement of the licensing policy can help in generating sales. We are going to develop a LicenseManager class that produces secure serial numbers based on the customer environment and the license type. The class will use an asymmetric algorithm to ensure that only the software vendor can issue the serial numbers. Even if you do not need to implement license management, you will benefit from reading this section because it demonstrates a practical use of Java security and cryptography APIs.

Deciding on the licensing design requires consideration of the most effective way to prevent licensing policy abuse without sacrificing the customer's experience with the product. For instance, issuing a license that unlocks commercial product features without tying it to the end user's environment is unsafe. This kind of license might be easier to issue because it does not require the user sending the information to the product vendor, but it can turn into a distribution nightmare if somebody places the license on the Internet. You should attach the license to a parameter in the customer environment such as the hostname, IP address, or domain name. That way, even if the license surfaces on the Internet, it will not work in an environment for which it was not issued. Another important consideration is the ability to enable restricted features of the product through the license file without having to maintain and build multiple versions of the software. Expiration time, embedded into the license file, can be useful if the vendor wants to issue a temporary license for product evaluation.

For instance, if Chat had commercial potential, we could have distributed a free edition with limited functionality that would allow sending plain-text messages to one user at a time. Then we could have implemented extra features such as HTML text, colors, buddy lists, smiley faces, and images support. Theoretically, we could have built two instances of Chat—the limited one and the full-featured one. But, in practice, maintaining that type of code is very difficult so, like most vendors, we prefer to keep one code base of the full-featured version. To restrict access to a commercial feature, we must insert checks in certain key parts of the code to test whether a license file exists and whether it allows that feature. If the checks fail, the feature is disabled. We then could offer Chat without a license file for a free download. If a user wanted to enjoy the advanced features of our wonderful application, he would have to purchase a license. After payment was received, we would issue a license based on the user's hostname and send the license file to him. The next time the user runs Chat, the application would read the license information and enable the purchased features.

The information about which features to allow and which ones to disable can be encrypted in the license file, but that makes the file hard to read and maintain. Storing the license parameters in plain text is easier, but that would be like dangling a piece of chicken in front of a hungry crocodile. For instance, a license can be issued for a specific host, but even the least-sophisticated user can copy the license file to another host and change the value of the hostname. The cleanest solution is to produce a secure digital signature based on the license parameters and store it in the license file together with the parameters in plain text. The signature is then generated by a licensing utility using a private key of an asymmetric algorithm. At startup, the application would use a public key of the algorithm and the signature to verify the authenticity of the information to be read from the license file. Only if the verification succeeds would the license restrictions be removed.

STORIES FROM THE TRENCHES

WebCream is a popular tool for Java enabling the dynamic conversion of Swing GUI applications and applets into interactive HTML Web sites. It is a commercial product distributed by CreamTec. We have decided to make the standard edition of WebCream free to persuade developers to evaluate it. The standard edition is a full-featured version capable of complete conversion. To promote the purchase of the commercial licenses, limitations were imposed on the number of concurrent users and some of the advanced customization features.

Initially, we were building three different editions from a slightly different code base. With multiple platforms and installer versions, the building of the releases was taking more than a day. To simplify the maintenance and to meet the aggressive schedules, we decided to maintain the same code base for the commercial and free editions. The commercial features were simply locked in the free edition and become unlocked only if a license file is found. The license file contains the encrypted information about the hosts that the license allows, the number of concurrent users, and the access to the commercial features. This approach has greatly simplified the distribution and management of multiple editions.

Creating a License File

Let's proceed with the development of a generic license manager and use it with Chat. For simplicity, we will use the Java properties file format for the license file. The licensing will be based on three parameters: the hostname, IP address, and expiration date. Because I didn't want to spend time writing all those money-generating features of Chat, this simple example is good enough to illustrate the approach. Create a new file called chat.license in CovertJava/distrib/conf that looks as shown in Listing 19.11.

LISTING 19.11   Chat License File

```
host=localhost
ip=172.24.109.159
expires=2005/1/1
serial=
```

Use your hostname and IP address and leave the value of the serial property blank for now—we'll get to it later. We must code two classes, one for the license generation and another for verification. We do not want to ship the license generation code with the application distribution, so two classes are necessary. Because both classes have to read the license information from a file, it would make sense for one of them to extend the other. Let's start with the LicenseManager class in the covertjava.protect package. We'll define member fields for the license properties (see Listing 19.12).

LISTING 19.12   LicenseManager Declaration

```
public class LicenseManager {
    private String host;
    private String ip;
    private Date expires;
    ...
}
```

Then we'll give it a constructor that takes the license filename as a parameter and populates the internal fields with the license information, as shown in Listing 19.13.

LISTING 19.13   LicenseManager Initialization

```
public LicenseManager(String licenseFileName) throws Exception {
    this.licenseProps = new AppProperties(home+File.separator+licenseFileName);
    this.host = licenseProps.getProperty("host");
    this.ip = licenseProps.getProperty("ip");
    String expiresString = licenseProps.getProperty("expires");
    this.expires = this.dateFormat.parse(expiresString);
    ...
}
```

To protect the license parameters from modifications, we need to produce a digital signature. All JCE algorithms work with arrays of bytes, so we'll add a `getLicenseString()` method that returns a unified representation of all the license properties. The source code for this method is shown in Listing 19.14.

LISTING 19.14   Unified Representation of License Properties

```
protected String getLicenseString() throws Exception {
    return this.host + this.ip + this.expires;
}
```

For now, we can leave the `LicenseManager` class and start working on `LicenseGenerator`. `LicenseGenerator` should extend `LicenseManager` and provide methods to generate the digital signature. We will use base64-encoded digital signature as the serial number. To generate a signature, we also need a pair of keys for use with the asymmetric algorithm. The keys can be generated using JDK's keytool utility or programmatically using Java security APIs. With keytool, the keys can be generated and exported with just a few commands, but we'll take the programmatic approach for academic interest. First, we need to decide on the algorithm to use and the key length. The standard choices for asymmetric encryption are the DSA and RSA algorithms. Both offer adequate protection with the right key size, but we'll use DSA because it is natively supported by Sun JCE, which is shipped with the JRE. The key size directly affects the complexity of encryption: The longer the key, the harder it is to crack. Every bit doubles the cracking time. Whereas 16-bit keys can be cracked by a modern CPU in a matter of minutes, 1024-bit keys are deemed impossible to crack because, even using all the silicon power on earth, the time required to crack one would run into millions of years (or so they say). Because we are not doing real-time decryption, we'll use the 1024-bit key size. The code in Listing 19.15 shows a method of `LicenseGenerator` that generates a pair of keys.

LISTING 19.15   Generation of Keys for the DSA Algorithm

```
public void generateKeys() throws Exception {
    KeyPairGenerator keyGen = KeyPairGenerator.getInstance("DSA");
    SecureRandom random = SecureRandom.getInstance("SHA1PRNG", "SUN");
    random.setSeed(System.currentTimeMillis());
    keyGen.initialize(1024, random);
    KeyPair pair = keyGen.generateKeyPair();

    String publicKeyPath = home + File.separator + "conf"
                                + File.separator + "key_public.ser";
    byte[] bytes = pair.getPublic().getEncoded();
    FileOutputStream stream = new FileOutputStream(publicKeyPath);
```

```
    stream.write(bytes);
    stream.close();
    ...
}
```

The implementation first obtains an instance of the DSA key pair generator. The generator needs to be initialized with the key size (1024 bits) and a random numbers provider (we use Sun's SecureRandom). After initializing the generator, keys are generated via a call to generateKeyPair(). After the pair is generated, the remaining task is to save the public and private keys to disk. Listing 19.15 shows how the public key was saved to the key_public.ser file in the Conf directory. The remaining part of the method that is not shown in Listing 19.15 saves the private key to the key_private.ser file in the same way.

Obviously, we want to generate the keys only once. LicenseGenerator is given a main() method that calls generateKeys() or generateSerialNumber(), depending on the command-line parameters. We've already seen the implementation of key generation, so let's look at generating the serial number. As mentioned earlier, the serial number is generated as a base64-encoded digital signature for the unified license properties. The generateSerialNumber() method shown in Listing 19.16 does just that.

LISTING 19.16   Generating a Serial Number

```
public String generateSerialNumber() throws Exception {
    String licenseString = getLicenseString();
    byte[] serialBytes = licenseString.getBytes(CHARSET);
    serialBytes = getSignature(serialBytes);
    BASE64Encoder encoder = new BASE64Encoder();
    return encoder.encode(serialBytes);
}
```

The bytes of the serial number string are passed to the getSignature() method, the output of which is then converted to a string using the BASE64Encoder class. This brings us to the implementation of digital signing with the DSA algorithm, which is shown in Listing 19.17.

LISTING 19.17   Digital Signing with DSA

```
private byte[] getSignature(byte[] serialBytes) throws Exception {
    String privateKeyPath = home + File.separator + "conf" +
                                File.separator + "key_private.ser";
    FileInputStream stream = new FileInputStream(privateKeyPath);
    byte[] encodedPrivateKey = new byte[stream.available()];
    stream.read(encodedPrivateKey);
```

LISTING 19.17   Continued

```
    PKCS8EncodedKeySpec pubKeySpec= new PKCS8EncodedKeySpec(encodedPrivateKey);
    KeyFactory keyFactory = KeyFactory.getInstance("DSA");
    PrivateKey key = keyFactory.generatePrivate(pubKeySpec);

    Signature dsa = Signature.getInstance("SHA1withDSA");
    dsa.initSign(key);
    dsa.update(serialBytes);
    return dsa.sign();
}
```

We are signing the license information using the private key to ensure that nobody else can generate licenses. The private key is read from a file into a byte array (encodedPrivateKey). We then convert the binary representation into an internal ASN.1 representation using the PKCS8EncodedKeySpec class from the java.security.spec package. The key representation is then converted into an instance of PrivateKey using the DSA key factory. With the key and the serial number bytes on hand, we obtain an instance of the secure hash with the DSA algorithm (SHA1withDSA), supply its parameters, and generate the digital signature using the sign() method. Running the license generator script licenseGenerator.bat for the chat.license configuration file in the distrib/conf directory produces the following output:

```
C:\CovertJava\bin>licenseGenerator.bat -serial distrib/conf/chat.license
License information read:
    host=localhost
    ip=172.24.109.159
    expires=Sat Jan 01 00:00:00 EST 2005
Serial=[MC0CFBiEzKka0pnEQSlDyKxbHy+gE1+zAhUAlxPlWyAXcCDcoWSRY/Kk/xAkvTQ=]
```

We now need to copy the generated serial number and paste it as the value of the serial property in the chat.license file. The license generation is complete.

Verifying the License File

We have to enhance the Chat application to read the serial number and verify that the license parameters have not been tampered with. Because the serial number we use for Chat is actually a digital signature of the parameters, we need to code a method that uses the public key from the generated key pair to verify that signature. Let's add a method called verifySerialNumber() to the LicenseManager class that we coded earlier. To verify the digital signature generated using the private key, the method must use the public key. The license properties and the serial number were read from the license file in the LicenseManager constructor and stored in the member variables. The source code for verifySerialNumber() is shown in Listing 19.18.

LISTING 19.18   Verifying the Serial Number

```
public void verifySerialNumber(String keyFileName) throws Exception {
    String keyFilePath = this.home + File.separator + keyFileName;
    FileInputStream stream = new FileInputStream(keyFilePath);
    byte[] encodedPubKey = new byte[stream.available()];
    stream.read(encodedPubKey);
    X509EncodedKeySpec pubKeySpec = new X509EncodedKeySpec(encodedPubKey);
    KeyFactory keyFactory = KeyFactory.getInstance("DSA");
    PublicKey publicKey = keyFactory.generatePublic(pubKeySpec);

    byte[] licenseData = getLicenseString().getBytes(CHARSET);
    String encodedSig = this.licenseProps.getProperty("serial");
    if (encodedSig == null ¦¦ encodedSig.length() == 0)
        throw new InternalError("Serial number is missing");
    BASE64Decoder decoder = new BASE64Decoder();
    byte[] serialSig = decoder.decodeBuffer(encodedSig);

    Signature signature = Signature.getInstance("SHA1withDSA");
    signature.initVerify(publicKey);
    signature.update(licenseData);
    if (signature.verify(serialSig) == false)
        throw new InternalError("Invalid serial number");
}
```

The method first reads the contents of the public key file and uses the X509EncodedKeySpec class with the DSA key factory to convert the binary representation of the key into an instance of the PublicKey interface. Then the unified representation of the license parameters returned by getLicenseString() is converted to an array of bytes. The serial number is read as the value of the serial property from the license file and, if it is not missing, the number is decoded from base64 encoding using the BASE64Decoder class. An instance of the SHA1withDSA signing algorithm is obtained and supplied with the public key and the license data. Finally, a call to the verify() method of the signature algorithm is used to test whether the serial number data is a correct digital signature for the license data. If the verification fails, an exception is reported using InternalError.

To integrate the license verification with Chat, we need to add the invocation of verifySerialNumber() to ProtectedChat's main() method. Because we already have an instance of LicenseManager in main(), we just add the block of code shown in Listing 19.19.

LISTING 19.19 Invoking License Verification

```
public static void main(String[] args) throws Exception {
    ...
    // Check license information
    licenseManager.verifySerialNumber("conf/key_public.ser");
    if (licenseManager.isHostAllowed() == false)
        throw new Exception("Host is not allowed by the license");
    if (licenseManager.isLicenseExpired() == true)
        throw new Exception("The license is expired");
}
```

If the verifySerialNumber() method of LicenseManager does not throw an exception, the hostname and license expiration date verification are performed. The hostname verification is a simple string comparison between the name of the host that was read from the license file and the name of the host running Chat. The expiration date verification is an equally simple comparison between the current system date and the read license expiration date. Only if both verifications are successful do the commercial features of Chat become enabled. As long as the code in LicenseManager and ProtectedChat is not hacked, we have a pretty secure licensing mechanism.

An interesting approach to insert the licensing checks is to use bytecode instrumentation, described in Chapter 17, "Understanding and Tweaking Bytecode." Rather than manually invoking the methods of LicenseManager throughout the application classes, a post-processor utility can be developed that decorates the key methods of the application with the license verification code. The utility would run after the source code is compiled but before it is put into a distribution JAR. The inserted bytecode would throw an exception or return an error if the license were invalid or if the feature were not allowed. This provides a clean separation between the application logic and licensing code.

Web Activation and License Registration

Using the licensing mechanism described in the previous section provides a great deal of protection against piracy. However, if the license verification is hacked, the proliferation of the compromised product can be hard to track, especially if it surfaces on the Internet. A good strategy is to duplicate the invocation of the license verification methods throughout the application code. In the sample code, the Chat application only instantiates and uses LicenseManager in ProtectedChat's main() method. For extra protection, you should call the same methods in the MainFrame or ChatServer code. Yet another measure of protection is activation and registration via the Web.

The idea behind Web registration is that each time the application is run, it connects to the vendor's Web site and checks whether the license information is still valid. This enables the vendor to track the number of installed versions and to turn off the licenses or builds that are known to be hacked. Establishing an online connection to the vendor provides additional benefits, such as the possibility of automatic updates and collection of usage statistics.

Online connection should not be viewed as the primary method of activation and registration, though. Products can be installed and run in a controlled, isolated environment behind company firewalls that completely block access to the Internet. Sending a customer's information to the vendor's Web site can also lead to privacy concerns.

Quick Quiz

1. What are the differences between a message digest, encryption, and signing algorithms?

2. What is the difference between symmetric and asymmetric algorithms?

3. How would you protect the contents of an email sent via the Internet? Which JCE classes would you have to use?

4. Which measures can be taken to protect the application content from hacking?

5. We have used a message digest algorithm to compute the checksum of Chat's distribution files. Would it be more secure to use a symmetric or an asymmetric algorithm for the checksum? Why?

6. What are the logical steps required to obtain a digital signature using a symmetric algorithm?

7. What are the logical steps required to obtain a digital signature using an asymmetric algorithm?

In Brief

- Cryptography provides a means of converting readable information into incomprehensible code that can be transmitted openly and then transformed back into its original form.

- Encryption is the process of encoding readable information into code, and decryption is the process of extracting the readable information from the code.

- Message digest algorithms do not modify the contents of the message. Rather, they produce a unique hash based on the message contents and a secret key.

■ Encryption/decryption algorithms hide sensitive information that can be intercepted by a third party. The message contents are modified using a secret key, producing output that is virtually impossible to convert back to the original contents without the key.

■ Signing refers to generating a relatively short digital signature based on arbitrarily sized data using a private key of an asymmetric algorithm. The signature is produced by the sender and is transmitted with the message. Authenticity is ensured through the use of asymmetric algorithms in which only the sender has the private key.

■ Java Cryptography Architecture (JCA) provides a complete and robust implementation of cryptography services and algorithms.

■ Encryption, message digests, and signing algorithms can be used to secure the communication between the layers of a distributed application.

■ Most security algorithms require parameters such as the password or keys. They typically operate on binary data.

■ After bytecode obfuscation, ensuring the integrity of distribution files is the most important measure that protects the application from hacking.

■ The most effective way to implement licensing that unlocks commercial features is to provide a text-based license file with a digital signature produced by an asymmetric algorithm.

Commercial Software License

LICENSE AGREEMENT FOR CREAMTEC'S WEBCREAM SOFTWARE PRODUCT

IMPORTANT. READ CAREFULLY: This WebCream End-User License Agreement ("License" or "Agreement") is a binding contract between you and CreamTec ("CreamTec") for CreamTec's WebCream ("Software" or "Product"), which includes computer software and may include related media, printed materials, and "online" or electronic documentation. Upon installing the software product, you agree to be bound by the terms of this License. Any installation or use of the WebCream Product will signify acceptance of, and your agreement to be bound by, this License. If you determine that you do not agree to the terms of this License, do not install or use the Product and if you received the Product by other than electronic means, return it immediately to CreamTec.

CREAMTEC LICENSE

WebCream means the current or future CreamTec's WebCream product and any additional modules, if any, licensed to you from CreamTec, that are installed on computer(s) acting as server(s). Additional software components may have been distributed to you along with the Product. Except as otherwise specifically stated in a separate license agreement provided with any such component, such additional components are subject to this License. The Product is protected by copyright laws and international copyright treaties, as well as other intellectual property laws and treaties. The Product is licensed, not sold.

1. GRANT OF LICENSE. This License grants you the following perpetual, non-exclusive and non-transferable rights:

a) Installation and Use—Subject to the test server, back-up and disaster recovery rights stated elsewhere in this License, you may install the Product where the application is located based on the number of concurrent users per application according to purchased license restrictions.

b) Business Use—Once installed in accordance with this License, you may use the Product only in the conduct of your own or your Affiliates' business and may not, directly or indirectly use the Product to process the work of any third party. "Affiliates" means any entity controlled by, or under common control with, you, the individual or entity purchasing this License.

c) Other Restrictions on Use—Your rights under this License shall not include the right to grant sublicenses or transfer (including transfer by rental or lease) the Product or any part thereof. Any attempt to grant sublicenses or transfer any rights shall be considered a breach of this Agreement. You may not create derivative works from, reverse engineer, decompile, or disassemble the Product except to the extent the foregoing restriction is expressly prohibited by applicable law.

d) Disaster Recovery and Backup—You may maintain the Product on a separate disaster recovery site provided that the installation is solely for the purposes of backup and emergency use. In addition, after installation of the Product pursuant to this License, you may keep the original media on which the Product was provided solely for archival purposes or for reinstallation of the Product in accordance with the terms of this License.

2. SUBSEQUENT RELEASES. A Product labeled as a subsequent release (or similar term) replaces and/or supplements the product originally licensed, and following the subsequent release you may use the resulting Product only in accordance with the terms of this License. Such releases include enhancements and corrections of and modifications and additions to the Product. Releases also include later versions of the Product. For the first year of this agreement and upon payment of the annual maintenance fee every year thereafter, you will receive for your use all releases issued by CreamTec. Use of such releases will be governed by and subject to the terms of this Agreement relating to the reproduction and use of the Product.

3. OWNERSHIP. The Product is licensed, not sold. Title and copyrights in and to the Product, accompanying printed materials, and any copies you are permitted to make herein are owned by CreamTec.

4. DUAL-MEDIA SOFTWARE. You may receive the Product in more than one medium. Regardless of the type or size of medium you receive, you may use only the medium that is appropriate for your hardware devices. You may not loan, rent, lease, or otherwise transfer any unused medium to another user.

5. EXPORT CONTROLS. You agree and certify that no technical data received from CreamTec, nor the direct product thereof, will be shipped, transferred or exported, directly or indirectly, to any country in violation of any applicable law, including the United States Export Administration Act and the regulations thereunder.

6. TERMINATION. You may terminate this License by destroying or returning to CreamTec the Product and all copies thereof. If you fail to comply with any provisions of this Agreement, each of which is considered to be the essence of this Agreement, CreamTec may immediately terminate this Agreement if you do not pay maintenance fees when due or if you breach any provisions of this License and do not cure such breach within thirty days (30) of CreamTec's notification to you of such breach. Upon termination, you shall immediately cease use of the Product and, at the option of CreamTec, shall either promptly return to CreamTec all copies of the Product in your possession or destroy all such copies, and shall certify in writing that all such copies have been returned or destroyed.

7. LIMITED WARRANTY. CreamTec has no control over the conditions under which you use the Product and subsequent updates and does not and cannot warrant the results obtained by such use.

a) LIMITED WARRANTY. In addition to warranting that it has the right to grant the license contained in this Agreement, CreamTec warrants that the media on which the Product is delivered and any user manuals to be leased under the terms of this Agreement are free of defects in material and workmanship under normal use for a period of thirty (30) days following shipment. CreamTec further warrants that the Product and any subsequent updates will perform substantially in accordance with the accompanying written materials such as those specifications found in the user manual or documentation provided in effect as of the date of this Agreement for a period of thirty (30) days from the date of receipt. CreamTec does not warrant that the functions contained in the Product or in any subsequent update will meet your requirements or that operation of the Product will be uninterrupted or error free. This Limited Warranty does not cover any copy of the Product or update or any user manual which has been altered or changed in any way, or if failure of the Product has resulted from accident, abuse, or misapplication. CreamTec is not responsible for problems caused by changes in or modifications to the operating characteristics of any computer hardware or operating system for which the Product is procured, nor is CreamTec responsible for problems which occur as a result of the use of the Product in conjunction with software or hardware which is incompatible with the Product. To the extent allowed by applicable law, implied warranties on the Product, if any, are limited to thirty (30) days. Some states/jurisdictions do not allow limitations on duration of an implied warranty, so the above limitation may not apply to you.

b) CUSTOMER REMEDIES. CreamTec's entire liability and your exclusive remedy shall be the replacement by CreamTec of any magnetic media or user manual not meeting CreamTec's "Limited Warranty." In addition, while in no sense warranting that the operation of the Product will be uninterrupted or error free, CreamTec will make best efforts to supply you with corrected versions of the Product through updates to correct any errors which you find in the Product during the warranty period and which prevent the Product from substantially performing as described in the accompanying written materials. Any replacement Product will be warranted for the remainder of the original warranty period or thirty (30) days, whichever is longer. Outside the United States, neither these remedies nor any product support services offered by CreamTec are available without proof of purchase from an authorized source. You must notify CreamTec of any breach of warranty within the warranty period to be entitled to remedy.

c) TO THE MAXIMUM EXTENT PERMITTED BY APPLICABLE LAW, AND TO THE EXTENT CONTAINED IN THIS AGREEMENT OR ATTACHMENT TO THIS AGREEMENT, CREAMTEC AND ITS DISTRIBUTORS DISCLAIM ALL OTHER WARRANTIES AND CONDITIONS, EITHER EXPRESS OR IMPLIED, INCLUDING, BUT NOT LIMITED TO, IMPLIED WARRANTIES OR CONDITIONS OF MERCHANTABILITY, FITNESS FOR A PARTICULAR PURPOSE, TITLE AND NON-INFRINGEMENT, WITH REGARD TO THE PRODUCT, AND THE PROVISION OF OR FAILURE TO PROVIDE SUPPORT SERVICES. The above limited warranty gives you specific legal rights. You may have others, which vary amongst jurisdictions. The warranties contained in Subsection a) of this Section are made in lieu of all other express warranties, whether oral or written. Only an authorized officer of CreamTec may make modifications to this warranty or additional warranties binding on CreamTec, and such modifications or warranties must be in writing. Accordingly, additional statements such as those made in advertising or presentations, whether oral or written, do not constitute warranties by CreamTec and should not be relied upon as such.

d) Any statements made by a dealer or any other third party other than CreamTec are not warranties and cannot be relied on by you. CreamTec shall not be liable for any claimed non-conformance of the Software Product under Article 35(2) of the United Nations Convention on Contracts for the International Sale of Goods, even if that Convention were to be determined applicable to this license and the underlying transactions.

e) LIMITATION OF LIABILITY. TO THE MAXIMUM EXTENT PERMITTED BY APPLICABLE LAW, IN NO EVENT SHALL CREAMTEC OR ITS DISTRIBUTORS BE LIABLE FOR ANY SPECIAL, INCIDENTAL, INDIRECT, OR CONSEQUENTIAL DAMAGES WHATSOEVER (INCLUDING, WITHOUT LIMITATION, DAMAGES FOR LOSS OF BUSINESS PROFITS, BUSINESS INTERRUPTION, LOSS OF BUSINESS INFORMATION, OR ANY OTHER PECUNIARY LOSS) ARISING OUT OF THE USE OF OR INABILITY TO USE THE PRODUCT OR THE FAILURE TO PROVIDE SUPPORT SERVICES, EVEN IF CREAMTEC HAS BEEN ADVISED OF THE POSSIBILITY OF SUCH DAMAGES. IN ANY CASE, CREAMTEC'S ENTIRE LIABILITY UNDER ANY PROVISION OF THIS LICENSE SHALL BE LIMITED TO THE AMOUNT ACTUALLY PAID BY YOU FOR THE PRODUCT. Because some jurisdictions do not allow the exclusion or limitation of liability, the above limitation may not apply to you.

8. US GOVERNMENT RESTRICTED RIGHTS. The Product and documentation are provided with RESTRICTED RIGHTS. Use, duplication, or disclosure by the Government is subject to restrictions as set forth in subparagraph (c)(1)(ii) of the Rights in Technical Data and Computer Software clause at DFARS 252.227-7013 or subparagraphs (c)(1) and (2) of the Commercial Computer Software—Restricted Rights at 48 CFR 52.227-19, as applicable.

9. TERM. This Agreement is effective from the date of its execution to a date of one year from that date unless terminated earlier by either party because of the default of the other party in any obligation under this Agreement.

10. ANNUAL MAINTENANCE FEE. On the date of the anniversary of this Agreement, you shall pay an annual maintenance fee. Payment of the fees entitle you to continued use of the Product as well as product updates, releases and technical support. Failure to pay the annual maintenance fee constitutes breach of this Agreement and shall be the basis for immediate termination of this Agreement.

11. RENEWAL OF LICENSE. The License granted under this Agreement and the terms of this Agreement shall be automatically renewed upon the continued payment of the annual maintenance fee unless either party notifies the other in writing of an intent to terminate or a request to modify terms at least sixty (60) days prior to the expiration date of this Agreement. In the event no notice of termination or request to modify is sent by either party, this Agreement, its license and terms, shall be renewed for the term of one year. If either party notifies the other of an election to terminate sixty (60) days prior to the Agreement's expiration date or if the parties cannot agree on the proposed modifications, the License will terminate upon the expiration of the Agreement.

12. TAXES. You are required to pay all local, state and federal taxes (but excluding taxes imposed on CreamTec income) levied or imposed by reason of the transactions contemplated in this Agreement. You shall promptly pay to CreamTec an amount equal to any such tax(es) actually paid or required to be collected by CreamTec.

13. INDEMNIFICATION. CreamTec, at its own expense, will indemnify, defend and hold Licensee harmless from all damages, costs and awards arising from any third party action to the extent that it is based on a claim that the Product or any subsequent update used within the scope of this Agreement infringes any patent, copyright, license, trade secret, or other propriety right, provided we are immediately notified in writing of such a claim. CreamTec, at its own expense, will defend any action brought against Licensee or CreamTec to the extent that it is based on a claim that the Product or any subsequent update used within the scope of this Agreement infringes any patent, copyright, license, trade secret, or other propriety right, provided we are immediately notified in writing of such a claim. CreamTec shall have the right to control the defense of all such claims, lawsuits, and other proceedings. In no event shall you settle any such claim, lawsuit or proceeding without CreamTec's prior written approval. CreamTec shall have no liability for any claim under this Section if a claim for patent, copyright, license, or trade secret infringement is based on the use of a superseded or altered version of the Product if such infringement would have been avoided by use of the latest unaltered version of the Product available as an update.

14. ARBITRATION. If you acquired this product in the United States, this Agreement is governed by the laws of the Commonwealth of Virginia. If this product was acquired outside the United States, then local law may apply. Except for the right of either party to apply to a court of competent jurisdiction for a temporary restraining order, a preliminary injunction, or other equitable relief to preserve the status quo or prevent irreparable harm, any controversy or claim arising out of or relating to this Agreement shall be settled by binding arbitration administered by the American Arbitration Association and pursuant to its rules, and judgment upon the award rendered in such arbitration may be entered in any court of competent jurisdiction.

15. GENERAL. This Agreement will inure to the benefit of CreamTec, its successors, and assigns. Each party acknowledges that it has read this Agreement and understands it, and agrees to be bound by its terms, and further agrees that they are the complete and exclusive statement of the agreement between the parties which supercedes and merges all prior proposals, understandings, and all other agreements, oral and written, between the parties relating to this Agreement. If any provision of the Agreement is deemed invalid by a court of competent jurisdiction, such provisions shall be enforced to the maximum extent permitted and the remainder will remain in full force.

Should you have any questions concerning this License, or if you desire to contact CreamTec for any reason, please contact us: CreamTec, 2400 Clarendon Blvd. #406, Arlington, VA 22201, or email us at sales@creamtec.com.

Resources

Utilities and Tools

Name: FAR

URL: `http://www.rarsoft.com/`

License: Shareware (version 1.70)

Description: File and archive manager that replaces a combination of Windows Explorer + Notepad + CMD.EXE.

Name: Total Commander

URL: `http://www.ghisler.com/`

License: Shareware (version 6.02)

Description: File and archive manager that replaces a combination of Windows Explorer + Notepad + CMD.EXE.

Name: WebCream

URL: `http://www.creamtec.com/webcream/`

License: Commercial (version 5.0.0)

Description: Converts Java GUI applications into interactive HTML Web sites on-the-fly.

Decompiling

Name: JAD

URL: `http://kpdus.tripod.com/jad.html/`

License: Freeware (version 1.5.8e2)

Description: Fast decompiler of Java class files written in C.

Name: JODE

URL: `http://jode.sourceforge.net/`

License: GPL (version 1.1)

Description: Java library containing a decompiler and an optimizer for Java.

Obfuscating

Name: Zelix KlassMaster

URL: `http://www.zelix.com/klassmaster/`

License: Commercial (version 4.1)

Description: Very powerful obfuscator that supports control flow obfuscation.

Name: ProGuard

URL: `http://proguard.sourceforge.net/`

License: GPL (version 2.1)

Description: Java class file obfuscator.

Name: RetroGuard

URL: `http://www.retrologic.com/retroguard-main.html`

License: GPL (version 1.1)

Description: Java class file obfuscator.

Tracing and Logging

Name: Log4J framework

URL: `http://logging.apache.org/log4j/`

License: Apache (version 1.2.8)

Description: Framework for outputting log messages and managing log files.

Debugging

Name: Omniscient Debugger

URL: http://www.lambdacs.com/debugger/debugger.html

License: GPL (version release of September 6, 2003)

Description: By recording each state change in the target application during the execution, it enables the developer to navigate backward in time to see the values of variables and objects.

Profiling

Name: JProbe

URL: http://www.quest.com/jprobe/

License: Commercial (version 5.0.0)

Description: Complete suite for Java code tuning (profiler, threadalizer, memory debugger).

Name: OptimizeIt

URL: http://www.borland.com/optimizeit/

License: Commercial (version 5.5)

Description: Complete suite for Java code tuning (profiler, threadalizer, memory debugger).

Name: JProfiler

URL: http://www.ej-technologies.com/products/jprofiler/overview.html

License: Commercial (version 2.4)

Description: All-in-one Java profiler, threadalizer, and memory debugger.

Load-Testing

Name: JUnit

URL: http://www.junit.org/

License: Common Public License (version 3.8.1)

Description: Simple framework for writing unit tests in Java.

Name: JMeter

URL: `http://jakarta.apache.org/jmeter/`

License: Apache (version 1.9.1)

Description: Java desktop application designed to load test functional behavior and measure the performance of Web and server applications.

Name: LoadRunner

URL: `http://www.mercuryinteractive.com/products/loadrunner/`

License: Commercial (version 6)

Description: Advanced load-testing tool that predicts system behavior and performance.

Eavesdropping

Name: TCPMon (Apache AXIS)

URL: `http://ws.apache.org/axis/`

License: Apache (version 1.1)

Description: A tunneling GUI utility that shows the contents of messages. It can be used for eavesdropping on HTTP-based protocols.

Name: HTTP Sniffer

URL: `http://www.effetech.com/`

License: Commercial (version 3.5)

Description: A powerful tool to monitor and analyze Internet traffic as well as advanced information inside packets of various protocols, such as HTTP, FTP, SMTP, POP3, and Telnet.

Name: Ethereal

URL: `http://www.ethereal.com/`

License: GPL (version 0.9.13)

Description: Used for network troubleshooting, analysis, software and protocol development, and education. It can be used for eavesdropping on virtually any communication protocol.

Name: P6Spy

URL: `http://www.p6spy.com/`

License: Apache (version 1.2)

Description: Open source framework for applications that intercept and optionally modify database statements. It can be used for JDBC eavesdropping.

Bytecode Tweaking

Name: jClassLib Bytecode Viewer

URL: http://sourceforge.net/projects/jclasslib/

License: GPL (version 1.2)

Description: Tool that visualizes all aspects of compiled Java class files and the contained bytecode.

Name: BCEL

URL: http://jakarta.apache.org/bcel/

License: Apache (version 5.1)

Description: The Byte Code Engineering Library is intended to give users a convenient possibility to analyze, create, and manipulate binary Java class files.

Name: ASM

URL: http://asm.objectweb.org/

License: BSD (version 1.4.2)

Description: High-performing Java bytecode manipulation framework.

Native Code Patching

Name: PE Explorer

URL: http://www.heaventools.com/

License: Commercial (version 1.94)

Description: GUI utility that enables you to view, analyze, edit, fix, and repair the internal structures of PE files with the click of a button.

Name: Function Replacer

URL: http://execution.cjb.net/

License: As-Is (version 1.0)

Description: Utility replacing an exported function in one DLL with an exported function from another DLL.

Name: IDA Pro

URL: http://www.datarescue.com/

License: Commercial (version 4.6)

Description: IDA Pro is the leading multioperating system, multiprocessor, interactive disassembler.

Name: Detours Library

URL: http://research.microsoft.com/sn/detours/

License: Microsoft Research License (version 1.5)

Description: Detours is a library for instrumenting arbitrary Win32 functions on x86 machines. Detours intercepts Win32 functions by rewriting target function images.

Name: OllyDbg

URL: http://home.t-online.de/home/Ollydbg/

License: Free to use; registration required (version 1.09)

Description: 32-bit assembler-level analyzing debugger for Microsoft Windows. Emphasis on binary code analysis makes it particularly useful in cases where source is unavailable.

Name: libelf

URL: http://www.gnu.org/directory/libs/misc/libelf.html

License: LGPL (version varies depending on platform)

Description: Allows you to read, modify, or create ELF files in an architecture-independent way.

Protection from Hacking

Name: Bouncy Castle JCE

URL: http://www.bouncycastle.org/

License: Free with AS-IS license (version 1.22)

Description: Java library providing an implementation of various security and encryption algorithms.

Name: Cryptix JCE

URL: http://www.cryptix.org/

License: Free with AS-IS license (version varies depending on subpackage)

Description: Java library providing an implementation of various security and encryption algorithms.

Quiz Answers

Chapter 1

1. Decompiling classes, using effective tracing, cracking code with debuggers, using profilers for runtime application analysis, eavesdropping, and reverse engineering.

2. Decompiling classes, hacking non-public methods and variables, replacing and patching application classes, manipulating Java security, hacking application resources and UI elements, controlling class loading, replacing and patching core Java classes, intercepting control flow, understanding and tweaking bytecode, and total control with native code replacement.

3. Replacing and patching application classes, using effective tracing, and eavesdropping.

4. Windows Explorer, Notepad/TextPad, CMD.EXE, FTP client, and WinZip/Other archiver.

Chapter 2

1. Recovering the source code that was accidentally lost, learning the implementation of a feature, troubleshooting an application or library that does not have good documentation, fixing urgent bugs in third-party code for which there is no source code, and learning to protect your code from hacking.

2. Debugging options specified using -g. The more debugging information is included, the better the decompiled code.

3. Because Java source code is compiled into intermediate bytecode rather than the machine code, and because a well-defined mapping exists between the source code operators and keywords and the generated bytecode.

4. There is no way to protect the code from decompiling, but obfuscation can make understanding the decompiled code almost impossible.

Chapter 3

1. Besides the legal protection offered through copyrights and patents, bytecode obfuscation provides an effective means against decompiling.

2. Name mangling, encoding Java strings, and changing control flow.

3. Decompiling and using a good debugger.

Chapter 4

1. Creating a helper class in the package of the class that has the protected or package visible member; using the Reflection API with a security manager.

2. Setting a security manager that grants required permissions and then accessing the private member using the Reflection API.

3. The helper class works well for nonsystem classes but requires being on the boot class path for the system classes; this technique cannot be used for private members. The Reflection API does not require boot class path manipulation and can access private data members, but it is slower and needs certain permissions.

Chapter 5

1. Navigating the classes starting from the entry point, text search for a known string or a class name, and call stack of an exception or a thread dump.

2. Because Java strings are stored as plain text inside the binary bytecode. Text search does not work for string constants if the strings were encoded by an obfuscator.

3. Using the `dumpStack()` method of the `java.lang.Thread` class.

4. The patched classes must be found before the original classes and be loaded with the same class loader.

Chapter 6

1. Tracing does not require an application to be running in debug mode. Trace messages are inserted into the source code permanently.

2. Because traces are designed to provide a human-readable history of operations performed by the application, they are easier to read than decompiled Java code. Examining traces gives you an understanding of the implementation and the control flow of the application.

3. Reloading the configuration file at runtime is important because it enables you to avoid restarting the application.

4. Every use of the + operator on Java strings results in the expensive operation of allocating a new buffer and copying the argument strings into it.

Chapter 7

1. `java.lang.SecurityManager`.

2. Permission represents access to system information or a resource.

3. First, the `java.policy` file is loaded from the `lib/security` directory of the JRE installation directory. Then the `.java.policy` file is loaded from the user's home directory.

Chapter 8

1. Snooping enables you to know the exact values of the various runtime environment parameters. It takes guessing out of the equation.

2. Values of system properties, installed security manager, and various memory and network information.

3. Native applications do not have the restrictions of the JVM and therefore can obtain more detailed information on the host system. Java applications can interface with the native modules using JNI or simple configuration files.

Chapter 9

1. When working with large applications that do not use tracing, when the application source code does not provide a clear understanding of internal logic, or when the application was aggressively obfuscated.

2. Conventional debuggers display the information only for the current moment, and as soon as the moment is gone, the information is irrevocably lost. To be effective, conventional debuggers require strategically placed breakpoints throughout the code.

3. Omniscient debugging enables you to record the state of the executing program and then go back in time to examine the states. The idea behind the omniscient debugger is to record as much information as possible about the threads, variables and their values, standard input and output streams, and loaded classes.

4. The logic can be located by navigating to the code from a known starting point. The starting point can be a call to System.out, a start of a thread, or a name of a method. A text search can be used to find a starting point based on a known string.

Chapter 10

1. Investigate heap usage and garbage collection frequency; find and fix memory leaks; find locking and data race problems in multithreaded applications; and investigate the application at runtime to gain a better understanding of its internal structure.

2. The full garbage collection starts from the roots of the object tree and identifies all the objects that can be reached from the root. The objects that are unreachable from the root are marked for garbage collection. Applications with large trees of objects require a lot of processing time.

3. Lingering objects prevent the memory from being reclaimed by garbage collection. If an object has a reference to it, it is not eligible for the garbage collection, even if it is never used again.

4. Using a profiler is the most effective way to find and fix memory leaks. It can be done by browsing the reference tree or finding all paths to the root in a heap snapshot.

5. The two most common problems are data race conditions and deadlocks.

6. Running an application in a profiler that collects execution statistics such as the method time, method number of calls, cumulative time, and average objects per method.

Chapter 11

1. The purpose of load testing is to assess how system performance meets the service level requirements under load.

2. *Simultaneous* means the clients that are sending a request at the same time, and *concurrent* means the clients that maintain a conversation with the server but are sending requests around the same time.

3. RMI.

4. The `assertTrue()` method needs to be used with a `false` parameter to tell JUnit that a test has failed.

5. HTTP and FTP. JMeter can also be used to test databases, Perl scripts, and Java objects.

6. A test plan can have thread groups, listeners, configuration elements, assertions, preprocessors, post-processors, and timers. A thread group can additionally have logic controllers and samplers.

7. By adding listeners such as View Results Tree and Assertion Results.

8. JUnit is a simple framework that requires programming of tests. It has no automation and provides no support for testing complex Web applications. It is good for low-level unit testing of code. JMeter is a tool with a sophisticated GUI and various test plan building blocks. It can automate the testing of Web applications, but it treats the application as a black box.

Chapter 12

1. Unpack all the library classes and do a text search for `Unknown error` in all files. If the string is hardcoded in a `CLASS` file, decompile the source, change the string text, recompile the source, and install the patch. If the string is found in a configuration file, change the string in the file.

2. Find out which GIF or JPEG file is used in the About dialog box by unpacking the Chat distribution and viewing the image files. Edit the image file, save it, and repackage Chat.

3. First, check all the configuration files to see whether the setting is configurable. If it is not, search the class files for the message displayed when the limit on the concurrent connections is reached. If a class file is found, decompile it and use it as a starting point to find the class that imposes the limit. After the class is found, check the code to see whether the limit is hardcoded.

Chapter 13

1. The general approaches to eavesdropping require intercepting the message exchange between the client and server. This can be achieved by placing an intermediary that traces the communication or by listening to network broadcast protocols.

2. Because HTTP is text based. Wide adoption of HTTP has resulted in a proliferation of tunneling and sniffing tools.

3. HTTP communication can be protected by running HTTP over SSL (HTTPS).

4. Network sniffing is possible by running a host in promiscuous mode where it accepts all packets traversing the network regardless of their destinations.

5. By eavesdropping on the underlying network protocol that is used to transport the serialized object data.

6. Installing a logging proxy or a wrapper around the real JDBC driver.

Chapter 14

1. A class loader loads and initializes classes and interfaces in the Java virtual machine.

2. A bootstrap class loader is implemented in native code and used to load the core Java classes, such as `java.lang.Object` and `java.lang.ClassLoader`.

3. An extensions class loader is used to load the extension libraries typically from the `lib/ext` directory of JRE. The JAR files placed in that directory are automatically available to Java applications.

4. Classes that have the same name and that have been loaded by the same class loader.

5. For runtime class reloading, for runtime bytecode decoration, and to provide a clean separation between logical components (such as Web applications) executing in the same JVM.

6. No, due to security considerations.

7. Because `DecoratingClassLoader` overrides the `findClass()` method that is called only if the class is not found by the chain of parent class loaders. If the class is found on the `CLASSPATH`, it is loaded by the application class loader.

Chapter 15

1. To answer this question, think about your professional work and see whether you've had to implement a tedious workaround for a problem or a bug in the core classes.

2. The patching of core classes requires manipulation of the boot class path because the core classes are always loaded by the bootstrap class loader.

3. Because the boot class path is where the bootstrap class loader gets the list of paths from which to load system classes.

Chapter 16

1. It is recommended to catch `java.lang.Throwable` because system errors are reported as unchecked exceptions. A good design solution is to have a try-catch block at the top of the call stack on main application threads that logs checked and unchecked exceptions.

2. A custom stream can be coded that persists the data into a database. Then the system error stream can be redirected to the custom stream using the `System.setErr()` method.

3. By installing a security manager that throws a security exception from its `checkExit()` method.

4. The Java application can add a shutdown hook. When the hook is called, the application closes all connections.

5. Events such as class loading, method entry and exit, thread start and end, and others.

Chapter 17

1. There is no dependency on having the source code, ability to generate/instrument byte-code at runtime, and easier automation.

2. Opcode identifies the JVM instruction in the bytecode. To pass the parameters, values are pushed onto the operand stack.

3. `(Ljava.lang.String;C)[Ljava.lang.Object]`.

4. `cp_info`, `field_info`, `method_info`, and `attribute_info`.

5. `JavaClass`, `Field`, `Method`, `ConstantPool`, `ClassGen`, `FieldGen`, `MethodGen`, `ConstantPoolGen`, `InstructionFactory`, `InstructionList`, and `Instruction`.

6. Code attribute.

Chapter 18

1. JNI allows the invocation of methods from a dynamically loaded native library. It provides a layer of abstraction between the JVM and the OS.

2. The method needs to be declared as native in a Java class, and the native library must be loaded in the class's static initializer. The javah utility should be used to generate a C header file; then the method body should be coded in a C implementation file. The C implementation file should be compiled and linked into a DLL that should be placed on the binary path of the Java program.

3. Patching a Java method declaration is simple to use and is portable, but it might not work if some code from the native library still needs to be called. Substituting native libraries is tedious, although not overwhelmingly difficult, to implement and does not require low-level patching. However, it might not be effective for DLLs with a large number of exported functions and might not provide enough flexibility in calling the original native code. Patching native code offers the ultimate power and flexibility but is difficult to write because the work is done at the lowest level; also, it's not portable across platforms.

4. .text section.

5. Because the machine code that implements the patch is written by the utility over the original function code. The code size depends on the name lengths and can be up to 100 bytes, which is larger than many simple C functions.

6. Yes, CALL can be used, but then the parameters need to be pushed on the stack again so the replacement function return executes correctly. Using a CALL instead of a JMP also requires a RETN instruction in the detour code to return the control back to the caller.

7. Detours is more reliable and should work for all versions of JDK and PE files. It offers a lot more flexibility via in-memory function interception and the capability to call the original function via a trampoline.

8. COFF and ELF.

9. Use the same approach as on Windows. Locate the binary code in the executable file based on the file format. Disassemble the function code and implement a detour in the assembly language. The detour can delegate to the new logic appended to the same file or to a function dynamically loaded from a shared library.

Chapter 19

1. A message digest protects only the integrity of the message; encryption protects the contents of the message; and signing protects the integrity of the message and ensures the authenticity of the sender through a trusted certificate authority.

2. Symmetric algorithms use the same key for encryption and decryption; asymmetric algorithms use a pair of keys (public and private) to provide one-way encryption.

3. Use encryption to convert the body of the email into unrecognizable content, and then apply base64 encoding to convert bytes into printable characters. You should use `javax.crypto.Cipher` for the algorithm, a concrete class that implements `java.security.spec.KeySpec` for the selected cipher, and `javax.crypto.SecretKeyFactory` to convert the key specification into a key.

4. Obfuscation, sealing application JAR files, asserting the source of the critical classes, and protecting the distribution files by verifying the checksum.

5. Using an asymmetric algorithm is more secure because the checksum can be calculated using the private key and verified using the public key. That way, nobody except the vendor can issue the checksum. In the sample Chat protection, the message digest algorithm is supplied with the parameters that can be obtained from the decompiled code.

6. A pair of keys needs to be generated or obtained for the given algorithm. Generating a signature requires an instance of a `PrivateKey` class for the private key and an instance of a `Signature` class for the given algorithm. The instance of the `Signature` class is given the key and the data to be signed, and then the `sign()` method is called to obtain the signature.

7. Verifying the signature requires an instance of the `PublicKey` class and a `Signature` class for the given algorithm. The algorithm instance is given the public key and the data, and then its `verify()` method is called with the signature data as a parameter.

Index

Symbols

+ (plus sign) operator, string concatenation, 67

A

B

C

H

hackers, decompiling, 25

hacking

    Apache Log4J logging API, 66

    bytecode, 209-211

    classes, 5

    commercial application protection, 7

    protection from, 27-28

    UI (user interface) elements/resources, 121

        configuration files, 125

        images, 123-125

        text, 122-123

hash, 202

heap usage, profiling, 90-92

helper classes, package-visible members, 44-45

Hibernate, 167

hierarchies

    class loaders, 140-142

    custom class loaders, 145

hooks, shutdown hooks (Java Virtual Machine), 160

HTML (Hypertext Markup Language), 44

HTTP (Hypertext Transfer Protocol), eaves-dropping

    application protection, 132

    network sniffers, 130-131

    tunnels, 128-129

HTTP Sniffer, 131, 236

HTTPS (Hypertext Transfer Protocol Secure), 132

Hypertext Transfer Protocol. *See* HTTP

I

IDA Pro Web site, 198, 237

IDEs (integrated development environments), 10

IIOP (Internet Inter-Orb Protocol), 133

images

    hacking, Chat application, 123-125

    searching, 123-125

implementing licensing, files, 217-218

    creating, 219-222

    verifying, 222-224

input streams, RMI (Remote Method Invocation) protocol eavesdropping, 133

installations, security managers (JVM), 159

instantiating, custom class loaders, 145-147

instructions, JVM (Java Virtual Machine), 167-168

instrumenting methods (bytecode), 175-179

integrated development environments (IDEs), 10

intellectual property (IP), protection of, 28

intercepting control flow

    JVM (Java Virtual Machine) shutdown, 160

    JVMPI (Java Virtual Machine Profiler Interface), 163

    methods, 160-163

    system errors, 155-156

    system streams, 156-158

    System.exit() calls, 158-159

Internet Inter-Orb Protocol (IIOP), 133

IP (intellectual property), protection of, 28

J

K-L

M

machine code, PE (Portable Executable) format, 192

maintenance, applications (obfuscation), 35-36

managers, security

bypassing security checks, 72-73

installing (JVM), 159

protected operations, 70

managing files, 7-9

mangling names, obfuscation, 29-30

memory, managing (Java Virtual Machine), 78

memory leaks, troubleshooting, 92-96

menu bars, Chat application, 11

Mercury Load Runner, 111

message digest algorithms, 203, 212-214

message processing code, Chat applications, 84-86

MessageInfoComplex code, 16-20

messages, debug. *See* tracing

method descriptors, 168-170

Method Traces panel (Omniscient Debugger), 84

methods

call stacks, application logic navigation, 58

instrumenting (bytecode), 175-179

intercepting, dynamic proxy, 160-163

native

declaring, 187

patching, 190-191

System.exit(), intercepting calls, 158-159

Microsoft Detours library, 196-198

Mocha decompiler, 15

multiple DES (DESede) cipher algorithm, 205

N

name mangling, obfuscation, 29-30

name patterns, Zelik KlassMaster obfuscator, 40

names, classes (Chat application), 56

naming conventions, troubleshooting (obfuscation), 35

native code, patching, 185

JVM (Java Virtual Machine), 186-189

native methods, 190-191

Unix, 198-199

Windows

Function Replacer utility, 194-196

Microsoft Detours library, 196-198

Portable Executable (PE) formats, 191-194

native libraries

loading, 187

native methods, patching, 190

native methods

declaring, 187

patching, 190-191

navigation, application logic (Chat application), 58

NetBeans Web site, 10

network sniffers

HTTP (Hypertext Transfer Protocol) eavesdropping, 130-131

RMI (Remote Method Invocation) eavesdropping, 133-135

networks, locating information (runtime environment), 79

nodes, test plans (JMeter tool), 111-112

T

X-Z

Your Guide
to Computer
Technology

www.informit.com